POLITICAL GASTRONOMY

EARLY AMERICAN STUDIES

Series editors: Daniel K. Richter, Kathleen M. Brown,
Max Cavitch, and David Waldstreicher

Exploring neglected aspects of our colonial, revolutionary,
and early national history and culture, Early American Studies
reinterprets familiar themes and events in fresh ways.
Interdisciplinary in character, and with a special emphasis on
the period from about 1600 to 1850, the series is published in
partnership with the McNeil Center for Early American Studies.

A complete list of books in the series
is available from the publisher.

POLITICAL GASTRONOMY

Food and Authority
in the English Atlantic World

Michael A. LaCombe

PENN

UNIVERSITY OF PENNSYLVANIA PRESS

PHILADELPHIA

Published by
University of Pennsylvania Press
Philadelphia, Pennsylvania 19104-4112
www.upenn.edu/pennpress

Printed in the United States of America on acid-free paper

10 9 8 7 6 5 4 3 2 1

Library of Congress Cataloging-in-Publication Data
LaCombe, Michael A.
    Political gastronomy : food and authority in the English
Atlantic world / Michael A. LaCombe. — 1st ed.
        p. cm. — (Early American studies)
    Includes bibliographical references ad index.
    ISBN 978-0-8122-4418-2 (hardcover : alk. paper)
    1. North America—History—Colonial period,
ca. 1600–1775. 2. Food—Political aspects—North
America—History. 3. Great Britain—Colonies—Amer-
ica—History—17th century. 4. Great Britain—Colo-
nies—America—Social conditions. 5. Colonists—North
America—Attitudes 6. Indians of North America—
Food—Political aspects. 7. Indians of North America—
First contact with Europeans. I. Title. II. Series: Early
American studies
E46.L33 2012
973.2—dc23

                                        2011045999

For Christa, Sophia, and Vivian

The table constitutes a kind of tie between the bargainer and the bargained-with, and makes the diners more willing to receive certain impressions, to submit to certain influences: from this is born political gastronomy. Meals have become a means of governing, and the fate of whole peoples is decided at a banquet.

—Jean Anthèlme Brillat-Savarin, *The Physiology of Taste, or, Meditations on Transcendental Gastronomy*, trans. M. F. K. Fisher

Contents

Introduction

Hungry, wet, and weary, a small group of English men rowed into the Carolina Sounds in the summer of 1584. They had arrived less than a month earlier, sent to explore the region and make contact with its native population. After a few tentative encounters with Carolina Algonquians, the English party decided to leave the safety of their ships and set out for the village of Roanoke.

As they watched the English approach, Roanoke's Algonquian inhabitants displayed the same mixture of curiosity and apprehension as their approaching guests. Most of the small group standing on shore were women, who had been cooking, tending fires, and minding children until they saw the English approaching. Among them was a woman whose clothing, hair, and bearing distinguished her from the rest. The wife of Granganimeo, a prominent man, and sister-in-law of Wingina, the Carolina Algonquians' overall leader, she had visited the English ships a few days before with her husband and children. In her husband's absence, she arranged a warm welcome for these uninvited but important guests: a fire, a bath, a meal, and a place to sleep.

Interactions like this one were not uncommon in the early period, and it was no accident that food lay at the center of each. Granganimeo's wife believed that a woman of her station was obligated to offer hospitality, and her guests shared these assumptions. This meant that as the English travelers sat and rested, warmed themselves, and ate (gesturing for more helpings of various dishes, smiling and nodding politely to their hostess, and offering comments to each other on the meal), they were also taking part in a form of communication. Everyone present at this meal knew that it was an important occasion and that meanings were being shared along with foods, and everyone conducted him- or herself accordingly. However vast the gulf of culture, religion, history, and technology that separated English from Indians, a table brought them surprisingly close together.

Political Gastronomy explores what food meant—and *how* food meant—to

Figure 1. This engraving, titled "The arrival of the Englishemen in Virginia," was prepared by the workshop of Theodor de Bry to accompany the 1590 edition of Thomas Harriot's *A briefe and true report.* Roanoke Island is shown surrounded by canoes and a fishing weir. On the island itself, the village of Roanoke is surrounded by fields of maize, as are the two other native villages depicted. In the forests of Roanoke Island, Algonquian hunters are shown pursuing deer, while on the mainland grapevines of the sort Arthur Barlowe described offer another image of plenty. Courtesy Rare Book and Manuscript Library, University of Pennsylvania.

these men and women and many others like them. Food is as ubiquitous in the written accounts of early America as the labor associated with it was in daily life. When Indians and English produced food, exchanged it, ate it, or described their experiences, they conveyed dense and interlaced messages about status, gender, civility, diplomacy, and authority.

The 1584 Roanoke voyage was intended to find a likely site for an eventual settlement, and in his manuscript account of the voyage Arthur Barlowe claimed success. Reporting to the voyage's backers, who included the influential young courtier Sir Walter Ralegh, Barlowe described islands "so full of grapes, as the very beating, and surge of the Sea overflowed them, of which we founde such plentie, as well there, as in all places else, both on the sande, and on the greene soile on the hils, as in the plaines, as well on every little shrubbe, as also climing towardes the toppes of the high Cedars, that I thinke in all the world the like aboundance is not to be founde." The forests were, Barlowe went on, "full of Deere, Conies, Hares, and Fowle, even in the middest of Summer, in incredible aboundance." Tangled vines heavy with fruit and forests teeming with game offered a tempting image of opportunity: a fertile landscape not fully exploited by its native population where English travelers and potential settlers might feed themselves with minimal labor.[1]

Barlowe also hoped to make contact with the native population of the Sounds, and on the third day of Barlowe's explorations, a group of three Carolina Algonquians paddled ashore within sight of the English ships. One of this group "came along the shoare side towards us" and "walked up and downe uppon the point of the lande next unto us," which the English understood as an invitation for a small party to row ashore to meet him.[2]

Noting that the man watched the English approach, "never making any shewe of feare, or doubt," Barlowe signaled that although these two groups had never met, they knew about each other, expected to meet, and had prepared accordingly. Even if they had not encountered Indians firsthand, the members of the voyage had read or heard accounts of others' encounters and expected to conduct their own. Some among the native population of the Carolina Sounds had firsthand knowledge of Europeans, having encountered Spanish or French travelers, shipwrecked sailors, or marooned privateers. The rest had learned what they knew (as most Europeans had) through secondhand reports.[3]

Barlowe described the encounter that took place after the English party reached shore in terms readers like Ralegh, and the investors he hoped to attract, would have found very promising: "And after he had spoken of many things not understoode by us, we brought him with his owne good liking, aboord the shippes, and gave him a shirt, a hatte, and some other things, and made him taste of our wine, and our meate, which he liked very well." In the absence of language (which Barlowe acknowledged in an unusually forthright way), the interaction between the English party and this Algonquian man centered on an offer of food, the single most meaningful and mutually understood form of symbolic communication. Just as he did in describing "incredible aboundance," Barlowe intended to convey a specific (though unrelated) meaning to his readers through references to food. For the English to offer this Algonquian man food, and for him readily to accept that offer, was a clear sign of not just a desire for an alliance but the beginning of one.[4]

A further layer or level of meaning in Barlowe's account of this encounter derived from the Indian man's conduct afterward, when "hee fell to fishing, and in lesse then halfe an howre, hee had laden his boate as deepe, as it could swimme." The man then returned to the place where the two groups had first met and "devided his fishe into two partes, pointing one part to the shippe, and the other to the Pinnesse: which after he had (as much as he might,) requited the former benefits receaved, he departed out of our sight." To Barlowe and his readers, this man's actions demonstrated that Indians and English shared an understanding of what had taken place, that the Algonquian man had accepted the meanings Barlowe intended to convey along with wine and food. Natural abundance and a native population peacefully inclined toward the English were important signs for Barlowe's readers. This episode served as further proof of these points and in addition evidence that the Carolina Algonquians understood that their interactions with the English had begun to establish bonds of mutual trust and reciprocity.[5]

Barlowe's party was introduced to an Indian leader only a day after this encounter, and in Barlowe's narrative the relationship between the two meetings was implicit but clear. Barlowe was describing his success in securing an increasingly close and trusting relationship with the native inhabitants of the region. The Carolina Algonquians told the English that Wingina, their leader, had been injured in a battle and could not meet with them. In his place appeared Granganimeo, described as "the Kings brother," who was accompanied by "fortie or fiftie men, very handsome and goodly people, and in their behaviour as mannerly and civill as any of Europe." Presented with "Chamoys, Buffe, and Deere skinnes," all valuable commodities, the English party "shewed [Granganimeo] all our packet of merchandize." Of "all things that he sawe," Barlowe went on, "a bright tinne dish most pleased him, which

Figure 2. The teeming marine life of the Carolina Sounds and various techniques for fishing are the subject of another engraving from the 1590 edition of Thomas Harriot's *A briefe and true report*. On the left, an elaborate weir captures fish, while simpler weirs in the center and right channel fish where Algonquian men in canoes and wading spear them. The fish in the canoe were presumably netted, perhaps when they were drawn to the light of the fire burning in the center of the canoe. Courtesy Rare Book and Manuscript Library, University of Pennsylvania.

hee presently tooke up and clapt it before his breast, and after made a hole in the brimme thereof and hung it about his necke." To those of his readers with knowledge of the early travel literature, Barlowe's description followed a pattern already familiar: an exchange of animal skins for metal goods.[6]

Barlowe's diplomatic achievements were not yet finished. "After two or three daies," Granganimeo came "aboord the shippes, and dranke wine, and ate of our meate, and of our bread, and liked exceedingly thereof," as the earlier visitor had. This meeting was followed by an extraordinary visit from Granganimeo, his wife, and their children, all of whom came aboard the English ships. After this unmistakable sign of trust, "[Granganimeo] sent us every day a brase or two of fat Bucks, Conies, Hares, Fish the best of the world. He sent us divers kindes of fruites, Melons, Walnuts, Cucumbers, Gourdes, Pease, and divers rootes, and fruites very excellent good, and of their Countrey corne, which is very white, faire and well tasted."[7]

These occasions serve to punctuate Barlowe's narrative, plotting an increasingly close relationship between English and Indians at Roanoke, and food is the only feature they all share. In one sense, this list of foods repeated earlier themes, namely the region's natural abundance and friendly native population. But this case added additional meanings Barlowe's readers were eager to hear. The arrival of such a broad range of foods "every day" was a clear sign of a strong and ongoing alliance between Indians and English, in which the Algonquians demonstrated their willingness and ability to feed the visitors. Even more, the range of foods offered, reflecting considerable labor by men (fish and game animals) and women (fruits, nuts, and vegetables), suggested a productive and orderly Algonquian society. And by specifying that these foods had been personally sent by Granganimeo, Barlowe described that society as under the control of an effective leader, one with the authority to dispose of the foods his people produced in exchanges.[8]

The peaceful, productive, and orderly society Barlowe encountered in the Carolina Sounds was even more vividly portrayed with reference to the idealized European past. Barlowe wrote that he "found the people most gentle, loving, and faithfull, void of all guile, and treason, and such as lived after the manner of the golden age." This rich cultural reference, familiar to all of Barlowe's readers, was also illustrated with reference to food: "The earth bringeth foorth all things in aboundance, as in the first creation, without toile or labour. The people only care . . . to feede themselves with such meat as the soile affoordeth." Barlowe's ecstatic portrait of Roanoke's native population concluded with specific praise for their simple and nourishing diet. He wrote that "their meate is very well sodden, and they make broth very sweet, and savorie." Even their cookware and dishes were worthy of Barlowe's praise: "their vessels are earthen pots, very large, white and sweete: their dishes are woodden platters of sweete timber." Food again conveyed the richest symbols for Barlowe's message of peace, simplicity, health, order, and bounty.[9]

The climax of Barlowe's account was his description of the hospitality his party enjoyed at Granganimeo's house, the episode with which we began. Rowing ashore near the village of Roanoke, Barlowe's party met Granganimeo's wife, who "came running out to meete us very cheerefully and friendly." First, she ordered some of her people to carry the English to shore on their backs while others drew the English boat ashore. Then, she and other women "caused us to sitte downe by a great fire, and after tooke off our clothes and washed them, and dried them againe." More extraordinary still, "some of the women pulled off our stockings and washed them" and "some washed our feete in warme water." Meanwhile, Granganimeo's wife "tooke great paines to see all things ordered in the best maner shee could, making great haste to dresse some meate for us to eate."[10]

Barlowe went on to describe the meal the English were offered in Granganimeo's house: "After we had thus dried our selves, she brought us into the inner roome, where shee set on the boord standing along the house, some wheate like furmentie, sodden Venison, and roasted, fish sodden, boyled, and roasted, Melons rawe, and sodden, rootes of divers kindes, and divers fruites. . . . We were entertained with all love, and kindnes, and with as much bountie, after their manner, as they could possibly devise." Another list of foods, but with new layers of meaning at this point in Barlowe's narrative. This meal, prepared and served by Granganimeo's wife and eaten in his home, was the culmination of Barlowe's narrative of a growing friendship between his party and the Indians of the region. A meal like this one was the clearest way to signal "love, and kindnes" coupled with "bountie," evidence that Barlowe knew his readers would find persuasive.[11]

Barlowe might have told his readers about the Carolina Algonquians' willingness to host a settlement of English men in their territory in a variety of ways, but his layered descriptions of food suggested meanings that could not be otherwise conveyed. These meanings depended on the ways food plotted the progress of his narrative, on the cumulative effect of his descriptions, and on the deep resonances certain images—bountiful hospitality, a golden age of simplicity, health, and abundance—conveyed to English readers. Food, in

Barlowe's account as in many others, was everywhere, simultaneously conveying meanings to Indians and English, whether travelers or readers, about ecology, diplomacy, civility, gender, status, and power.

Political Gastronomy explores how men and women in the English Atlantic world—both Indians and English—conveyed and interpreted the intertwined symbolic meanings of food and how they manipulated those symbols in their struggles for precedence. During the early period of high hopes, false starts, and frail beginnings, nearly all leaders of English voyages and settlements struggled to establish themselves as strong and effective leaders with a legitimate claim to office. Middling men whose social position would not qualify them to hold powerful offices in England, leaders in the English Atlantic world faced a variety of challenges in this effort—from ordinary settlers, from peers and rivals, and from Indians—and responded in very different ways. Food lay at the heart of these challenges and would-be leaders' responses to them.

Two questions must be addressed at the outset. The first is how food can be said to have played any role in politics in the formal sense of courts, legislative assemblies, governors' councils, and the like. Formal institutions like these are a familiar feature of the scholarly literature on early America, but *Political Gastronomy* focuses on less tangible features of leadership, summed up in the term "authority." One of the early period's most salient features is the dynamism and fluidity of its political culture. Many English leaders found themselves faced with the need to secure legitimacy, and titles, offices, and royal patents alone were not always sufficient. So officeholders turned to more informal means, presenting themselves in public in a way that conformed to the expectations of peers and the commons and describing their actions in a way aimed to appeal to a metropolitan audience. Food was fundamental to this search for legitimacy. This is not to say that courts and legislatures were secondary: food was not the only site or occasion for political contests in the early period, nor was it always the most important site for the negotiation of relationships, whether among the English or between Indians and English. But food was always *a* site for such interactions, which gives it a unique value for historians.[12]

The second question focuses on "food" itself, a loose term that refers only in part to what one eats. Food is among the most richly symbolic elements of social life, conveying a variety of meanings relating to host and guest, giver and recipient, cook and diner, producer and consumer, and these meanings are linked to the most fundamental of all social relationships. Food had meanings that depended on whether or not it was present; who controlled, prepared, and presented it and under what circumstances; whether it was a plant or an animal, bread or meat. The paths food took from the soil, streams, and forests of England to the tables of the people who lived there delineated the social order itself. Tracing these paths is akin to tracing the circulation of blood in a body politic.[13]

Each of these social practices and relationships contributed meanings for early English travelers and settlers and for the native peoples they encountered in the Americas. In cases like the meal offered to Barlowe's party, basic similarities between English and Native American food customs yielded similar meanings for both groups; in others, widely different cultural associations led to very different meanings. But despite the gulf that separated the two groups in most areas, both English and Indians understood that foods conveyed fundamental messages when they passed from one group to the other or were shared at a meal. In other words, even when they did not grasp the nuances of this symbolic communication, all parties understood that they were communicating and even, in many cases, the basic substance of what they were communicating. When Barlowe offered his Indian visitor food and wine, for example, the man understood the obligation conferred by this gift, reciprocating with fish. When an English party visited her home, Granganimeo's wife honored them with abundance and variety while in equally unmistakable terms conveying her own household's status through the foods she offered.

Its multivalence is one of food's most fascinating qualities, and at the heart of food's many meanings lies a unique combination of dense symbolism with the basic human need for nutrition. These aspects are impossible to separate: the human body's need for calories made food a daily concern in the early period, and its symbolic richness linked these daily occasions to larger social and political meanings. To put it another way, food "had not only more than one meaning but more than one *kind* of meaning," and caloric and symbolic meanings always overlaid each other in the eyes of contemporaries.[14]

For hungry settlers across the English Atlantic world, ample food in any form meant nothing less than deliverance from hunger and the fear of starvation. The appearance of a supply fleet, for example, was a unique opportunity to display the pageantry of political power, which might include volleys of cannon fire as the ships entered the harbor, an honor guard with antique weapons gleaming, bowed and bared heads on all sides, an oration, a procession, a sermon, a seated figure dressed in rich robes. All of these elements were important to the pageantry of authority, but only food—only the barrels of grain and salted meat that would surely be lifted over the ships' sides and rowed ashore in full view—carried this double meaning.

Similarly, when native leaders appeared at the gates of an English settlement bearing a gift of venison, they intended to convey a dense set of symbolic messages connecting this particular animal to masculine skill in hunting and, by extension, warfare. Control of these animals—the ability to offer them in exchanges—was evidence of effective leadership on both sides. Therefore the act of eating such animals was a symbolic enactment of social relationships; in the English case, it separated the upper and lower reaches of society by virtue of their access to venison. But the significance of this food extended beyond the occasion on which it was exchanged, or served, or even eaten, to the metabolic processes by which it was digested. A diet that regularly featured such foods resulted in real physical differences in nutrition, fertility, longevity, height, and weight.

A natural place to begin peeling back these layers of meaning for the early modern English is where they themselves would have seen the roots of social relationships: daily life and household labor. Most Europeans of the period organized their lives according to the seasonal rhythms of agriculture and spent most of their waking hours producing food in one form or another. The cultural significance of this daily labor and the foods it produced was vast: in many ways the labor itself defined social roles based on age, gender, and social status. Hunting, fishing, gathering, planting, herding, harvesting, storing, preserving, preparing, and serving plants and animals at table—and cleaning up after meals—were each among the most highly gendered of all work, and when early modern English men and women performed this labor, they were also performing social roles. By doing so, they expressed meanings that extended well beyond the human need for sustenance.

Thomas Tusser's *Five hundreth points of good husbandry united to as many of good huswiferie*, a manual in verse for small landowners and substantial tenant farmers, embodied many of these assumptions in a way that clearly appealed to Tusser's contemporaries: the book went through eighteen editions between 1557 and 1599. Unlike other husbandry manuals, which were written for the gentry, Tusser's work painted an idealized image of an ordinary farm household, and its author instructed, reminded, and chided his readers about the diligence and hard work it would take to conform their own households to that image. To Tusser and his contemporaries, the ideal English household was cooperative yet patriarchal, unequal yet harmonious: a miniature model and the basic unit

of society itself. An orderly and productive farm indicated that the most basic
social relationships were functioning properly, that diligent labor by men and
women in their separate roles had produced a harmonious whole.[15]

On one level, Tusser's work stressed separate roles and distinct forms of
labor for men and women, adults and children, servants and masters. Male
labor focused on crops and fields, farm animals and tools, and local markets; female labor focused on gardening, dairying, brewing, and baking. This
labor was simultaneous and parallel, separated physically into male and female
spaces but part of the overall work of providing for the family. As important
as gender distinctions were to Tusser, the interdependence of the household's
members was even more important. When fattened animals were slaughtered
in late fall, for instance, they moved from barn to kitchen through the labor of
slaughtering and butchering, primarily work for men, and salting and smoking their flesh, primarily female labor. Similarly, grain, the product of male
labor, became the staff of life through the highly gendered labor of baking.
Dairy products—cheese, whey, and butter—provided the bulk of protein and
fat in the early modern English diet. These foods also combined male responsibilities for husbandry with women's (and children's) responsibility for the
twice-daily work of milking and the labor-intensive work of dairying, which
required specialized equipment and knowledge. From a perspective like Tusser's, freshly baked bread and sweet butter, or bacon, or beer, encapsulated a
properly ordered household, whereas rancid butter, spoiled meat, and moldy
bread were not just revolting but evidence of disorder.[16]

A household that was properly "governed," to use a revealing early modern term, was one in which each member played his or her distinct role properly. For Tusser, Christmas was the occasion to display a properly governed
household through the fruits of diligent husbandry and housewifery:

> Good bread & good drinke, a good fyer in the hall,
> brawne pudding & souse & good mustarde withal.
> Biefe, mutton, & porke, shred pyes of the best,
> pig, veale, goose & capon, & Turkey wel drest:
> Chese, apples & nuttes, jollie Caroles to here,
> as then, in the cuntrey, is counted good chere.[17]

The Christmas display of abundance embodied Tusser's vision of English
society completely. Servants and dependents were invited to share the household's bounty, manifesting the vertical ties that (in this case) bound the lower

and middle reaches of the English social hierarchy. Social peers of the host and hostess were not only invited but expected to extend invitations of their own, an ethic of "neighborliness" that bound the members of rural English communities with horizontal social ties. Each of these relationships found its purest expression in shared meals. As Tusser put it,

> Good wife, & good children, are worthy to eate,
> good servant, good laborer, earneth their meate.
> good frend & good neighbour, that fellowly gest:
> with hartely welcome, should have of the best.

It required a properly ordered society composed of properly governed households to produce a meal like this, and for Tusser the specific qualities and inequalities of English rural society were publicly displayed and affirmed on such occasions.[18]

Generalizations about Native American food habits are much more difficult, given the geographical and cultural diversity of Native American societies encountered by the English during the early period. Not all groups placed the same importance on agriculture, or even cultivated crops at all. The Iroquoian-speaking Hurons and Iroquois of the eastern Great Lakes and present-day upstate New York, for example, lived in hilltop villages surrounded by fields. These groups produced a surplus of food that was used to sustain these dense settlements, to provision military expeditions, and to trade with other groups. The Algonquian speakers of present-day eastern Québec and the Canadian Maritimes—Montagnais, Micmac, Abnaki, Algonkin, and other groups—lived in close proximity to the Iroquoian speakers but pursued very different subsistence strategies. Instead of agriculture, these groups relied primarily on fishing and hunting, perhaps trading their surplus of game for maize with groups like the Hurons. Farther north, salmon runs provided Arctic peoples with seasonally abundant food, which they supplemented with hunting, gathering, and fishing offshore for the rest of the year. Agriculture, a practical impossibility given the climate, played no part in the diets of these groups.[19]

Still, certain features were broadly shared by those Native American groups encountered by the English in the early period. Most of the Algonquian speakers of the Atlantic coast, from Florida to the Maritimes, had adopted the cultivation of maize in the centuries before contact. As was true

Figure 3. The town of Secotan is an image of orderly, productive agriculture. Fields of maize on the right are shown in three stages of growth.
Pumpkins or squashes adjoin a fenced kitchen garden in the center. Hunters at the top of the engraving pursue deer near a field of tobacco, and sunflowers grow on the left side of the engraving near another plot of tobacco.
Thomas Harriot, *A briefe and true report* (1590). Courtesy Rare Book and
Manuscript Library, University of Pennsylvania.

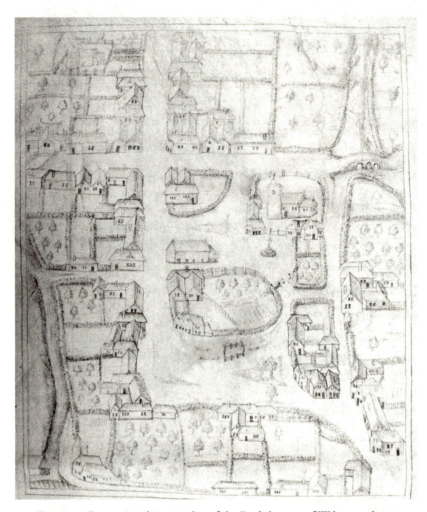

Figure 4. Comparing this 1565 plan of the English town of Wilton to the engraving of Secotan in Figure 3 reveals obvious similarities. Wilton's houses lie along orderly streets with separate fenced orchards, fields, and kitchen gardens. In both cases, the artist's intention was to convey a productive and properly ordered agricultural society. Courtesy the Earl of Pembroke and the Wiltshire and Swindon Archives, 2057/S/3/1.

for Tusser, the daily labor of producing and preparing food embodied and legitimated Native American gender and status distinctions.

A field planted with maize along with beans and squash is often called a *milpa*, from this combination's origin in central Mexico. Known elsewhere as the Three Sisters, *milpa* agriculture slowly spread northward through eastern North America, complementing crops domesticated earlier and seasonal fishing, hunting, and gathering. The year after Arthur Barlowe wrote his descriptions of the Carolina Sounds, Sir Walter Ralegh sent another expedition to the region that included John White, who was instructed to provide visual evidence of the region's landscape and native population. White's watercolors were the basis for copperplate engravings produced by the workshop of Theodor de Bry to accompany the 1590 edition of *A briefe and true report of the new found land of Virginia* by Thomas Harriot. The village of Secotan, for example, provides a snapshot of this process. Maize grows alongside tobacco, sunflowers, and pumpkins, three crops independently domesticated earlier in the Southeast. This image of an orderly and productive farming village would have resonated with English readers who, whether or not they had also read Thomas Tusser, viewed quite similar images as reflections of their own idealized social hierarchy.

There were important differences between the two, deriving from the fact that Algonquians did not live in settled agricultural communities like Secotan for the entire year. Instead, most relied for subsistence on seasonal migrations to exploit sources of food when and where they were most abundant. In early spring, Algonquians gathered in villages like Secotan near the coast or the banks of inland rivers to exploit the abundant spawning runs of smelt, alewives, salmon, and sturgeon and migrations of ducks and geese northward along the Atlantic seaboard. This was a period of intense activity and abundant food, and labor was divided according to gender in terms that Thomas Tusser would have recognized. Men for the most part did the work of hunting and fishing, and women dressed the game, cleaned the fish, preserved some of it, and prepared the rest.[20]

During the months of April and May, the first corn crop was planted. Here too, labor was highly gendered. Men helped clear new fields, which was done by girdling trees and leaving them standing. When the trees died, sunlight could reach the soil between their trunks. Beyond this, agriculture was work for women in Algonquian society, quite the opposite of the English experience. Women planted their crops in hills using simple tools like pointed sticks and hoes, and women weeded the cornfields in the spring. After this, fields needed little attention.

Once the crops were in, women in inland Algonquian groups foraged for wild plants, berries, and (in the fall) nuts. Beginning in the late summer, the residents of Secotan harvested the first of three crops of maize. Groups farther north could expect fewer harvests, but their first corn also ripened in late summer. For coastal groups, men fished offshore in canoes and speared fish closer to land. Men also built and tended fish weirs, while women gathered shellfish in tidal flats and dried the catch in smoke to preserve it. Late summer and early fall was another busy season. The waterfowl migrations were reversed, which offered animal protein in brief abundance, and crops were harvested and stored, usually in covered pits. Beginning in October, villages like Secotan dispersed, moving inland and dividing into smaller groups.

Agricultural labor and the crops it produced were identified with women everywhere in Algonquian society, and the foods produced in late fall and winter—mostly by hunting—were similarly identified with men. Strengthening this association, fall and winter were not only the season for hunting but also for war. By the end of winter, grain stores had been depleted, and the game animals that provided a crucial supplement were as lean as the men who hunted them. As spawning fish returned to the rivers and the first ducks and geese appeared overhead, Algonquian villages again appeared in the same areas, often on the same sites, as the previous year, and the seasonal round repeated.

The correspondences Barlowe described between English and Algonquian assumptions, and which appeared in visual form in the de Bry engravings, had their roots in the similar labor required to produce food no matter where it grew, ran, swam, or flew. But the similarities went further and deeper. Secotan's inhabitants and Tusser's readers subsisted on more or less the same daily meal: a one-pot stew of grain, herbs, vegetables, and (when available) meat or fish. Two more engravings that accompanied the 1590 edition of Harriot highlight these similarities. The first shows a stew of maize, fish, and other ingredients simmering in a thin-walled clay pot. Underscoring the similarities to European pottages, Harriot's text compared the dish to a "gallimaufrye, which the Spaniarde call, olla podrida." Another engraving shows a man and woman eating together from a dish of cooked maize, suggesting that the foods Algonquian men and women provided separately were shared at family meals that differed only in minor points from those described by Tusser.[21]

Formal meals were far more likely than daily meals like these to feature

VMMA induſtria figulina vaſa eorum femina parare norunt, eaque capacia admodum & tenuia, vt ne figulus quidem currente rota meliora conficere poſſit; huc illuc ea transferentes tanta facilitate vt nos aheneam lebetem. His maſſa luti impoſitis, ne cadant, ligna circumponunt, quibus inceſis illorum quiſpiam ſummam curam adhibet, vt ignis circumquaque æqualis ardeat: vaſe ab ipſis aut eorum mulieribus aqua repleto, iniiciunt fructus, carnes, piſcesque, & ſimul omnia percoqui ſinūt inſtar laſtaurocacabi, quod Hiſpani olla podrida appellāt. Jn lances deinde transfuſa cœtui apponunt, atque ſimul in hunc modum genio indulgent, in victu tamen moderati, ne in morbum incidant. Utinam eorum exemplum imitaremur: immnes enim eſſemus a tam variis morbis quos ſumptuoſis & intempeſtiuis conuiuiis nobis accerſimus, noua condimenta & gula irritamenta ſemper excogitantes, vt ſaturi fiamus.

Figure 5. Carolina Algonquians prepare a typical meal of maize and fish simmered in a clay pot. Thomas Harriot, *A briefe and true report* (1590). Courtesy Rare Book and Manuscript Library, University of Pennsylvania.

Æc est eorum victus ratio: Storea Icirpea humi strata, cibum in eius meditul-
lio collocant, deinde in orbem assident viri ab vna parte, feminæ ab altera.
Cibus est mayzi grana elixa, eo quo superiore libro scripsimodo, boni admodum
saporis, ceruina aut alterius animalis caro & pisces: sobrii tamen sunt in victu
& potu, inde diuturno tempore viuunt, cum naturæ vim non inferant.

C

Figure 6. A Carolina Algonquian man and woman share a meal of cooked maize. A tobacco pouch, pipe, nuts, fish, shellfish, and cobs of maize are in the foreground. Thomas Harriot, *A briefe and true report* (1590). Courtesy Rare Book and Manuscript Library, University of Pennsylvania.

the choicest foods and rarest ingredients and to display social distinctions of status and gender. As evidenced by the feast offered to Barlowe by Granganimeo's wife and the feast offered by Tusser's fictional household to its Christmas guests, this was also true of both Indians and English. Nearly all English travelers found that food played an important role in early encounters and dominated many of them. Because of the inescapable connections between hospitality and the social standing of host and guest, such occasions were potentially fraught. Even in England, hosts were sensitive to slights, signals that the relative social positions of host and guest were perceived differently by both sides, and this was only more true in the Americas. English and Indian leaders closely observed each other's manners and customs, searching for meanings in a host's placement of his guests, his offer or withholding of particular foods, whether he washed his hands (and if so, whether he included others in this ritual), and a number of other possibly meaningful actions and objects. Although the nuances of this symbolic language could be lost in translation (and often were), Barlowe's account again shows that both sides clearly understood the seriousness of the occasion and, to varying degrees, grasped the meanings their counterparts sought to convey.

Recognizing the frailty of their initial efforts at settlement, that their claims could not proceed as if Indians were not there, most English leaders were careful to conform their behavior to native expectations as much as possible. Indians were neither a screen onto which English leaders might project their vision of authority and dominance nor a passive audience for English claims of authority. To describe early encounters in such a way suggests that they were conducted on English terms, when in fact English officials often had to allow for the presence of powerful, outspoken native leaders who sought to make similar claims in a similar way.[22]

Therefore, even on the frequent occasions when the parties encountering each other on the beaches of the Americas had never experienced such an encounter, both sides proceeded from the assumption that, in certain broad areas, their cultural assumptions overlapped. This perception of mutual understanding, however limited in actual fact, explains how it is that English travelers like Barlowe without any personal experience with Indians or the Americas could approach interactions surrounding food with the assumption that they understood and were understood. Early encounters were taut, contested negotiations, dynamic occasions limited by language but facilitated by symbolic expressions. Food was at the center of these occasions, a welcome gift, a common gesture, and a readily understood medium through which the two sides might convey a range of meanings.

Food in these many forms and meanings is the subject of the chapters that follow, a perspective that brings into focus features of the early period otherwise invisible, misunderstood, or overlooked. First, when English elites struggled with each other for precedence or negotiated with Indian leaders, they could not always rely on formal institutions, offices, and titles as props to their claims of legitimacy. Instead, they often made use of public occasions and appealed to ordinary men and women to support these claims, which shifts our understanding of the period's political culture onto new ground. *Political Gastronomy* argues that food lay at the heart of these public assertions of legitimacy in the early period.

A second and related point is that food always remained more than the sum of its symbolic resonances, however rich. The chief reason food played such a vital role in public assertions of legitimacy was that it combined biological necessity with symbolism. In other words, food was never *just* a symbol to be employed as a means of staking a claim to authority, whether by leaders in the English Atlantic world or writers who described their actions. Unlike other symbols of power, food had to be physically present—and ultimately consumed—in order to convey its full meanings, and when it was not, other symbolic assertions of legitimacy rang hollow. Further, because it is a daily necessity, food and the occasions associated with it—distributing rations, for example—could not be avoided and their meanings could not be downplayed, even when those meanings undermined a leader's efforts to assert his legitimacy. In this way, food's inescapable materiality provides a sure route to correcting an overemphasis on textual or symbolic claims to authority.[23]

The daily life of the early English settlements, especially those aspects of daily life that surrounded food, were dominated by Indians, a third feature that emerges clearly from this perspective. Indians were not important only when they negotiated formal treaties, entered churches, or appeared in combat. Their "existential centrality" to early settlers is more easily claimed than shown, but focusing on food makes this fact abundantly clear.[24]

Fourth, English understandings of food were broadly shared across the Atlantic scope of settlement. Not only did the English travel, trade, chart, fight, proselytize, and attempt settlements from Guiana to the Arctic, these efforts were all part of a coherent whole. In addition to bringing together regions more usually described as distinct, this approach incorporates the sixteenth-century efforts to explore and settle the northernmost parts of North America along with the more familiar seventeenth-century settlements. These early efforts drew massive investment, generated enormous interest, and left behind volumes of manuscript and printed sources that later travelers drew on (and sometimes carried with them).[25]

This approach is not without its limitations. Stressing the similar assumptions, strategies, and responses that marked English projects and the texts that described them unavoidably flattens the diversity of Native American cultures encountered by the English during the period in question. Similarly, this approach flattens both the regional diversity that made English travels and settlements in Newfoundland and Bermuda, to take two examples, so different and the many important changes that took place between 1570 and 1650. To embrace such a broad range of places, peoples, and events requires such compromises (and others), and to name them is not to wholly excuse their absence. But this book's purpose lies in exploring and explaining a feature of the early period whose importance has not yet been acknowledged.

Beginning with the broadest assumptions with which English travelers approached these encounters, *Political Gastronomy* progressively narrows its focus, chapter by chapter, in order to uncover the meanings passing back and forth at meals like the one Barlowe shared with his Algonquian hostess. English assumptions about food and leadership informed their choices of governors, admirals, and other officials for early voyages and determined how they equipped those voyages. Once they reached the Americas, these assumptions informed the ways English leaders conducted themselves in exchanges like those Barlowe described and how they interpreted Indians' conduct. When describing these occasions, English writers like Barlowe tried to shape their readers' perceptions with specific rhetorical strategies, and English elites often made use of similar strategies in their struggles with each other for primacy. Food lay at the heart of all these assumptions, encounters, strategies, and texts. The culmination of *Political Gastronomy*, the most symbolically rich of all stages, were formal meals like the one Barlowe described.

In one sense, this is a story limited to the early period of settlement, when the threat of hunger and the inability to impose English claims to authority on native groups necessitated negotiation. But by suggesting a richer understanding of the political culture of these years, *Political Gastronomy* contributes to recent scholarship that argues against a narrative of futility and dysfunction for the early period, replacing that familiar story with one of experimentation, a process of trial and error that eventually resulted in a durable model for

English settlement. By suggesting changes to the narrative of English origins, *Political Gastronomy* joins with other scholarship to reassert the continuities linking the early period to later events. What is more, the political culture of the early period did not dissolve after 1650, or 1700, and neither did food's importance. Although some of its expressions changed, food remained a reservoir of rich meanings connected to gender, social inequality, and political leadership.

In these ways, food offers historians a critical standpoint that sidesteps the question of whether England's settlements in the Atlantic world were dysfunctional in order to reveal what contemporaries envisioned as an appropriate social order, how that order should be manifest in everyday life, and how to respond when experiences diverged from the normative vision. This is not to say that food had only one meaning shared by the many parties involved, but because nearly every early settlement had problems supplying itself at the outset, food was a central concern everywhere. Everyone knew that hunger raised political questions as well as practical ones, and that these questions would play out in daily negotiations taking place across the English Atlantic world.

Chapter 1

"Commutative Goodnesse": Food and Leadership

One of the earliest and most weighty decisions facing the backers of England's early colonies was choosing a leader, and most writers on the subject were in agreement on the fundamentals. Richard Eburne, for example, wrote that "Governours and Leaders of the rest" should be chosen from "men of Name and Note." In other words, leaders were expected to be men whose "power and authoritie, greatnesse and gravitie, purse and presence" supported their claim to lead. The circularity of Eburne's reasoning—that "authoritie" and "greatnesse" qualified a man for positions that conferred precisely these qualities—derived from assumptions widely shared by the early modern English. Since all hierarchy had its roots in "the very order of Nature," as Eburne put it, one of these assumptions was that the powers of office and the qualities that legitimated a claim to hold it were mutually supporting.[1]

Another basic assumption was that the legitimacy of a leader could be seen in his ability "to order and rule, to support and settle the rest." William Strachey, a Virginia Company official who traveled to the Chesapeake in 1609, echoed these remarks when he described "order and governement" as "the onely hendges [hinges], whereupon, not onely the safety, but the being of all states doe turne and depend." Without them, he asked, "what society may possibl[y] subsist, or commutative goodnesse be practised"? To the early modern English, social order was the result of proper "governement," in Strachey's terms. The right sort of leader produced a harmonious society built on reciprocal ties binding the commons and their leaders to the benefit of all.[2]

These assumptions underlay all discussions and descriptions of leadership in the early period, and food was central to any image of an effective leader, whether Native American or English. Arthur Barlowe's descriptions of Granganimeo's authority over the Carolina Sounds, to take one example, were dominated by the varied and abundant foods he alone was able to provide the English travelers. Just as abundance was a sign of proper government, dearth encapsulated the opposite.

Nearly all of the familiar features of English society were absent in the early Atlantic world, and as a result disagreements soon emerged among English travelers, settlers, and metropolitan officials. The scholarly literature often infers a lack of coherence, not to mention competence, from these disagreements and the violence, hunger, disease, and death that marked nearly every settlement's first years. And yet given the substantial investment required, every feature of the early English settlements was carefully planned, then monitored and adjusted to maximize the chances of success. The choice of a leader was of paramount importance to a settlement's stability and profit, and the question received careful attention. But since no one could claim a record of success in building a profitable English settlement in the early period, there were no clear models to follow.

In their search for effective leaders, all those concerned recognized that some improvisation would be necessary. The leaders appointed to govern England's first efforts at settlement were not surprised to find themselves without the familiar props with which to stage a demonstration of their authority, but they were not entirely without guidance or precedent. They drew on others' experience and volumes of manuscript and printed sources to derive lessons that they thought would ensure peace, health, stability, and profit. The first English settlements in the New World represented the fruition of earlier efforts as much as the start of an English presence in the Americas, and English leaders set sail knowing they would have to observe carefully, adjust their expectations when necessary, and above all learn from their mistakes. Despite their differences, the backers and officials of all early projects shared the same assumptions about leaders' authority and the same goal of peaceful, orderly, and prosperous settlements. Just as it was for Thomas Tusser and Arthur Barlowe, abundant food was the most potent sign of these larger meanings.

The popularity of Tusser's *Five hundreth points of good husbandry* signals the extent of agreement on the normative model of English society that he sketched. The sort of rural household Tusser described, a social microcosm whose prosperity and order were encapsulated in the varied and abundant foods it produced, would take generations to establish in the Americas, not months or years. So would the horizontal and vertical social ties that interlinked such households on occasions like Christmas feasts. Rural elites, who in England played a vital role in mediating disputes and administering justice, were almost wholly absent in the early settlements, as were churches, whose hierarchy paralleled and supported secular inequalities. Even women, whose labor was essential to Tusser's idealized household, were rare. Since the hierarchies that structured English society were so tightly interwoven, the absence of churches, landlords, and (especially) families had sweeping effects.

Tusser among many others viewed the household, ruled by father, husband, and master, as the foundation of English society. A man's authority over his family was reproduced on a larger scale by the leaders of English villages, parishes, towns, and counties and culminated in the monarch's authority over the kingdom as a whole. All social inequalities, all reciprocal bonds between inferiors and superiors, stemmed from the same divine ordering. Richard Brathwaite summed up with a familiar metaphor: "As every mans house is his Castle, so is his family a private Common-wealth, wherein if due government be not observed, nothing but confusion is to be expected." The magistrates of the Massachusetts Bay settlement similarly proclaimed that "A family is a little common wealth, and a common wealth is a greate family."[3]

The contemporary understanding of the connection between these very different relationships was not metaphorical. A father was the king of his family and a king the father of his subjects: the source of these two claims to authority was the same divine "order of Nature" that Eburne described. Accordingly, household government was linked directly in English law to the formal levels of government. Nathaniel Butler, governor of Bermuda, defined petty treason as the murder "by an inferior" of his or her "superior," one who "hath a dominion, and a kind of majestie and regalitie as it wer, in ruleinge over the sayd partie." The examples Butler gave were a child murdering a parent, a servant his master or mistress, or a wife her husband. Petty treason represented an attack on the same structure of hierarchy and authority that supported and legitimated the monarch: a threat to any one of these hierarchical relationships was a threat to the whole edifice that supported monarchical power.[4]

English writers often described social relationships by reference to the human body, pointing out that the health and success of the entire organism depended on direction by a head but also on the strength and cooperation of its various parts. Gardening and horsemanship were other metaphors for authority, examples in which order and beauty were produced by the skill, knowledge, and control of a single person. Each expressed the same vision of society and authority. Whether the lower orders of society were akin to horses, flowers, or feet, they could not be orderly or productive without the direction of the higher orders, the "commutative goodnesse" William Strachey described as characterized by "order and governement." As Kevin Sharpe has pointed out, it "might take a considerable imaginative leap for us to comprehend that bee-keeping might be or become an ideological act," but government of bees and of a kingdom expressed the same fundamental truths.[5]

One of these was that inequality was part of the natural order and necessary for a stable, harmonious, and prosperous society. The result of a leader's effective exercise of authority was not submission or obedience for its own sake but the mutual benefit of rulers and those subject to them. One of the most tangible symbols of this unequal yet harmonious interdependence was food, produced by the labor of the lower orders but abundant owing to the government of those at the top.

These idealized descriptions provided elites with a comforting set of assumptions: that the social hierarchy was rooted in a divine plan and therefore was immutable in its basic contours and that their place at its higher reaches was secure. But in practice, the social relationships of early modern England were neither as static nor as consensual as these descriptions suggest. Elites often found that their claims to precedence and their ability to exercise the powers of political office—in other words, their authority—required the consent of ordinary people, and this was never more true than during periods of widespread hunger.

One of the distinctive features of early modern English politics was the fact that the monarch and Privy Council depended on lesser officials in the localities to interpret and implement royal policies. Local elites might serve as "deputy lieutenants, JPs, town magistrates, sheriffs and grand jurors," while their "middling and even more humble" neighbors could expect to serve as "constables, beadles, tithingmen, nightwatchmen, vestrymen, overseers of the poor, trial or petty jurors, or even perform a stint in the militia or trained bands."[6]

Although the authority of a leading official like a justice of the peace or lord lieutenant was granted by the monarch, the social standing that qualified a man to hold such an office had its roots in the local community. In part, this explains the circularity of Richard Eburne's reasoning that officials should be chosen from among those who already have "greatnesse" and "authoritie." These characteristics of office also meant that a man's authority was rooted in local ties as much as connections to powerful superiors. By mediating the desires of those above him in the hierarchy with local assumptions about the proper role of those in authority, an officeholder solidified his claim to local status and effective leadership. In this way, local elites might be named to more powerful offices, which opened up new patronage opportunities, augmented local standing, and improved chances for further honors.[7]

Just as Tusser's Christmas feast signaled a prosperous and properly ordered household, abundance of food was a sign of a properly ordered commonwealth. Dearth was among the most powerful signs of the opposite, a challenge local officeholders struggled to explain and address in the late Tudor period. The nature of the problem was complex. A rapid rise in England's population in the second half of the sixteenth century occurred as elites engrossed larger landholdings and enclosed common lands. As a result, England's larger, younger population had a much harder time finding access to land and livelihoods than had previous generations, which contributed to unprecedented geographic mobility. Alongside these economic and demographic trends, the "Little Ice Age" contributed to lower crop yields and shorter growing seasons. When harvests failed in 1586, 1594–98, 1623–24, and 1630, the situation seemed to many to have reached crisis proportions.[8]

To contemporary elites, the nature of these social and economic changes was opaque, and their response was based on fear of instability, on a perceived rent in the social fabric symbolized by the increasing visibility and mobility of the poor. The response at the highest levels of government was to treat vagrancy as a "status crime." Even absent any criminal actions committed by vagrants themselves, vagrancy violated elites' normative social vision, which expected that every able-bodied young man would be rooted to a community, a family, a parish, a landlord, a master. The "masterless men" roaming the countryside posed a threat to the social order because they were not subject to "government" in the all-embracing early modern sense of the term.[9]

The response of the Privy Council and the monarch was premised on the assumption that vagrancy was an individual failing worthy of punishment. The idle poor, meaning the able-bodied, were to be punished as criminals and the deserving poor supported by their local community. Crucially, this distinction between idle and deserving poor was made at the local level, by local officeholders based on local considerations of how much relief was available and whether or not those seeking it could make a claim on the resources of their neighbors. The role of local officeholders in this process was to respond to perceived threats to social order and stability in a way that resonated with

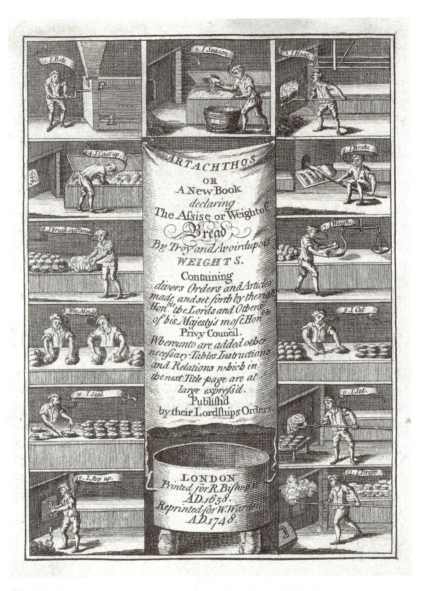

Figure 7. Surrounding the title of John Penkethman's *Artachthos* (London, 1638; repr. 1748) are a series of illustrations depicting the various stages in baking bread, from bolting the flour (top left) to drawing the baked loaves from the oven (bottom right). Penkethman's text described the Assize of Bread, the English law that specified the permissible weight for a loaf of a given price. Courtesy Rare Books Division, The New York Public Library, Astor, Lenox and Tilden Foundations.

the widely shared assumptions of reciprocal obligation, to reconcile elite demands for order with the commons' demands for relief.[10]

The purest expression of these assumptions was the dearth orders, issued by the monarch to guarantee the availability of grain during times of scarcity. In the medieval period, when landlords often collected rents in grain and other foods, elites were expected to distribute the stored food under their control to those subject to their authority, an enactment of the reciprocal obligations thought to underpin society as a whole. In the early modern period, rents were more likely paid in cash, but elites' role in guaranteeing the availability of food in the monarch's name remained. In place of grain stores under manorial control, local elites oversaw the operation of grain markets within their jurisdiction. According to the dearth orders, grain was only to be transported on market day, to ensure that private sales did not circumvent the public market. Before the market opened, local officeholders met with sellers to establish a price for the grain. Those who needed grain to feed their households were given the first opportunity to purchase small quantities as soon as the market opened, and commercial buyers could enter the market only afterward to buy larger amounts.[11]

As was true of any statute, the effectiveness of the dearth orders depended on the efforts of local officeholders. But it was especially important in this case that those efforts be undertaken in public, in full view of what Frank Whigham has called the "enfranchising audience" of the local community. By exercising the powers of their office in public, local elites demonstrated that the commons' assumptions of reciprocity held true, that leaders cared for ordinary people and would act in times of need to ensure their well-being. Officeholders' conduct on these occasions was closely watched. The expectations of the commons had to be considered in a leader's performance of his duties, since ordinary people were hardly passive observers, especially during times of dearth. Officials understood that just as a successful performance of office might augment social standing, the reverse was also true.[12]

When harvests failed, urban areas that relied on grain markets and distant suppliers were most severely affected, as were smallholders, tenants, and farmers of marginal land. Not everyone suffered the effects of dearth equally, a fact that was plain for everyone to see, and the conclusion contemporaries most often drew from these observations was that the causes of scarcity lay in unequal distribution, not inadequate harvests. Blame was usually placed on greedy middlemen profiting from their knowledge of markets and others' hunger. When hunger bordered on famine, the commons took action

THE

Defcription and Ufe

of

The Table of Affife

or

Weight of Bread.

He Table being digefted in 20 pages or fides, every page conteyneth 3 parts or divifions, whereof the firft towards your left hand fheweth the price of a Quarter of wheate in the market, the reft fhew the Affife or weight of the feverall forts of Bread by *Troy* and *Avordupois* weights, to wit, of the halfe penny white, the penny white, the penny wheaten and the penny houfhold, as their feverall Inftitulations or words on the heads of each part or columne doe evidently declare, what is to be noted.

Under the word *Troy.*

O. fignifies Ounces, P. Penny weight, and the figures thereunder refpectively placed doe fignifie fo many Ounces and Penny weights.

Under the word *Avoirdupois,*

O. fignifies Ounces, D. Drams, and the figures thereunder refpectively placed fignifie fo many Ounces and Drams.

Againe, 73 (being a denominator) fignifies a dram broken

or

---

or divided in 73 parts and the figures thereunder (being Numerators) doe fignifie fo many parts of a dram fo broken or divided.

Laftly   Under the words *Troy* and *Avordupois.*

Nu. fignifies Numerators, and in the next columne towards your right hand, De. fignifies Denominators, the figures under De. fignifying a penny weight *Troy* broken or divided into fo many parts; and the figures under Nu. in *Troy* weight doe fignifie fo many parts of a penny weight fo broken or divided. The figures under Nu. in *Avordupois* weight fignifying fo many parts of one part of a Dram in 73 divided.

Now for the Ufe of this Table.

Suppofe, when the fecond wheate, (which is the fecond wheat being unground) is fold for iiiil. the Quarter in the market, you would know what the Affife or weight of Bread fhould be in London, or any other City, Borough or Corporate Towns where white, wheaten and houfhold are ufually baked and fold.

In it felfe, confidering that the Baker there is allowed by the wifdom of the State, and viz. for the baking of a Quarter of wheate, fo much above the price of the fecond wheat in the market. Looke in the 27 page of the Table under the word (Price) for iiiil. viz. and directly againft it you fhall finde the weight of the halfe penny white by *Troy* weight is 1 ounce 19 penny weight and 15 parts of a penny weight in 43 divided. By Avoirdupois weight 2 ounces, 1 dram and 18 parts of a dram in 73 divided, and 7 parts of one part of the 73 in 43 divided. Of the penny white, by *Troy* weight 3 ounces 18 penny weight and 30 parts of one penny weight in 43 divided. By *Avordupois* weight 4 ounces 2 drams and 36 parts of one dram in 73 divided and 14 parts of one part of 73 in 43 divided. Againe, looke in the 18 page of the Table under the word (Price) for iiiil. viz. and directly againft it you fhall find the weight of the penny wheaten by *Troy* weight, 5 ounces 18 penny weight and 2 parts of 4 penny weight in 43 divided. By *Avordupois* weight 6 ounces 3 drams 54 parts of a dram in 73 divided. Of the penny houfhold, by *Troy* weight 7 ounces 17 penny weight and

D 2   17.

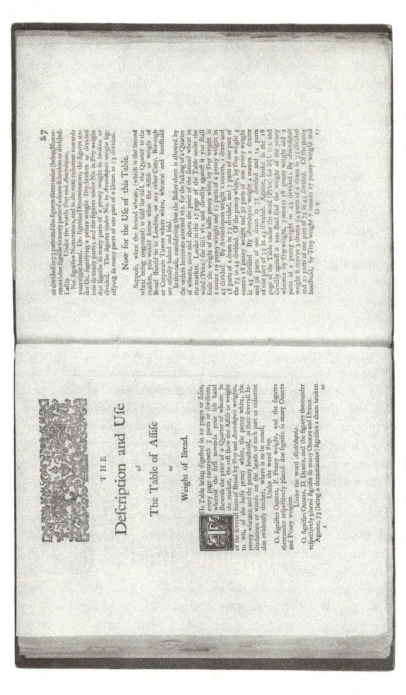

Figure 8a. Pages from John Penkethman's *Artachthos* give instructions for determining the weight of a loaf of bread based on the market price of wheat. John Penkethman, *Artachthos* (London, 1638; repr. 1748), 26–27. Courtesy Rare Books Division, The New York Public Library, Astor, Lenox and Tilden Foundations.

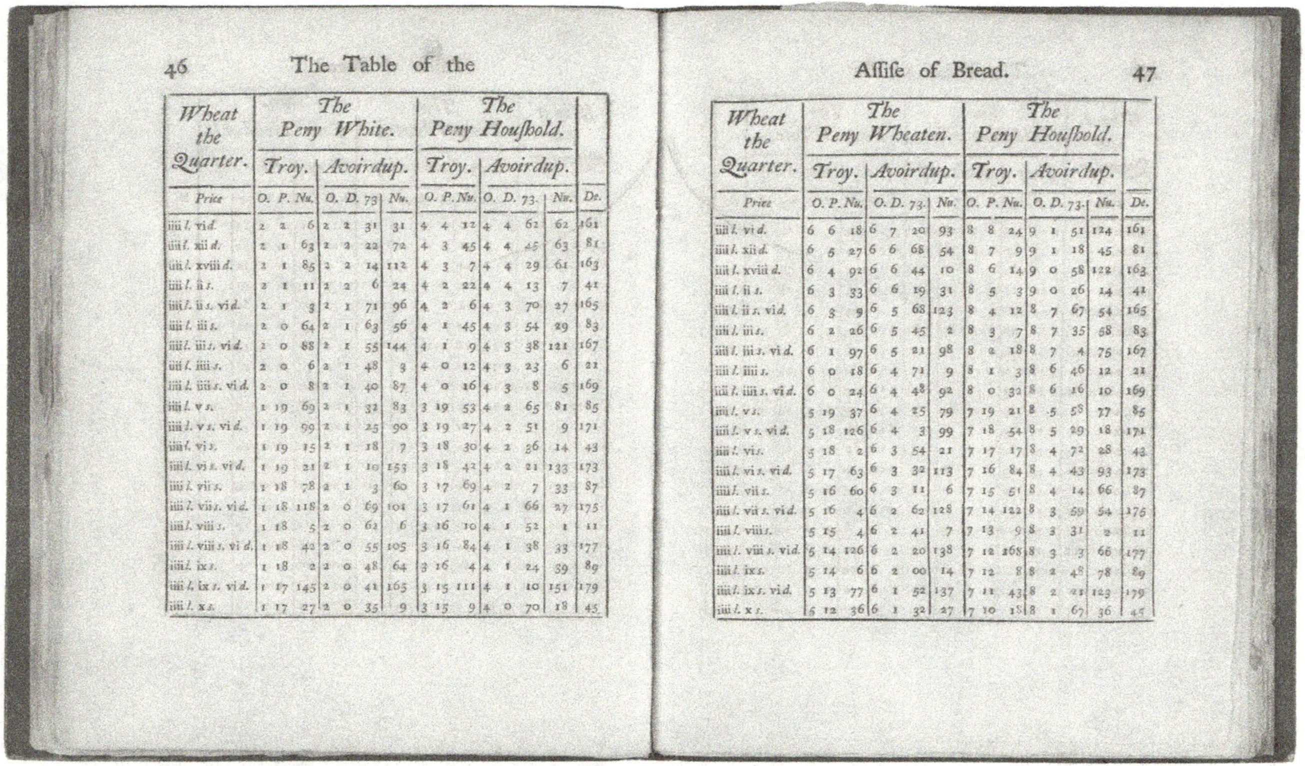

Wheat the Quarter.	The Peny White.							The Peny Houſhold.							
	Troy.			Avoirdup.				Troy.			Avoirdup.				
Price	O.	P.	Nu.	O.	D.	73	Nu.	O.	P.	Nu.	O.	D.	73.	Nu.	De.
iiii *l.* vi *d.*	2	2	6	2	2	31	31	4	4	12	4	4	62	62	161
iiii *l.* xii *d.*	2	1	63	2	2	22	72	4	3	45	4	4	45	63	81
iiii *l.* xviii *d.*	2	1	85	2	2	14	112	4	3	7	4	4	29	61	163
iiii *l.* ii *s.*	2	1	11	2	2	6	24	4	2	22	4	4	13	7	41
iiii *l.* ii *s.* vi *d.*	2	1	3	2	1	71	96	4	2	6	4	3	70	27	165
iiii *l.* iii *s.*	2	0	64	2	1	63	56	4	1	45	4	3	54	29	83
iiii *l.* iii *s.* vi *d.*	2	0	88	2	1	55	144	4	1	9	4	3	38	121	167
iiii *l.* iiii *s.*	2	0	6	2	1	48	3	4	0	12	4	3	23	6	21
iiii *l.* iiii *s.* vi *d.*	2	0	8	2	1	40	87	4	0	16	4	3	8	5	169
iiii *l.* v *s.*	1	19	69	2	1	32	83	3	19	53	4	2	65	81	85
iiii *l.* v *s.* vi *d.*	1	19	99	2	1	25	90	3	19	27	4	2	51	9	171
iiii *l.* vi *s.*	1	19	15	2	1	18	7	3	18	30	4	2	36	14	43
iiii *l.* vi *s.* vi *d.*	1	19	21	2	1	10	153	3	18	42	4	2	21	133	173
iiii *l.* vii *s.*	1	18	78	2	1	3	60	3	17	69	4	2	7	33	87
iiii *l.* vii *s.* vi *d.*	1	18	118	2	0	69	101	3	17	61	4	1	66	27	175
iiii *l.* viii *s.*	1	18	5	2	0	62	6	3	16	10	4	1	52	1	11
iiii *l.* viii *s.* vi *d.*	1	18	42	2	0	55	105	3	16	84	4	1	38	33	177
iiii *l.* ix *s.*	1	18	2	2	0	48	64	3	16	4	4	1	24	39	89
iiii *l.* ix *s.* vi *d.*	1	17	145	2	0	41	165	3	15	111	4	1	10	151	179
iiii *l.* x *s.*	1	17	27	2	0	35	9	3	15	9	4	0	70	18	45

Wheat the Quarter.	The Peny Wheaten.							The Peny Houſhold.							
	Troy.			Avoirdup.				Troy.			Avoirdup.				
Price	O.	P.	Nu.	O.	D.	73.	Nu.	O.	P.	Nu.	O.	D.	73.	Nu.	De.
iiii *l.* vi *d.*	6	6	18	6	7	20	93	8	8	24	9	1	51	124	161
iiii *l.* xii *d.*	6	5	27	6	6	68	54	8	7	9	9	1	18	45	81
iiii *l.* xviii *d.*	6	4	92	6	6	44	10	8	6	14	9	0	58	122	163
iiii *l.* ii *s.*	6	3	33	6	6	19	31	8	5	3	9	0	26	14	41
iiii *l.* ii *s.* vi *d.*	6	3	9	6	5	68	123	8	4	12	8	7	67	54	165
iiii *l.* iii *s.*	6	2	26	6	5	45	2	8	3	7	8	7	35	68	83
iiii *l.* iii *s.* vi *d.*	6	1	97	6	5	21	98	8	2	18	8	7	4	75	167
iiii *l.* iiii *s.*	6	0	18	6	4	71	9	8	1	3	8	6	46	12	21
iiii *l.* iiii *s.* vi *d.*	6	0	24	6	4	48	92	8	0	32	8	6	16	10	169
iiii *l.* v *s.*	5	19	37	6	4	25	79	7	19	21	8	5	58	77	85
iiii *l.* v *s.* vi *d.*	5	18	126	6	4	3	99	7	18	54	8	5	29	18	171
iiii *l.* vi *s.*	5	18	2	6	3	54	21	7	17	17	8	4	72	28	43
iiii *l.* vi *s.* vi *d.*	5	17	63	6	3	32	113	7	16	84	8	4	43	93	173
iiii *l.* vii *s.*	5	16	60	6	3	11	6	7	15	51	8	4	14	66	87
iiii *l.* vii *s.* vi *d.*	5	16	4	6	2	62	128	7	14	122	8	3	59	54	176
iiii *l.* viii *s.*	5	15	4	6	2	41	7	7	13	9	8	3	31	2	11
iiii *l.* viii *s.* vi *d.*	5	14	126	6	2	20	138	7	12	168	8	3	3	66	177
iiii *l.* ix *s.*	5	14	6	6	2	00	14	7	12	8	8	2	48	78	89
iiii *l.* ix *s.* vi *d.*	5	13	77	6	1	52	137	7	11	43	8	2	21	123	179
iiii *l.* x *s.*	5	12	36	6	1	32	27	7	10	18	8	1	67	36	45

Figure 8b. A selection from the Assize of Bread giving the weight of, from left to right, a halfpenny loaf of white bread, a penny loaf of white bread, a penny loaf of wheat bread, and a penny loaf of household bread according to the market price of wheat per quarter (eight bushels). The first two columns are mislabeled. John Penkethman, *Artachthos* (London, 1638; repr. 1748), 46–47. Courtesy Rare Books Division, The New York Public Library, Astor, Lenox and Tilden Foundations.

according to their understanding of the problem. Suspecting that middlemen were to blame, crowds were most likely to take action not simply when food was scarce but when grain was being moved from or through their communities in times of dearth. On such occasions, groups formed to demand that local officials regulate the distribution of grain in the area under their control and stop its transportation.[13]

For example, in 1596 Sir Ferdinando Gorges, captain and commander of the fort at Plymouth (and later in life a promoter of English settlements in Maine), reported to his patron Sir Robert Cecil that crowds had threatened to seize grain being moved through Plymouth's port. Gorges wrote, "had not your warrant of staye Come as it did," the "necessitie of the poore woulde have inforced theim to have offered som owtrage, bothe uppon the shippe and goodes." Gorges's letter makes plain both the fact that the residents of Plymouth viewed themselves as entitled to the grain moving out of their city's port and that Cecil's order to stay the shipments restored public order.[14]

As investors and officials named leaders, wrote charters and instructions, and fitted out ships to make the transatlantic journey, they drew on these assumptions about food and a leader's authority. But everyone involved recognized that leaders would have to improvise when faced with unexpected challenges in unfamiliar surroundings. The most glaring daily reminder of this fact was the relative absence of women, and therefore of orderly households, in most early settlements. Some leading men felt it necessary to bring their wives if at all possible. Sir Thomas Gates sailed for Virginia in 1611 with his wife and daughters. Henry Ashton, governor of Antigua, urged the Earl of Carlisle to take up his claim to the West Indies personally and to bring along his wife. As the Virginia House of Burgesses put it in a petition to the Virginia Company, "in a newe plantation it is not knowen whether man or woman be more necessary."[15]

The Virginia Company's response to this problem in 1621 was recruiting women of reputable character and transporting them to the Chesapeake in hopes that their presence would "tye and roote the Planters myndes to Virginia by the bonds of wives and children." Newfoundland, another largely male settlement, also sought women in order to ensure stability and a more permanent footing. Richard Whitbourne wrote that in addition to fishermen "some others may goe to be as Servants in the voyage, which may be Tradesmen, and their wives; who will labour fitly in the fishing, whiles it lasteth, and afterwards continue there to plant." The situation in the early settlements was not unprecedented: many early settlements were similar to seasonal fishing camps or military expeditions, in which the division of labor was not exclusively associated with gender. But as their leaders tried to root their settlers more permanently, or as those settlers found themselves without women for extended periods of time, a solution was obviously needed.[16]

Women were needed in the settlements because English society was unthinkable without the rural households Tusser described, but even absent their roles as wives and mothers women were needed to perform specific and highly gendered labor, especially in connection with food. Governor Edward Wynne, for example, wrote from Newfoundland to England asking the settlement's backers to send "a couple of strong maids, that (besides other worke) can both brew and bake." The desire here was clearly for skills, not marriage partners, although the "strong maids" would have had excellent chances for marriage in early Newfoundland. Father Andrew White brought women servants along with him to Maryland to do the washing for his party. Virginia's settlers wrote to England asking for women to fill another traditional and vital role: that of nursing the sick. For lack of women, the writer claimed, the company's "poore Tenantes that have nothing dye miserablie through nastines & many departe the World in their owne dung for want of help in their sicknes." The letter went on, "Wherefore for prevention I could wish women might be sent over to serve the Company for that purpose for certayne yeares whether they marry or no."[17]

Even so, women remained scarce in Virginia, and to compensate the Virginia Company sent to the colony "markams workes of husbandry & huswifry bound togeather and . . . the like of Gowges &c." By reaching for the works of Gervase Markham and Barnaby Googe, Virginia's leaders admitted in part that their settlers' English experiences were inadequate to the task they faced. Markham's works doubtless included *Countrey Contentments*, published in 1615 with later editions under the title *The English House-wife*, and *The English Husbandman* (1613), if not other selections from this prolific author. Googe's work in question was *Foure Bookes of Husbandrie*, first published in 1577 with the most recent edition in 1614. Given the challenges of planting in the New World, Markham's advice on soil, farm equipment, and animal husbandry must also have been valuable. But more revealing is the fact that the settlers needed instruction on the unfamiliar tasks of "huswifry": brewing, baking, cooking, and preserving food.[18]

The image of Jamestown's early settlers leafing through the pages of housewifery manuals suggests that men might do the work of cooking and

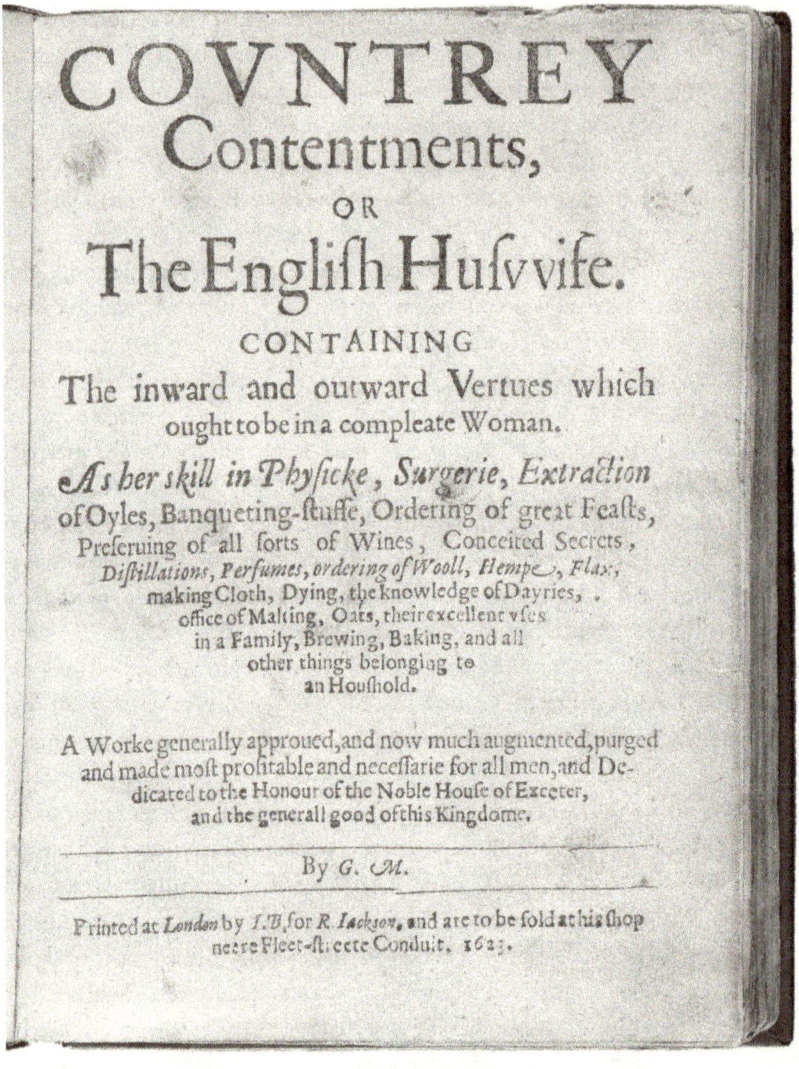

COVNTREY
Contentments,
OR
The Englifh Hufvvife.

CONTAINING

The inward and outward Vertues which
ought to be in a compleate Woman.

As her skill in Physicke, Surgerie, Extraction
of Oyles, Banqueting-ftuffe, Ordering of great Feafts,
Preferuing of all forts of Wines, Conceited Secrets,
Diftillations, Perfumes, ordering of Wooll, Hempe, Flax,
making Cloth, Dying, the knowledge of Dayries,
office of Malting, Oats, their excellent vfes
in a Family, Brewing, Baking, and all
other things belonging to
an Houfhold.

A Worke generally approued, and now much augmented, purged
and made moft profitable and neceffarie for all men, and Dedicated to the Honour of the Noble Houfe of Exceter,
and the generall good of this Kingdome.

By *G. M.*

Printed at *London* by *I.B.* for *R. Jackson*, and are to be fold at his fhop
nerre Fleet-ftreete Conduit, 1623.

Figure 9. The title page of Gervase Markham's popular housewifery manual
Countrey Contentments (1623) suggests the variety of skills expected of
English women, including medicinal knowledge, brewing, baking, and
dairying. Skills like these were in short supply in most early settlements.
Courtesy The Huntington Library.

baking when women were absent, but only in unusual circumstances. When women were present, English men proved extremely reluctant to do work they associated with women. One powerful example comes from early Plymouth. In many early settlements, servants and single men were placed in the households and under the government of older, often married men. These ad hoc "families" underscore both the importance of the household to more formal levels of government and the improvisations that marked most settlements. Massachusetts Bay governor John Winthrop was not unusual in having a large "family" that included many members not related to him by blood or marriage. In Virginia in 1621 (and probably before), improvised families were a way to absorb the large number of company tenants—servants with indentures binding them to the Virginia Company—into existing households. There was nowhere else for these men to stay and no other way to ensure their good conduct than by, in effect, delegating responsibility to established men in the settlement. In Plymouth, the situation was very similar: servants and single men were placed in other men's homes and under their government. But Plymouth's governor William Bradford was faced with unexpected opposition on this point.[19]

One way Plymouth was distinct from other English settlements was in the terms of its patent, which stated that all property—land, houses, and improvements—was to be held in common for seven years. After this, everything was to be divided among the investors, both those who had advanced money and those who had traveled to settle. This meant that all the work Plymouth's settlers did building houses and barns, clearing and fencing land, and raising animals would be shared out after seven years in proportion to one's initial investment. In 1623 Plymouth's settlers protested what Governor William Bradford called the "Common Course and Condition" for a variety of reasons, but Bradford described the roots of Plymouth's discontent as lying in a desire for landownership. Accordingly, Bradford granted temporary possession of small plots to individuals and (nuclear) families. These plots were small, and they could be neither sold nor inherited, but according to Bradford, the result was a noticeable increase in food production and a marked decrease in dissent. Bradford may well have followed the example of the Virginia Company, which beginning in 1616 also distributed small plots to individual settlers in hopes of increasing food production. However he came to his decision, the solution Bradford proposed has shaped subsequent scholarly interpretations: since a form of property in land defused the conflict, the thinking goes, its causes were primarily based in a desire by English migrants to hold land. Certainly most English officials in the New World followed Virginia's example in recognizing the importance of landownership to social stability.[20]

A closer look at Bradford's discussion of this episode reveals that private landownership was not the primary area of concern. Mary Beth Norton has shown that ideas about gender and household government—particularly women's responsibility for preparing and serving food—underlay many of the disagreements. Additional concern was raised about how distinctions among Plymouth's settlers were reflected in the distribution of the common food stores. One cause of "confusion and discontent," Bradford claimed, was the forced equality common labor and common supplies brought about in the settlement. "The aged and graver men," Bradford wrote, "to be ranked and equalized in labours and victuals, clothes, etc., with the meaner and younger sort, thought it some indignity and disrespect unto them." Without familiar cues of status, Plymouth appeared uncomfortably homogeneous from the perspective of "aged and graver men" accustomed to deference. These men resented that their social standing was not reflected in the quantity and quality of their food rations and even, possibly, the way meals were prepared and served. Bradford remarked that "Upon the point all being to have alike, and all to do alike," younger men "thought themselves in the like condition" as men who would have been their social superiors in England, "and one as good as another." Bradford recognized that this conclusion undermined the "mutual respects" on which the social and political hierarchy of England and Plymouth depended.[21]

According to Bradford, dissatisfaction was also voiced by the "meaner and younger sort" as well. Bradford wrote that the "strong, or man of parts, had no more in division of victuals and clothes than he that was weak and not able to do a quarter the other could; this was thought injustice." Here again, food, not land, lay in the foreground of the settlers' complaints, which once again focused on the quantity and quality of rations distributed from the common stores. The "weak" Bradford referred to in this quotation were likely the same "aged and graver men" who protested Plymouth's equal division of the common stores for very different reasons. In this case, healthy and strong young men, who did the bulk of the settlement's physical labor, claimed the right to more food for themselves.[22]

Not only did Plymouth's "young men, that were most able and fit for labour and service" protest the "injustice" of receiving the same rations as less able men, they also "did repine that they should spend their time and strength to work for other men's wives and children without any recompense." The settlement's young, single men were supporting older, married men's households, helping to support women and raise children that would be of no benefit to them later in life. This arrangement would have been familiar, and fair, if these younger men had some "recompense," as servants and apprentices did in England. But under the terms of the Plymouth patent, none of the settlers were accumulating property of any kind, not to mention wages.[23]

Here again, the "aged and graver men" had a very different perspective. Bradford wrote that "for men's wives to be commanded to do service for other men, as dressing their meat, washing their clothes, etc., they deemed it a kind of slavery, neither could many husbands well brook it." In this case, husbands protested the presence of single men in their households who expected to rely on the labor of their wives. Bradford's distribution of land resolved this issue by giving each of Plymouth's husbands control of his household's labor, restoring governance over their wives and children. The repeated mentions of food during the course of these disagreements, as a marker of status and gender distinctions and a defining feature of household government, are a sign of how intertwined food was with daily life, household government, and politics on a formal level in the early settlements.[24]

When Bradford wrote that because of the similar living conditions of Plymouth's settlers, some "thought themselves in the like condition, and one as good as another," he suggested another unique characteristic of early English settlements, one encapsulated in his own position as governor. Bradford's middling social rank, like that of many men who held positions of authority in the early settlements, belied Eburne's assumption that leaders would be "men of Name and Note," and in particular men of "purse and presence." In similar terms, Sir Thomas Smith defined a gentleman as a man "who can live idly and without manual labour and will bear the port, charge and countenance of a gentleman."[25] Dressing and acting the part of a leader, in a range of public spaces including "the household, the hunting field, the parish church, quarter sessions and assizes," as one study has put it, was only half the equation. The other half was the acceptance by the local community of a claim to gentle status, which was signaled by standing when an official entered a room, removing one's hat, and similar gestures. At meals, leading figures would expect to be served first, to be presented with the choicest parts of the choicest dishes, to eat and drink from vessels that indicated their status, signs that doubtless lay at the heart of Plymouth's struggles over status and precedence. Just as gentle status was confirmed by a man's treatment by his peers, to "deny public gestures of respect," even on ordinary occasions like these, "was in effect to deny a claim to authority."[26]

English officials of widely varying rank expected continually to receive such signs that peers and inferiors had accepted their authority. But men like William Bradford lacked the social status that would ordinarily support a claim to hold the powerful office of governor and lacked experience in presenting the proper image of a leader. Robert Gray, in a promotional tract entitled *Good Speed to Virginia*, felt the need to advise colonial officials on a point that their metropolitan counterparts would have regarded as obvious. Gray wrote that "there must be a speciall care in the Magistrate how to carry himselfe in his place and order: for herein consists the verie maine matter of the successe of this businesse." Naming men of humble origins to powerful offices was a necessary step when men of high rank were few, but it opened the question of an officeholder's authority in unusual ways.[27]

Often, the first signs of trouble were not long in coming. All English voyages of settlement carried at least two men with exclusive claims to authority: the commander of the fleet and the leader of the proposed settlement. In most cases, the admiral held supreme authority until the voyage had reached its destination, when the governor took command of the settlement and the men and equipment assigned to it. Provisions, as one might expect, were a crucial issue. In most cases, these were under the control of the admiral, who had first claim to adequate supply for his return voyage. Whatever stores remained were left under the control of the governor. Nathaniel Butler commented on the frequency and destructiveness of clashes between "sea and land-commandours," which he claimed was "a qualetye over common to the English." According to Butler, these clashes tended to produce "a separation of the company," no matter how desperate the circumstances. Even worse, the "sea and land-commandours" could move from mutual "jealousies" to "disgraceing one another, and crossinge their designes."[28]

A remarkable example comes from Martin Frobisher's 1578 voyage to Baffin Island. The voyage was intended to secure huge piles of what was thought to be gold- and silver-bearing ore, which raised the stakes of the voyage considerably. According to one English traveler, there was "heynous contention" between Frobisher and Captain Edward Fenton, who had been named lieutenant general and governor of the proposed settlement. In a typical example of this sort of conflict, "Captaine Furbusher sayd to Captaine Fenton that he had none Aucthoritye at all in anye matter but by him," and before long the sailors and the "gentlemen" had nearly come to blows. In an extreme case, these disagreements culminated in an exchange of gunfire.[29]

Metropolitan officials anticipated that this sort of conflict would arise and took elaborate precautions to avoid it. A common strategy was to conceal the names of the man or men appointed to lead the settlement until after arrival. The backers of Frobisher's 1578 expedition included in their written instructions the following elaborate plan "for the succession of the Generall governour of this whole voiage yf he should fortune to die for avoydinge of stryffe & kepinge of peace & fryndship." The plan called for "the names of iiii gentlemen [to be] privatlie sett downe." These men were named to succeed Frobisher, the governor general, "one after the other." The names were "wrytten in paper included in balls of wax, sealed with hyr Majesties sygnett and put into boxes, locked with severall keys." These elaborate precautions were intended to prevent peeking, which it was feared might lead to the sort of clashes that eventually broke out between Fenton and Frobisher. It bears emphasizing that when sailors and gentlemen, "sea and land-commandours," exchanged bullets to settle the question of precedence, none of their contemporaries interpreted this as evidence of failure, social breakdown, or incompetence. However striking these disagreements to modern eyes, they indicated how important signs of respect were to English officials. The elaborate, almost ridiculous precautions taken to avoid them are clear evidence that metropolitan officials understood the nature of these disagreements and were willing to improvise a solution that seemed reasonable to all concerned.[30]

Precautions like this might keep the peace during the voyage (although not for Frobisher), but the basic problem reemerged as soon as the ships made landfall: how to secure the legitimacy of a leader chosen from men of basically equal rank. John Robinson, pastor of the Pilgrims' church in Leyden, addressed a letter to the Plymouth settlers on just this subject. Since none of the settlers was of "speciall eminencie above the rest," Robinson argued that the Plymouth colonists must choose their leaders based on other criteria. But Robinson argued that after their election, leaders must be treated with the respect their office deserved, whatever their social status beforehand. John Winthrop made precisely the same point: that although the choice of leaders lay in the hands of the Massachusetts Bay freedmen, once "being called by you," Winthrop claimed, the magistrates "have our Authoritye from God." When he was named governor, Winthrop naturally "furnished my selfe with servants and provisions accordingly in a farr greater proporcion than I would have done, hadd I come as a private man or as an Assistant onely," fitting out his person and, equally important, his table in a way that suited his new station.[31]

The Virginia Company took this a step further in one instance by securing a knighthood for George Yeardley at the time of his appointment as governor in 1618. Thomas Warner was hastily knighted for the same reasons in 1629, soon after his appointment as governor of Saint Christopher (Saint Kitts). But these steps did not fix the underlying problem. In a petition to the Virginia Company, the planters of Virginia echoed Eburne in asking for a man of status to lead the plantation, declaring it "an approved truithe, that Great Actions are carryed with best successe by such Comanders, who have personall Aucthoritye & greatness answerable to the Action." Contradicting the sentiments of Robinson, the planters went on to say that "all cannott be select." A "Comanders Eminence, or Nobillitye" would, the planters argued, "by Nature . . . yeild a willing submission withowt contempt, or repyning." But the same "Aucthoritye conferrd upon a meane man," one merely "selected owt of their owne Ranke, shall nevar be able to compell" the same submission and respect. The petition goes on to insist that this request was not meant "to derogate from the Governor who nowe holds the Place," the very same Sir George Yeardley whose knighthood had apparently failed to secure the appropriate "Reverence" and "willing submission."[32]

William Bullock, who inherited an estate in Virginia's Warwick County from his father Hugh, reached the same conclusions. Bullock wrote in 1649 that since "Government is no other then the extraction of power into the hand of one or more," it stood to reason that "those in whom the power rested, ought to be for wisdome, justice, and integrity, drawn from the very quintessence of the people." Instead, the Virginia Assembly's "great Port" was "maintained by an Adventurers purse" rather than their own.[33]

Improvised arrangements like these clearly show that the situation in the Americas had no precise analogue in the English experience. Since there was no generally agreed-on set of qualifications for a leader, and since few if any men had a clear record of relevant accomplishments, the choice of leaders was largely subjective. This opened a further dimension to the question of authority in the English Atlantic world, the rhetorical efforts to characterize certain leaders as worthy of the offices, men, money, and supplies entrusted to them. Interested parties pressed the case of one would-be official or another, claiming that his experiences, abilities, and knowledge were adequate to the task at hand (and his rivals' claims were not). Accordingly, one goal of many early written accounts was to sketch a portrait of English leaders conducting themselves in unfamiliar circumstances according to familiar expectations. By doing so, texts represented their authors' knowledge as authoritative, their experiences as expertise widely applicable to the unfamiliar environment and challenges of the Atlantic settlements.[34]

Often rival claims held up quite different images of a leader as a model, but in every case food was as fundamental to these images as it was a tangible sign of effective leadership. Even in England, different languages of politics were used to describe what sort of man was best fitted for leadership, how he should conduct himself as a leader, and what the effects would be. These languages shared a great deal with Tusser's idealized vision, but each was based on slightly different assumptions and referred to different images of a leader. As Winthrop did by fitting out a table to suit the office of governor, some colonial officials hoped to display their own status and social separation from their inferiors through the foods they ate, how, where, and with whom they ate them, and the way they distributed the common stores. Others effaced social differences by joining ordinary settlers in their daily labor and at their daily meals. Many officials intoned the biblical injunction that those who do no work should not eat; other writers emphasized the Christian duty of charity and hospitality. But in each case, they revealed that food was an essential aspect of leadership and the texts that sought to legitimate it.[35]

The patriarchal vision of a hierarchy based in birth and inscribed on the landscape provided one common set of symbols and references. The analogies and metaphors that elites used to describe the social order—a human body, a beehive, a family—encapsulated both this patriarchal vision of society and a remedial vision of how to restore society's proper functioning. Authors discussed the need to excise diseased tissue, to encourage surplus population to form its own "hive" in the settlements, and to employ stern discipline to correct the waywardness of youth. Ideas like these, elite responses to the fear of social breakdown represented by poverty and vagrancy, contributed to the criminalizing of the "wandering poor" embodied in the poor laws.[36]

Elites' understanding of the problems facing early settlement projects was also shaped by humanism, which gained increasing influence in England during the sixteenth century. From an education based on the study of classical authors, especially the writings of Cicero and Tacitus, Elizabethan humanists developed a language of politics that focused on the interlinked threats of individual moral decline and despotic government. According to classical writers and their early modern translators and interpreters, tyranny proceeded almost naturally from the pursuit of base ends on the part of citizens and leaders alike: the sacrifice of the common good to private wealth, ambition, and luxury. Slavery and despotism could be countered only by citizens' active service of the commonwealth, the fundamental humanist virtue known as the *vita activa*.[37]

Although a humanist education was available only to the elite, the humanist vocabulary linking politics and morality was familiar to those without this education. By observing and emulating the language and conduct of those at the upper reaches of the social order, officeholders lower down the social scale made humanism a shared set of "beliefs, rituals, and social practices that provided alternative frames of reference within which contemporaries conceived of the operation of power." Humanism was a "language of duty" whose references to virtue and corruption, the *vita activa* and luxury were understood by English officials of nearly any social standing and education. This language was equally useful in praising a man's abilities and assigning blame: both promoters and critics of England's early settlements made use of the language of luxury, virtue, and corruption to make their case.[38]

Humanism was attractive to those involved with travel and settlement for specific reasons. Some of the Roman writers from whom humanists drew their ideas specifically discussed the Roman experience with colonies. Early modern writers found a clear analogy between their efforts to civilize and convert Native Americans and the Roman conquest and colonization of Europe, which spread Roman civilization to Britain. These historical references had negative overtones as well. As some classical writers noted, the Roman treatment of conquered peoples was a clear indication of the empire's descent into tyranny. Tacitus held up the primitive virtues of both the German tribes and ancient Britons as a counter to Roman luxury. In the *Germania*, he suggested that the Germans, and not the Romans, were exemplars of virtue. In the *Agricola*, the military virtues of the Britons were ultimately sapped by the "demoralizing temptations of arcades, baths, and sumptuous banquets." In this way the English experience with colonization resonated with a humanist discussion of virtue and corruption.[39]

Another reason for the attraction of humanism for promoters of English settlements was the central importance of rhetoric to both enterprises. Writing was one form of the *vita activa* valued by humanists, a laudable contribution to the commonwealth on the part of its citizens. This was especially true of those promoting settlement in the Americas. Since English colonial projects were funded and organized by private backers rather than the Crown, rhetoric was vital in attracting the investors needed to launch a voyage of discovery or settlement. With the goal being to replicate the Roman example of civilization through conquest, or to advance England's wealth and glory, writers served important ends.[40]

Although humanism derived from specific texts and a specific education and employed a recognizable language of politics, it is important not to mischaracterize it as an exclusive or rigid doctrine. Not everyone who received a humanist education presented himself in this light, and no one did so on every occasion. Authority in the early modern English Atlantic world had many possible bases: textual, religious, aristocratic, and military, for example, and each of these was characterized by different kinds of knowledge, different sorts of responsibilities, and different languages for asserting and contesting claims to authority. The choice of how to present oneself and how to describe one's actions was partly a strategic decision aimed at securing the patronage of a specific man or group.

The term "idleness" illustrates how the patriarchal and humanist languages of politics were used to explain the circumstances of the early English settlements and how the same term, central to both languages, meant very different things in each. "Idleness" was commonly used by contemporary writers to describe what had gone wrong in early America. Plymouth's Edward Winslow offered several reasons for his own inability to command the labor of his subordinates, including "self-love" and "the base disposition of some drones." The accusation of "self-love" was a charge that settlers lacked the virtue necessary to dedicate themselves to the common good, phrased in a humanist language of political and social obligation. Winslow made the same point in slightly different terms when describing "three things [that] are the overthrow and bane . . . of plantations": the "vaine expectation of present profit," the "ambition" of leaders who seek only "a transitory base honour in themselves," and the poor selection of colonists. In many cases, settlers failed to work diligently toward seemingly self-evident goals: fortifying settlements; clearing fields and planting crops; fishing, hunting, and gathering food. But "idleness" is more than a descriptive term for the behavior of ordinary settlers. To contemporaries, "idleness" accounted for a breakdown in the obedience due to leaders by referring to the behavior of ordinary settlers.[41]

To encourage their inferiors to diligent labor, and in hopes of convincing metropolitan backers that they did not share the "idleness" of ordinary settlers, Winslow and many other leaders "followed men to their labors" in an effort to lead by example. Captain John Smith led Virginia's gentlemen off to work by setting his own day's labor as the standard others must follow. Perhaps influenced by Smith's example, Virginia's president and first leader, Edward Maria Wingfield, claimed that he "never hid" his own hands "from labor." Bermuda governor Richard Moore worked alongside his settlers, and for his part Moore may have been influenced by the example of Sir George Somers. While shipwrecked on Bermuda in 1609–10, Somers "laboured from morning untill night" building a ship, "as duelie as any workeman doth labour for wages."[42]

Smith claimed to have spent time studying Machiavelli, and it was perhaps there that he learned virtuous men "are of such reputation and so much example that good men desire to imitate them and the wicked are ashamed to hold to a life contrary to them." Smith's self-presentation was clearly phrased in the language of humanism, as a leader who hated "basenesse, sloath, pride, and indignitie, more then any dangers . . . that loved action more then words, and hated falshood and covetousnesse worse then death." Smith's example countered Sir Thomas Smith's definition of a gentleman as one "who can live idly and without manual labour." By crossing this stark line, leaders signaled that desperate circumstances—especially hunger—required that they improvise a demonstration of "commutative goodnesse," since they could not live up to its usual terms by guaranteeing the food supply as spelled out in the dearth orders.[43]

Similar descriptions of leaders joining the commons told a different story when phrased in the patriarchal language of politics. When, for example, John Fitzherbert wrote in 1530 that by a strict interpretation of the biblical injunction that those who do no work should not eat, "the kynge/the quene/nor al other lordes spirituall & temporall sholde nat eat/without they sholde labour the whiche were uncomely/& nat convenyent for such estates to labour." Fitzherbert clearly believed that although "work" was required of each of society's different parts, this injunction was not meant to imply that nobles and commons should do the same sorts of labor.[44]

Writing of Virginia, the *True Declaration* reported that gentlemen worked in the settlement in an inspirational and supervisory role befitting their station, not the actual labor Smith demanded of them: "Nor should it be conceived, that this busines excludeth Gentlemen, whose breeding never knew what a daies labour meant; for though they cannot digge, use the square, nor practise the axe and chizell; yet may the stayde spirits of any condition finde how to employ the force of knowledge, the exercise of counsell, the operation and power of their best breeding and qualities."[45]

William Strachey wrote that Virginia governor Sir Thomas Gates joined his settlers at work in just this way, with his "speech and authority" rather than any actual physical labor. Nevertheless, his presence was welcome: "How contentedly," Strachey claimed, "do such as labor with us go forth when men of rank and quality assist and set on their labors!" Elaborating elsewhere on the patriarchal vision of a leader insisting on separation from the commons at the same time his "waies and carriage" inspired those whose duty it was to labor, Strachey signaled the public nature of English politics: "examples at all times prevaile farre above precepts, men beeing readier to bee led by their eies, then their eare, for seeing a lively pattern of industry, order and comlinesse, wee are all of us rather swayed unto the same by a visible object, then by hearing much more in wel instructed Arguments." By the force of his example—though not his actual labor—a leader could sway ordinary men and women to obedience without compulsion. As Smith had, Strachey may have been influenced by Machiavelli in this regard.[46]

Sometimes, Strachey's optimism was misplaced, and settlers refused to work, or did so reluctantly. Puritan minister and Virginia Company investor William Crashaw responded to Virginia's early troubles by blaming its settlers as "the scumme and skouring of the streetes . . . raked up out of the kennels" of London. By doing so, Crashaw made use of the rhetorical figure of "idleness" that underpinned the poor laws, explaining the troubling failure of apparently qualified elites to ensure a stable and prosperous settlement in the Chesapeake by blaming the criminal "idleness" of its settlers.[47]

Strachey's patriarchal assumptions are plainly seen in the way he understood "idleness," but this was not the only way it was understood. Captain John Smith, equally fond of the term, described "idleness" as a disease of Virginia's gentlemen, who refused to do any actual labor. Insisting on leading by inspiration rather than actual example, Smith argued that Virginia's gentlemen had abandoned humanist virtue, the *vita activa*.

Both men agreed on the symptoms of "idleness" and on its course. In both the patriarchal and humanist languages, starvation was the inevitable outcome of a society poisoned by idleness. As Thomas Tusser had suggested, abundant food was the result of diligent work by each member of the household in his or her own sphere. Nathaniel Butler, governor of Bermuda, claimed that the reverse was as true of colonies and kingdoms as it was of rural households when he wrote that "from no worck, no care, noe government, what could be had but privations, that is to saye noethinges"? William Strachey made a similar point: "if riot and sloth should both meet in any one of their best families in a country most stored with abundance and plenty in England," he wrote, "what better could befall unto the inhabitants, landlords, and tenants of that corner than, necessarily following, cleanness of teeth, famine, and death?" Strachey was especially clear that responsibility ultimately lay with leaders. To ensure "health, plenty, and all the goodness of a well-ordered state" required compelling "the headless multitude" to perform the labor required of them. Without government, in this sense, Strachey claimed, the commons would be unwilling "to sow corn for their own bellies."[48]

Both the humanist and patriarchal languages supposed that a leader would serve as a model, an inspiration, an embodiment of order. Perhaps the clearest example of this fact came in 1609, after Thomas West, Baron De La Warre, had accepted the title of governor of Virginia and agreed to travel to the Americas to govern the settlement personally. The written accounts of this very rare episode—one of very few cases in which a titled aristocrat held office in the New World—clearly illustrate the patriarchal ideal. Accounts of De La Warre's arrival and investiture optimistically assumed that Jamestown's troubles would fall away upon the arrival of a leader with, as Virginia's settlers later put it, "personall Aucthoritye & greatness answerable to the Action."[49]

De La Warre's arrival also illustrates the special role of food in displays and accounts of leadership, since his arrival in the Chesapeake, in the summer of 1610, came at the settlement's most desperate hour. Relations between the colonists and the Chesapeake Algonquians had collapsed. Without access to Indian supplies and unable to leave their fort to forage, Jamestown barely survived the winter of 1609–10: reports of cannibalism among the English in Virginia suggested a total breakdown, not just of political authority but of the most fundamental social bonds.

De La Warre's deputy, Sir Thomas Gates, arrived in the Chesapeake first, in the spring of 1610. Gates quickly recognized the magnitude of Jamestown's troubles and admitted the impossibility of continuing without hope of supply from the Chesapeake Algonquians or from home. Reluctantly, he ordered Jamestown abandoned in June, barely succeeding in preserving the settlement itself, which some of the fleeing colonists had wanted to burn to the ground as they left. But on their way out to sea, the fleeing settlers encountered Lord De La Warre's fleet, loaded with supplies. The new arrivals followed the survivors back up the James River and reestablished the settlement.

De La Warre was welcomed into the ruined fort, whose gates hung from their hinges and ordnance lay buried in the ditches beyond the walls, with elaborate ceremony befitting the occasion if not the surroundings. A color guard conducted him inside, where his commission as lord governor and captain general was read to the assembled settlers. De La Warre then accepted the patents, commission, and official seal of the settlement from Sir Thomas Gates.[50]

Then, in what was doubtless a pregnant moment, De La Warre rose to address the starving settlers, many of whom had tried to burn the fort to the ground days before. In his speech, De La Warre blamed the state of the settlement on their "many vanities and their idleness" and threatened ominously "to draw the sword in justice to cut off such delinquents which I had much rather draw in their defense to protect from enemies." De La Warre then shifted his emphasis, cheering the settlers "with the knowledge of what store of provisions I had brought for them." The language was patriarchal to the core, derived from the same assumptions that underpinned the poor laws and dearth orders alike. Idleness on the part of the commons was Jamestown's problem, and the solution was twofold. With a natural leader in place, his sword would defend the settlement and punish the idle, while the stores he brought would support his claim to lead by guaranteeing the survival of those who followed him.[51]

A later account of these events emphasized the role of food in bringing order to early Jamestown. Alexander Whitaker traveled to Virginia in 1611 as minister to the new settlement at Henrico. While there, he wrote a letter describing his experiences that was published by the Virginia Company in 1613 under the title *Good Newes from Virginia*. In his letter, Whitaker described De La Warre's arrival (which he did not witness) as a providential deliverance of the colony and a restoration of order. Whitaker drew clear connections between proper government, the orderly functioning of society, and the efficient distribution of food: "by Gods blessing," Whitaker wrote, the settlers "never wanting government, they never wanted bread, for him that would take paines and do his dutie." Whitaker's qualification exempted the idle poor from the reciprocal obligations of patriarchalism, as De La Warre had in his speech. Government, bread, and labor provided a sort of shorthand, an equation that laid out the principal bonds between society's upper and lower orders.[52]

To Whitaker, De La Warre's person and the stores he controlled represented a properly functioning society, with a titled aristocrat at the top of the social order whose authority to punish idlers and to reward diligent labor with food was unquestioned. The most serious threat to this ideal state came from idleness, a disease of the commons whose most salient symptom was failure to follow the orders and example of their superiors. The very different uses of the term "idleness" by men like Smith and De La Warre, combined with other examples—Frobisher's sealed orders and Yeardley's hasty knighthood—suggests that the leaders of England's first settlements confronted an uncomfortable fluidity regarding their most basic political assumptions. In their efforts to answer fundamental questions—What legitimated an official's claim to lead? What obligated the commons to accept those claims?—English leaders recognized the necessity of improvisation. They drew on rich assumptions regarding the character, qualities, and conduct of a leader, but as De La Warre and Smith both knew, at bottom the success of these claims depended on sufficient supplies of food.

Chapter 2

"Art of Authority": Hunger, Plenty, and the Common Stores

Whitaker's account of Lord De La Warre's arrival in the Chesapeake borders on the providential, and his description of De La Warre's installation as James-town's governor on the magical. Nevertheless, when he wrote of Virginia's colonists that "never wanting government, they never wanted bread, for him that would take paines and do his dutie," Whitaker drew on fairly ordinary assumptions. Leaders like De La Warre in England or (especially) in the Americas were expected to inspire the commons to diligent labor, and a leader's authority rested on his ability to punish idlers and feed the diligent when they could not feed themselves. When they distributed the common stores, leaders demonstrated that their authority had its basis in reciprocal relationships: guaranteeing survival in exchange for obedience and especially labor.[1]

Most early English settlements tested whether the converse of Whitaker's statement was also true: wanting bread, they called into question the authority of their leaders. Jamestown's infamous "starving time" is the best known example of a hungry settlement teetering on the brink of collapse until De La Warre's arrival put everything right, at least in Whitaker's eyes. But food's close association with authority, with "government," was not limited to times of famine and dearth.

When supplies of food were adequate and firmly under their control, English leaders were secure in their positions. Accordingly, most English projectors went to exorbitant lengths to supply their settlements with sufficient and familiar provisions, recognizing that travelers and settlers expected familiar foods like wheat to be part of their diet, often a substantial part. Part of the reason for this lay in fears rooted in humoral theories of climate, diet,

BVE arrostito intiero in publica piazza ripieno di diuersi Pollami, et altri animali comestibili da distribuirsi al volgo in occasione dell'allegrezze celebrate in Roma dall'Emin.mo R.mo Cardinal OVARD di NORFOLCIA e dall'Ill.mo Sig. Agente di sua MAESTA' BRITANNICA per la nascita dell'Altezza Reale di GIACOM PRENCIPE DI WALLIA Primogenito di GIACOMO SECONDO Re' della gran Bretagna e della Regina MARIA BEATRICE sue Consorte, Sacramenti, & & . . . .

Figure 10. An extravagant public feast given in Rome to celebrate the birth of James II's firstborn son clearly associates abundant food with kingship. Bread and wine are handed out to clamoring crowds surrounding an enclosure within which a crowned bull is turned on a spit and basted. In the right foreground, a crowd jostles for loaves of bread; in the left foreground, a man has overindulged in free wine. In the center, the heads of poultry and other animals, stuffed inside the bull, are visible. "Bue arrostito intiero in publica piazza ripieno di diversi Pollami . . ." (Rome, van Westernon, 1688).

and health that English bodies would be changed by foreign foods and a foreign climate. To live in a foreign environment required English travelers to overcome these fears, although when confronted with the need to eat strange plants and animals, food's most basic meaning—the caloric—was often the most important. Hunger regularly trumped fears of hybridity.

There is another important connection between what Whitaker summed up as government and bread. Adequate supplies of food could produce order in the early English settlements only when they were under the effective control of a leader. This was true when settlements faced scarcity (as at Plymouth and Jamestown) as well as the unusual case of Bermuda, whose leaders faced the unprecedented challenge of plenty. The leaders of all three settlements reached the same conclusion: if settlers did not depend on them for basic needs, leaders faced significant obstacles. Bermuda illustrates the important point that abundance could be as fatal to authority as dearth.

In 1609, the Virginia Company carefully considered the lessons of its first two years and decided that fundamental changes were needed for their investment to bear fruit. Jamestown needed a significant infusion of men and supplies and a single strong leader, a governor to replace the fractious and bitterly divided council. Improving their chances for success, the Virginia Company recruited Thomas West, Baron De La Warre, to take up this powerful office, and Sir Thomas Gates, a veteran of military service in the Low Countries, to serve as deputy governor until his arrival. To outfit the supply fleet that would bear Gates to Virginia, the Virginia Company lowered the share price of its stock, a move that attracted a number of new, smaller investors. This new investment fitted out the largest fleet to date, which sailed for the Chesapeake bringing a new leader, a new charter, roughly eight hundred new settlers, and provisions to expand on the foundation laid in the settlement's first two years.

The new charter had been carefully considered and the fleet more than adequately manned and supplied, yet from these promising beginnings followed nothing but disaster. The supply fleet was scattered by a storm. Gates, along with the other men sent to lead the colony, was shipwrecked on Bermuda and feared dead. As the remaining ships straggled up the James River to the frail settlement, new arrivals and the survivors of the first years struggled with each other for control. Meanwhile, hundreds of men, sickly and weak after their long voyage, crowded into the already cramped fort. The Chesapeake's punishing drought—these events occurred during the driest period in six hundred years—made it all but impossible for Jamestown's settlers to feed themselves on the small plots they had managed to clear. As food supplies ran low, the English began demanding provisions from the Chesapeake Algonquians and plundering their corn stores when they refused. Relations between English and Indians quickly deteriorated into open hostility, and the English settlers at Jamestown were soon imprisoned within their own walls.[2]

The desperate winter that followed has been known ever since as the "starving time," the most familiar example of food's close connections with politics in the early English Atlantic world. At Jamestown during these months, hunger drove the settlement to the brink of collapse. Chesapeake Algonquians killed settlers who ventured outside to forage in the woods for food, leaving some corpses "with their mowthes stopped full of Breade" to mock their desperate hunger.[3]

George Percy, son of the Earl of Northumberland, led Jamestown briefly during this period, and in his account of the starving winter of 1609–10, foods illustrated Jamestown's slow decline. Hungry English men (and a few women) were forced to eat strange and distasteful foods: "haveing fedd uponn horses and other beastes as long as they Lasted we weare gladd to make shifte with vermine as doggs Catts Ratts and myce." The Spanish ambassador to England, Don Alonso de Velasco, reported in 1610 that a batch of new arrivals had "died from having eaten dogs, cat skins and other vile stuff." The meaning was clear: to eat foods normally considered unfit was a sign that the norms of civilized life had been abandoned out of desperation, with potentially fatal results.[4]

Simply to eat a specific plant or animal does not always have these meanings. To eat proscribed foods out of necessity was a sign of extremity, but to eat these things voluntarily conveyed a quite different message. On a 1586 exploratory voyage near Roanoke, for example, Ralph Lane realized that the Carolina Algonquians would not trade with him for food. Rather than turn back immediately, his men suggested to Lane that if supplies grew desperately short, they could eat the expedition's two mastiffs, "upon the pottage of which with sassafras leaves (if the worst fell out) the companie would make shift to live two dayes," enough time to float back down river to the Roanoke settlement. For Lane, eating dogs was a sign that he and his men accepted hardship and sacrifice in the name of a larger goal. On a voyage into Chesapeake Bay, Captain John Smith inspired his men to continue by referring to Lane's example and in particular to the willingness of Lane's party to continue until the mastiffs were eaten. To eat dogs and cats without hesitation conveyed still another meaning to English travelers and readers—barbarism or savagery—but at bottom, all of these meanings rested on the importance of distinguishing between permissible and proscribed foods.[5]

According to Percy, after killing and eating every animal inside the fort and then boiling and eating their shoes and other leather goods, the starving settlers "weare inforced to search the woodes and to feede upon Serpents and snakes." Sir George Somers, admiral of the 1609 supply fleet, indicated the depth of hunger at Jamestown in a letter to the Earl of Salisbury by saying that the settlers "had eaten all the quick things that were there and some of them had eaten snakes or adders." Eating snakes, especially poisonous snakes, signaled that another line had been crossed, another step had been taken separating the starving from the norms of civilized life.[6]

The last step on this path was cannibalism. Percy recounted the infamous story of a man salting his wife's body to preserve it during the "starving time," and the Spanish ambassador to England reported to Philip II that "when one of the natives died fighting, they dug him up again, two days afterwards, to be eaten." Another account corroborates these stories and adds the nauseating detail that Jamestown settlers also ate human excrement. To eat these things signaled the extreme of desperation.[7]

Percy's account drew on other descriptions of famine, many of which also featured examples of cannibalism. These accounts echo Percy even in describing cannibalism's most extreme form, when family members eat one another. As one scholar of the subject has noted, the broad similarities like these ultimately derive from biblical accounts. In this light, descriptions of parents eating their children or men their wives are important "not as a particular example but as a universal type of famine." The story Percy meant to tell, a slow decline into desperate hunger, was plotted with foods: dogs, cats, and mice; then snakes; and finally human beings. Its larger importance to the story of political culture in the early English Atlantic world lies in the fact that images of food conveyed a range of meanings that other aspects of social life cannot. Percy could find no other way to describe famine than by reference to eating.[8]

Jamestown's desperate winter of 1609–10 is the most dramatic example of food's importance to political authority in the early English Atlantic world, one where authority disintegrated along with the most fundamental social relationships. But Jamestown's suffering was unique in many ways. By recruiting and equipping settlers in such large numbers to replace its losses, the Virginia Company operated on a scale unprecedented for the English at the time. Refusing to abandon its efforts as others had, the Virginia Company poured money and men into its project, hoping to find a viable model before the supply of either ran dry.[9]

A symbol far more broadly applicable to the English experience in the early period was the ship's stores that embodied Lord De La Warre's providential restoration of "order and government" to Jamestown. As long as the stores held out, leaders like De La Warre could order walls built and repaired, a guard posted, and hundreds of other crucial tasks performed because every day labor and obedience could be requited with a meal. Under circumstances like these, the meanings of food derived from more subtle distinctions than either starvation or salvation. The contents, quality, and quantity of the food stores were a central concern of every English voyage and settlement.

As early as Martin Frobisher's 1578 voyage, it was generally agreed that settlers should be provided with eighteen months' provision. These stores would feed them during the difficult first months, the so-called "seasoning" period when all travelers faced high mortality, and after that as they built houses and cleared fields. Only after this work was done could settlers be expected to survive from the produce of their own fields, animals, and labor.[10]

Naval stores served as the basis of most early settlements' supply. One scholar of naval provisions has stated that "meals for the ordinary seaman aboard British navy ships remained virtually unchanged from the Middle Ages to the mid-nineteenth century, depending as they did on three basic items: preserved meat, beer, and ship's biscuit." N. A. M. Rodger has reconstructed the terms agreed between the Crown and Edward Baeshe, appointed "General Surveyor of the Victuals of the Seas" in 1550. Baeshe agreed to provide a standard ration, which consisted of one pound of bread (biscuit at sea) and a gallon of beer per day. On the four "flesh days" of the week, each sailor would receive either two pounds of fresh beef, one-half pound of salt beef, or one-half pound of bacon. On the three "fish days" (Wednesday, Friday, and Saturday), the ration was one-quarter of a stockfish or four herrings plus four ounces of butter and one-half pound of cheese. In the late eighteenth century, these basic provisions were supplemented by others. Sailors in this later period expected two pounds of salt pork and four pounds of salt beef, two pints of dried peas, three pints of oatmeal, eight ounces of butter, twelve ounces of cheese, and one pound of ship's biscuit per week. Their drink was one gallon of beer per day.[11]

The question of which foods to bring on a voyage was largely a matter of which foods could be preserved to last two or three months in a ship's hold and a year or more afterward. The Virginia Company published a broadside in 1622 listing the essential provisions for travelers to the Chesapeake. The bare minimum according to this source was meal, peas, oatmeal, aqua vitae, oil, and vinegar. Beef, pork, fish, bread, peas, and oatmeal were the more ample provisions for Thomas James's near-fatal effort to find a Northwest Passage in 1633. On board ship, William Wood pointed out, most travelers would be unfamiliar with the routine naval stores provided for each traveler as part of the cost of passage: "salt beef, pork, salt fish, butter, cheese, peas, pottage, water gruel, and such kind of victuals, with good biscuits, and six-shilling beer." Wood recommended that travelers also "carry some comfortable refreshing of fresh victual," for example, conserves, wine, oil, prunes, sugar, eggs, bacon, rice, poultry, sheep (for meat and milk), and bread. Other sources amplified Wood's advice, suggesting that wealthier planters bound for New England bring meal, malt, salted beef and pork, dried peas, groats, butter, cheese, vinegar, distilled spirits, and mustard seed. Poorer planters were advised that they could do without the malt, beef, pork, alcohol, and salt. Subsequent migrants to New England, and to a lesser extent other settlements, could bring money with which to buy what they needed in the New World.[12]

Many accounts of voyages to the New World included lists like these, and most, if not all, agreed on the fundamental elements of the English diet in the Atlantic settlements, although prices and amounts varied somewhat. Sailors and settlers in the northern region generally received a ration of salt fish, and by providing salt and fishing tackle other settlements implied that this would be a staple of the diet.[13] The Virginia Company, facing constant complaints of short supply in the settlement, tried to standardize a ration for colonists in 1620, settling on three barrels of English grain per person per year, which amounted to roughly one bushel per month, or two gallons per week. If supplemental foods were available—ship's stores like peas, oatmeal, or biscuit or Indian crops like maize—the ration could be adjusted somewhat, to one pound of meal a day (roughly half the standard ration) plus a pint of peas or oatmeal. But it is clear from the Virginia Company's reports that a diet based on meal alone was a drastic measure.[14]

These rations were unfamiliar but not wholly foreign, since every English household preserved food for the winter by salting, pickling, and smoking flesh and barreling up grain. In the relatively abundant season between springtime and the harvest, each adult family member of a yeoman household in Stuart England could expect half a pound of butter, cheese, meat, or fish per day. Poorer households would subsist almost entirely on dairy products, supplemented only occasionally with meat. In addition, each adult member could expect one-quarter pound of "porridge meal," one pound of bread, some fruits and vegetables if available, and one gallon of skim milk, whey, beer, or cider.

In leaner times, two pounds of bread, nine ounces of dried peas, and three and one-half ounces of cheese would suffice. These foods were similar to those that accompanied most early voyages, with the exception of dairy products. But since all were dried or salted, the overall diet was lacking in what Wood called "comfortable refreshing of fresh victual." Notably lacking were the vegetables often underrepresented in reconstructions of the early modern English diet. Many of these rely on probate inventories, which often included butter, cheese, bacon, grain, and other preserved foods as marketable assets. Others infer foods from the presence of animals or equipment for dairying, malting, or other tasks. None of these sources account for the fresh vegetables common in the English diet, some of them raised in kitchen gardens and others growing wild. The lack of these foods on board ship would be felt immediately.[15]

Wood's remarks to travelers on smoothing their adjustment to a new diet was a sign that travelers understood and accepted that their diets would not be the same as in England, at least not at first. The Virginia Company underscored this point by providing for maize as a supplement to the usual rations. It was quite another thing to replace English with New World foods entirely. Although they were surrounded by plants and animals that sustained a native population uniformly described as strong and healthy, and although they were often forced by necessity to make a trial of American crops like maize, early travelers and settlers were skeptical that these foods could properly nourish English bodies.[16]

All New World foods were suspect, but maize was the focus of concern for a variety of reasons. Nearly all early descriptions of Native American society and culture mention maize. Many describe native origin myths surrounding it, underscoring the grain's centrality to the culture and diet of most (though not all) of America's native peoples. According to Roger Williams, the Narragansetts believed that maize and beans were gifts from the spirit world: "the Crow brought them at first an Indian Graine of Corne in one Eare, and an Indian or French Beane in another, from the Great God Kautántouwits field in the Southwest from whence they hold came all their Corne and Beanes." Thomas Morton reported that "Kytan," a deity living in the west, "makes corn grow, trees grow, and all manner of fruits." When Morton's informants died, they expected to go to Kytan's "house . . . where they eat all manner of dainties, and never take pains (as now) to provide it."[17]

The gift of these spirits was not only the foods themselves but the remarkable ways they supplemented and complemented each other. By itself, maize is deficient in two vital amino acids, and because it is also deficient in niacin, a B vitamin, a diet composed largely of maize can lead to pellagra. Beans provide the nutrients that maize lacks, making the combination perfect from a nutritional standpoint. Since beans fix nitrogen in the soil, they prolong the fertility of cornfields, which would otherwise be rapidly depleted. Finally, the two crops were more literally intertwined: planted among the corn, beans climbed the cornstalks as each plant grew.[18]

According to humoral theory, maize's close association with Native American culture and religion extended to Native American bodies. Medical theories derived from Hippocrates and elaborated by Galen were based on the four humors—blood, phlegm, black bile, and yellow bile—and their corresponding qualities of heat and moisture (blood was hot and moist, for example, black bile cold and dry). Disease was the result of a humoral imbalance, and medicine was the art of readjusting the humors to achieve a healthy balance. However, all human bodies did not have the same ideal balance of humors. Some people and groups were naturally dominant in one or another humor and were categorized by medical writers by the supposed effects of this humoral mixture: sanguine or phlegmatic, melancholy or choleric. Humoral composition, or temperament, varied over an individual lifetime, differed between men and women with the same diet and environment, and was different for rich and poor, laborers and leisured. Despite these variations, early modern authorities on health believed that certain climates induced in human bodies native to that climate a particular set of humoral characteristics and that these had a determining effect not only on human bodies but on nearly every aspect of life, including morality, religion, and politics.[19]

According to medical writers, climate had the same determining effect on people, plants, and animals, which meant that the animal and plant foods of a given region were perfectly suited to human bodies native to that region. Medical authorities warned that to live in a foreign climate and to subsist, even in part, on the foods it produced might transform English bodies, with a corresponding change in temperament. For this reason, English writers in the early period feared the effects of foreign environments and the foods native to them on English bodies adjusted to a very different set of environmental circumstances, finding native foods "unsatisfying or even dangerous."[20]

Although maize was the chief concern, other New World foods were described by English writers with suspicion. Some noted that just as New World plants might change the bodies of European men and women, these plants might change the bodies of European animals in a similarly profound way. Thomas Gage, an English Catholic who traveled to the Spanish New World and wrote an extensive account of his experiences, was unimpressed to say the least with his diet. In "Spain and other parts of Europe a mans stomack will hold out from meale to meale, and one meale here of good cheer will nourish and cherish the stomack foure and twenty houres," Gage wrote. But in America, Gage claimed, just "two or three houres after a good meale of three or foure severall dishes of Mutton, Veale or Beefe, Kid, Turkies, or other Fowles, our stomackes would bee ready to faint." Gage suggested that environmentalism could also work in a reverse fashion. He was served "hedgehog" on his travels (which must have been a different animal, since the hedgehog is not indigenous to the Americas). Gage wrote: "Of this meat I have also eaten, and confesse it is a dainty dish there though I will not say the same of a Hedgehog here; for what here may be poyson, there may be good and lawfull meate, by some accidentall difference in the creature it selfe, and in that which it feeds upon, or in the temper of the air and climate."[21]

Gage's confusion regarding why meats that "seemed as fat and hearty, excepting the Beefe, as ours in Europe" was cleared up by a "Doctor of Physick," who blamed its lack of "substance and nourishment" on the New World climate. The "pasture . . . is dryer and hath not the change of springs which the pastures of Europe have, but is short and withers soone away," Gage's informant told him. According to Gage's Spanish informants, Queen Elizabeth I had come to similar conclusions regarding the fruits of the New World, proclaiming "to some that presented unto her of the fruits of America, that surely where those fruits grew, the women were light, and all the people hollow and false hearted."[22]

William Bradford feared that the "change of air, diet and drinking of water" demanded by the Plymouth planters' settlement in a new climate "would infect their bodies with sore sicknesses and grievous diseases." A sudden change of climate and diet shared with disease the effect of changing the body's humoral balance. Suggesting the degree to which environment was thought to shape the natural world and human bodies, medieval and early modern medical authorities believed that a climate produced both diseases and their cures. John Josselyn suggested that a rattlesnake's heart was a remedy for its poison when eaten fresh, as was the application of a rattlesnake's liver to a bite. Captain John Smith's decision to eat a stingray that had injured his wrist may have been motivated by a similar belief that within the fish's body itself lay both poison and antidote. After the immediate pain of the sting was soothed by a "precious oile" applied by "Docter Russell," Smith's companions reported that he ate the fish for supper, "which gave no lesse joy and content to us then ease to himselfe."[23]

CHAP. 61.   Of Turkie Corne.

1 *Frumentum Asiaticum.*
Corne of Asia.

2 *Frumentum Turcicum.*
Turky corne.

¶ *The Kindes.*

OF Turky Corns there be diuers sorts, notwithstanding of one stocke or kindred, consisting of sundry coloured Graines, wherein the difference is easie to be discerned ; and for the better explanation of the same, I haue set forth to your view certain eares of different colours in their ful and perfect ripenesse, and such as they shew themselues to be when their skin or filme doth open it selfe in the time of gathering.

The forme of the eares of Turky Wheat.

3 *Frumenti Indici spica.*
Turky Wheat in the huske, as also naked or bare.

G 3

Figure 11. Illustrations and a description of maize, from John Gerard's *Herball* (1633). Courtesy Rare Book and Manuscript Library, University of Pennsylvania.

These examples underscore the need for caution in interpreting the meanings of food, or even attributing to food a single set of meanings. Snakes, which for Percy and Somers were evidence of Jamestown's desperation, might, Josselyn suggested, be eaten as a medicine. Smith's fish supper provides further evidence that food's meanings are not to be found according to one discourse alone, whether it be civility, hybridity, or disease. It is quite likely that, in addition to seeking a cure for the fish's poison, Smith ate his tormentor as a triumphant gesture to boost the morale of his crew, which it seems to have done. It is almost certain that Smith was hungry.

John Gerard's 1597 *Herball*, expanded by Thomas Johnson in 1633 and 1636, was the Elizabethan period's authoritative survey of the nutritive and medicinal qualities of plants and summed up contemporary notions of diet, climate, and temperament. According to Gerard, maize "doth nourish far lesse than either wheat, rie, barly, or otes," more familiar grains to English bodies. Although, Gerard pointed out, "Wee have as yet no certaine proofe or experience concerning the vertues of this kinde of Corne," it was decisive that "the barbarous Indians, which know no better, are constrained to make a vertue of necessitie, and thinke it a good food." Because of its suitability to barbarous Indian bodies, Gerard concluded, "we may easily judge, that it nourisheth but little, and is of hard and evill digestion, a more convenient food for swine than for man." Although he admitted no direct experience, Gerard definitively concluded that maize was not nourishing to English bodies simply because it was a staple in the diet of "barbarous Indians," and a food nourishing to such people could not be suitable for English men and women.[24]

However much they may have viewed maize with suspicion, nearly all English settlers were forced by necessity to try it. The English learned everything they knew about maize from the Indians, especially the Indian women whose work it was to plant and tend the crop. The author of the *Relation of Maryland* wrote that "The Indian women seeing their servants to bee unacquainted with the manner of dressing [maize], would make bread thereof for them, and teach them how to doe the like." At Plymouth, William Bradford recorded the English dependence on Squanto for knowledge of planting corn. In 1621, Bradford wrote, the Plymouth settlers "began to plant their corn, in which service Squanto stood them in great stead, showing them both the manner how to set it, and after how to dress and tend it. Also he told them, except they got fish and set with it in these old grounds it would come to nothing." Other sources from early Plymouth mention the use of fish as fertilizer and report that this was an Indian practice. Lynn Ceci has argued that

Squanto, who had been captured by an English vessel, brought to England, and escaped on his return to America, learned this technique in England. Regardless of the ultimate source of this technique, the Plymouth planters relied on their Algonquian hosts, especially women, for information about maize and presented the idea of using fish fertilizer as having Algonquian origins.[25]

One of the most common remarks early English writers made about maize was its spectacular increase in comparison to wheat. One of the earliest writers on the subject, Thomas Harriot, was also among the most enthusiastic. Harriot wrote that maize "is a graine of marveilous great increase; of a thousand, fifteene hundred and some two thousand fold." Other writers recorded more modest numbers but similar astonishment. Edward Waterhouse, who never visited America, completed this ecstatic description of corn: "their Maize (being the naturall Graine of Virginia) doth farre exceed in pleasantnesse, strength, fertilitie, and generalitie of use, the Wheat of England." Other writers were a bit less fulsome. William Bradford and Edward Winslow claimed that "our Indian Corne even the coursest, maketh as pleasant meat as Rice."[26]

Looking closely at these descriptions, one of the features of maize that convinced some that it was healthy for the English to eat was its "pleasantnesse." Taste—in the sensory sense—crops up very rarely indeed in the literature of travel and settlement, but when it does it is often connected with health, as is true in this case. Taste was diagnostic, evidence of a given food's suitability to a given body. Healthy foods could not be rank or coarse, just as dangerous foods would never be described as sweet or pleasant. Further signs whether New World foods were suitable for English bodies might be found by observing the reactions of Indians who tasted English foods. Among other things, a strong negative reaction might suggest stark differences between English and Indian bodies. William Wood, for example, wrote that when Algonquians "change their bare Indian commons for the plenty of England's fuller diet, it is so contrary to their stomachs that death or a desperate sickness immediately accrues, which makes so few of them desirous to see England." And Dionyse Settle remarked that three Inuits captured by Martin Frobisher's men "could not digest oure meate."[27]

Although Indian responses to European foods, and the reverse, might have a medical explanation, there were other possibilities open to early travelers and writers. It is not hard to imagine that Inuits used to a diet of fresh fish might indeed have trouble digesting pork salted a year or so before, especially if when they ate it the Inuits were prisoners lurching on the frozen deck of an English vessel surrounded by men who hadn't bathed in months. Similarly, if an English writer pronounced maize "pleasant meat," this meant he had eaten it and found it was not dangerous despite the alternative possibilities, which suggests clear limits to the pervasive anxiety about degeneration and hybridity. As was the case with Captain John Smith's fish supper, food might convey quite different meanings at the same time.

Maize received special attention and concern for other reasons. Staple foods carry deep cultural resonances that cannot be reduced to considerations of science and health, and wheat (especially wheat bread) filled this role in the early modern English diet. The lower and upper reaches of society differed in the types of bread commonly eaten and the degree of their dependency on bread for calories. But all English men, women, and children regarded wheat bread as the staple of their diet, and therefore maize posed a different sort of threat because it supplemented, or even supplanted, wheat.[28]

The efforts of the Virginia Company to supply its settlement with wheat from England suggest the importance with which the "staff of life" was regarded in the early period. The Spanish ambassador to England suggested the degree of the connection between wheat bread and health when he reported to Philip II in 1613 that the Jamestown settlers were "sick and badly treated, because they have nothing to eat but bread of maize, with fish; nor do they drink anything but water—all of which is contrary to the nature of the English." Captain John Smith made a similar point when he wrote that the struggling settlement was destitute of food with the exception of sturgeon, which Virginia's settlers ate so much of that they fell ill of a "surfeit." Similarly, when Sir Thomas Dale wrote to the Earl of Salisbury in 1611 that Jamestown's troubles were attributable solely to "the not haveing of sufficient of provision (and in that good kindes likewise)," he was referring not only to spoiled provisions but to the settlers' need to include maize in their daily diet. And Nathaniel Butler suggested that on Bermuda, it was a mark of deprivation that "not only the common sort but even the Governours own table . . . was for some monethes some meales found without bread." In these cases, settlers' health was endangered not by a lack of food but by the absence of the right foods, since human bodies then as now are quite capable of surviving on a diet of maize, fresh fish, and water.[29]

English settlers expected not only "sufficient of provision" but "good kindes likewise." Even in circumstances far less severe than Jamestown's starving winter, written accounts from the New World complained about the quantity and quality of rations. Richard Frethorne, in a 1623 letter to his parents, complained that "since I came out of the ship, I never at[e] anie thing but pease, and loblollie (that is water gruell) . . . [we] must Worke hard both earelie, and late for a messe of water gruell, and a mouthfull of bread, and beife, a mouthfull of bread for a pennie loafe must serve for 4 men which is most pitifull."[30]

Other servants facing similar conditions declared their indentures void as a result. Writing in 1631, Thomas Dudley reported to the Countess of Lincoln that servants sent to Massachusetts by the Massachusetts Bay Company had reluctantly been freed for lack of food. Dudley's grudging tone suggests that the servants had demanded their freedom since their masters had proven unable to live up to the terms of their contracts, which specified that servants would be provided for over the duration of their service. In 1636, the situation repeated itself in another new settlement, Saybrook. Servants there petitioned, complaining that the terms of their contracts were being broken by inadequate and insufficient provisions, including the lack of wheat bread. They wrote that "as for our diet our bread that is taken away our brakfast and our bere and so most of our diet is peass porig." Similarly, Nathaniel Eaton, the first master of Harvard College, was censured for providing his scholars with insufficient provision. William Wood wrote of the difficulty controlling servants without sufficient supplies: "Want of due maintenance," he wrote, "produceth nothing but a grumbling spirit with a sluggish idleness, whenas those servants which be well provided for go through their employments with speed and cheerfulness." The Virginia Company's instructions echoed Wood's use of the weighty term "idleness" in connection with the daily food ration. Advising Sir Thomas Gates to let his men "eate together at seasonable howers in some publique place," the Virginia Company advised him to make sure "there bee equality and sufficient that so they may come and retourne to their worke without any delay and have no cause to complaine of measure or to excuse their [i]dlenes uppon the dressinge or want of diett."[31]

These problems repeated themselves throughout the early English settlements, but the problem was more complex than the simple equation of hunger and discontent that characterized nearly every settlement at first and Jamestown in particular. The exceptional case of early Bermuda, where abundant food was available for the taking, adds an important final dimension to the linkages between food and authority in the early English settlements. Bermuda shows that what ultimately mattered in the equation of food and authority was not simply sufficient stores of food but whether the food supply lay under the effective control of leaders. In Bermuda, survival did not depend on effective leadership or on the sorts of self-presentations De La Warre staged on his arrival at Jamestown.

The *Sea Venture*, the flagship of the 1609 supply fleet bound for Virginia, carried De La Warre's deputy, Sir Thomas Gates. Gates, who carried Virginia's new charter, was accompanied by Admiral George Somers, the commander of the fleet, and William Strachey, the colony's secretary and the appointed recorder of the voyage. Separated from the rest of the fleet in a powerful storm, the *Sea Venture* nearly sank and was cast upon the dreaded shoals surrounding Bermuda. That group of islands, lying roughly six hundred miles off the coast of the Carolinas, had been known to sailors since the early sixteenth century, and the reefs encircling the islands had earned them a terrible reputation as the "Isle of Devils."[32]

When the shipwrecked English men and women, accompanied by two Chesapeake Algonquians on their way back to Virginia, waded ashore they found that the "Isle of Devils" was better described as a paradise. Bermuda has a temperate climate and no large predators. It also had no native population, lying well offshore and well north of the Bahamas. Because of its reputation, most European vessels steered clear of its reefs and shoals. Over the century or so since it was first discovered, hogs either had been released by Spanish visitors to the island or had swum ashore from shipwrecks. Finding themselves in the same favorable circumstances as the *Sea Venture*'s survivors, the hogs had bred prolifically. These, combined with the surviving native fauna, offered food in profuse abundance.[33]

One writer tried at length to describe what the castaways found on Bermuda, describing the islands as "the richest, healthfullest, and [most] pleasing land . . . as ever man set foot upon." He went on, "fish is there so abundant that if a man step into the water they will come round about him; so that men were fain to get out for fear of biting," and the fowl were similarly forward. On the islands, the English found thousands of "small birds so tame and gentle that, a man walking in the woods with a stick and whistling to them, they will come and gaze on you, so near that you may strike and kill many of them with your stick."[34] Strachey described calling to seabirds, who settled on men's arms, allowing them to heft several and choose the plumpest for dinner, and he was rapturous about the delicious and easy-to-catch turtles the English found on Bermuda. Even the most taciturn account of the islands' abundance, by Admiral George Somers himself, praised Bermuda as "the most plentifull place, that ever I came to, for fishe, Hogges and fowle."[35]

No account of early Bermuda betrays any anxiety about hybridity. Instead, these descriptions resonated with popular fantasies of the fantastic Land of Cockaigne, where food could be gained without labor. Combining rest and abundance, freedom from work and hunger, the situation Gates encountered on Bermuda was anathema to those hoping to establish a properly functioning social order with the threat of punishment and the promise of sustenance, the very equation De La Warre embodied.[36]

Popular fantasies of leisure and plenty were satirized in print as hopeless utopias. Sir William Alexander specifically addressed the Bermuda example as an illustration of what he hoped to be a general truth: "there is no Land where men can live without labour." Other writers were more caustic, for example, Joseph Hall, bishop of Exeter and Norwich, whose satirical *Mundus alter et idem* was published anonymously in 1605; an English translation was published under the title *The Discovery of a New World* in 1609. Hall satirized accounts of New World plenty in his fictional depiction of a newly discovered southern continent, which was divided into several separate lands and provinces. One of these, "Tenter-belly," was divided into the provinces of "Eat-allia," also known as "Gluttonia," and "Drink-allia," or "Quaffonia." Hall also described "Shee-land," or "Womandecoia," a (to him) dystopic region where women rule and a direct reference to Wingandacoia, the first name for the region around the Roanoke settlement. The fear uniting Hall, Alexander, and Strachey was that authority would disintegrate in these lands of popular fantasy because ordinary people did not depend on their leaders for food or defense. In other words, popular fantasies of abundance and rest suggest that in a world without hunger authority itself dissipated along with the roles and obligations that legitimated it: protection and sustenance on the part of leaders, obedience and labor from the rest.[37]

Most leaders who found themselves in this position did so through scarcity, not abundance. Edward Winslow wrote that Plymouth's "governors," by which he meant both himself and William Bradford, if not other leading men, "had nothing to give men for their necessities, and therefore could not so well exercise that command over them therein, as formerly they had done." Captain John Smith reached a similar conclusion based on his inability to convince, cajole, or coerce Virginia's settlers to work. Smith wrote that "Many did urge I might have forced them to it, having authority that extended so farre as death: but I say, having neither meat, drinke, lodging, pay, nor hope of any thing, or preferment . . . I know not what punishment could be greater than that they indured." For both Smith and Winslow, very different men leading very different settlements, the lesson was the same: without anything to offer

in return for labor, there was no way to bind settlers with reciprocal obligations in the way De La Warre did after his arrival, not even with punishment.[38]

Gates's experiences on Bermuda showed that authority was rooted in
a leader's *control* of the food supply, not simply its adequacy. According to
Strachey, "the major part of the common sort" wanted to stay on the islands
forever, "especially when they found such a plenty of victuals." The most compelling reason to stay, according to Stephen Hopkins, a separatist puritan, was
"abundance by God's providence of all manner of good food." This reasoning
was simple enough to Strachey, who understood that "in Virginia nothing but
wretchedness and labor must be expected, with many wants." The Chesapeake
had "neither that fish, flesh, nor fowl which here (without wasting on the one
part, or watching on theirs, or any threatening and art of authority) at ease
and pleasure might be enjoyed."[39]

Gates quickly realized the scope of his problem. Some among the shipwrecked English men and women on Bermuda quickly pointed out that although he was the duly appointed governor of Jamestown as clearly specified
in the 1609 charter, they were not in Virginia, and no one had been granted
authority to govern in Bermuda. Stephen Hopkins argued that Gates's "authority ceased when the wreck was committed," and the settlers "were all then
freed from the government of any man, and for a matter of conscience . . .
were therein bound each one to provide for himself and his own family."
Hopkins, along with his fellow puritans, physically withdrew from the rest
of the settlers. The sailors did so as well and, under the protection of Admiral
Somers, refused to recognize Gates as their leader.[40]

The long-term goal for both Gates and Somers was to build new ships
and complete their voyage to Virginia, but Gates needed first to solidify his
right to command. As a first step toward this goal, he and Somers declared
and demonstrated themselves willing to work alongside the ordinary settlers,
as we have seen. But men like Hopkins refused to accept the basic premise that
the survivors needed a leader at all, let alone new ships. Gates's recourse was
to what Strachey had called "art of authority," the means by which a leader
might compel obedience even absent the reciprocal relationships that were
understood to legitimate it.

Some, possibly influenced by Hopkins's speech, "conceived that our governor indeed neither durst nor had authority to put in execution or pass the
act of justice upon anyone," but Gates sentenced Hopkins to death just the
same. On the scaffold Hopkins tearfully begged for clemency, and no doubt
playing his own part with equal care, Gates reprieved him. Another settler,

named Paine, was not as fortunate. Paine's mutinous speeches and efforts to raid the storehouse had similarly led to a death sentence. He was granted his wish to be shot, as befitted a gentleman, rather than hanged as a common criminal. The "art of authority" in cases like these—a pardon on the one hand and a demonstrative execution at sundown on the other—could at least bolster a claim to legitimacy on the part of a leader, especially since both of the condemned men played their roles perfectly. But Gates's "art of authority" is not to be confused with legitimacy; in fact, the divisions among the English on Bermuda reached perhaps their widest point when Gates condemned a sailor to death for murder and his shipmates, "in despite and disdain that justice should be showed upon a sailor and that one of their crew should be an example to others," freed him and helped him escape. Worse still, Somers—who had at the very least an equal claim to preeminence on the islands—took the side of his condemned crewman.[41]

In this case, Gates's "art of authority" failed, weakening his claim further. Pleading his case to Somers, Gates wrote that both men had sufficient "authority in their places to compel the adversant and irregular multitude at any time to what should be obedient and honest." In other words, each man's social standing and office legitimated his right to rule and, if necessary, to punish. But more important, if they did not use this power to restore order, Gates wrote, "the blame would not lie upon the people (at all times wavering and insolent) but upon themselves, so weak and unworthy in their command."[42]

At bottom, Gates's problem was not the shipwreck, or the fact that his powers were limited to territory in Virginia, but the abundance of food his settlers found all around them. There is another revealing parallel with the Plymouth settlement, namely the truculent Stephen Hopkins. Roughly ten years later, Hopkins was a passenger on the *Mayflower* when the ship approached landfall on Cape Cod. Like Bermuda, Plymouth was clearly outside the borders of Virginia, making the patent granted to the Leyden separatists (also by the Virginia Company) technically worthless. And as on Bermuda, some "not well affected to unitie and concord" among the *Mayflower*'s passengers pointed out through "discontented and mutinous speeches" that the patent was no longer a sufficient basis for leaders to claim authority. But in Plymouth the settlers were faced with the necessity of building a settlement in the middle of a New England winter. They had to defend themselves from possible Indian attack, find enough food to survive, and begin searching for commodities that might offer a return to their investors. Under these very different circumstances, Plymouth's settlers demanded a formal covenant, the "Mayflower

Compact," and did not scatter to fend for themselves, which would have been a fatal mistake. Nevertheless, this sort of common cause could last only as long as Plymouth's leaders maintained control of the necessities of life.[43]

In the event, Gates was able to command his settlers to work in Bermuda, enforcing his authority with threats, punishment, and his own example. In April 1610, Gates finished construction of a small, decked sailing vessel, the pinnace *Deliverance*, and Somers and his men meanwhile built a smaller pinnace, which Somers perhaps revealingly named the *Patience*. The passengers of the *Sea Venture* finally finished their voyage in May, reaching Jamestown at the height of the "starving time."[44]

De La Warre's installation as governor under the second charter soon afterward was described by Whitaker as the end of a narrative that encompassed both Jamestown's starving time and Bermuda's abundance. For Whitaker, the end of his narrative demonstrated that, in contrast to both its desperation in the preceding months and the near collapse of authority on Bermuda, Virginia under the leadership of a titled aristocrat was stable and settled, well fed and properly governed. But in a larger sense, however correct the display of authority, and De La Warre's elaborate costume drama was certainly correct, the linkages to actual changes on the ground were tenuous. De La Warre's authority would survive only as long as the stores he brought, and as soon as they were gone his claim to leadership—unquestioned by Whitaker or by those actually present at De La Warre's installation as governor—began to crumble. Taken together, the promise Whitaker described in De La Warre's arrival and his difficulty in making good on that promise show the vital role food played, not just in sustaining life but in supporting a claim to authority.

Chapter 3

"By Shewing Power Purchasing Authoritie": Gender, Status, and Food Exchanges

In *An Encouragement to Colonies* (1624) Sir William Alexander both mocked the dreams of a life without labor inspired by early Bermuda and praised the more pragmatic leadership of Rene de Laudonnière, who led the French settlement at Fort Caroline in Florida. Alexander especially valued Laudonnière's efforts to find information "concerning the Savages, what their force was, what relation they had one to another, where they were friends or foes, how their pleasures were placed, and by what accounts they reckoned their gaines or losses." This sort of information about his Indian neighbors' diplomatic and economic relationships, their linked desires for goods and allies, Alexander wrote, allowed Laudonnière to be "alwaies ready as might stand best with the good of his affaires to assist, or oppose, to divide, or agree any partie, thus by shewing power purchasing authoritie, til he drew the ballance of all businesse to bee swayed where hee would as being Master of the Country."[1]

English leaders hoped to establish authority over Indians in the early years of settlement in just this way, and as Alexander suggested exchanges were one of the most important means to this end. Exchanges were common in the early period as a means to acquire food, which many early settlements desperately needed, and trade goods that might return a profit to the backers of English settlements. But in his encounters with Carolina Algonquians, Arthur Barlowe was neither the first nor the last English traveler to recognize that exchanges also offered a form of communication especially valuable when the language barrier was all but insurmountable. As Barlowe discovered and

Alexander reported, exchanges were one of the most important means to establish and maintain relationships in which English leaders hoped to establish their own preeminence. Native leaders were hardly passive participants on these occasions: although European goods were in most cases rare and valuable in the early period, native leaders were always keenly attentive to the meanings of their participation in exchanges. In many encounters English and Indian leaders each sought to assert preeminence in more or less the same terms.

Approaching exchanges in this way, unearthing the layers of meaning that passed back and forth along with kettles, hatchets, pelts, fish, and other objects, emphasizes the common ground between each side's exchange customs rather than what separated them. Accordingly, I use the broad term "exchange" whenever possible, instead of the familiar terms "gift giving" and "trade." These terms imply that Indians and English approached exchanges with radically different motivations, that Indians sought to establish social bonds and to exchange symbolic meanings by giving gifts, whereas the motivations of the English were to secure profitable trading relationships.

Instead, as historians in recent years have shown, English and Indians had some knowledge of each other, especially by the early seventeenth century. Both sides were familiar with the adaptations and improvisations necessary when traveling among strangers or hosting foreign travelers, even if not firsthand. Most important, all parties recognized that a meeting between leaders presented an opportunity for "purchasing authoritie," in the sense Alexander used the term, and little else. Although there were clear differences in the ways each side approached exchanges, and although they did not always understand the precise meanings they or their counterparts conveyed, leaders on both sides always understood that when they participated in exchanges, they were sending messages to their counterparts. English leaders consistently tried to shape these meanings, presenting themselves as strong leaders in a way intended to resonate with Native American understandings. The English were not imposing their will or dictating terms on these occasions but learning, improvising, and negotiating, often to the extent of conforming their own conduct to the expectations of their hosts.[2]

This portrait of early exchanges clearly bears the markings of a "middle ground" of flexible meanings, creative misunderstanding, and mutual accommodation. Yet for a variety of reasons, exchanges of food considerably narrowed the scope of this middle ground, making meanings far less flexible. For one thing, the cultural meanings associated with some foods—especially venison and other game animals—were more closely shared than with any other exchange object. And since both sides understood such gifts to embody messages of gender and status, the meanings that passed back and forth were often uncomfortable for the English to accept in the early period, a point that will be more fully addressed in Chapter 4.

Last, as always food embodied both symbolic and caloric meanings. Although nearly everything connected with food has symbolic resonance, no item offered in exchanges was more important than food to the hungry early English settlements. Since hunger and political authority were so closely associated for the English, a leader's authority was dependent in part on his ability to secure supply. This only raised the stakes in exchanges, layering the need for nutrition on top of the other meanings passing back and forth. In the symbolic language of exchange, English and Indian leaders negotiated political relationships: by showing power through the items they offered and received and their conduct while doing so, they purchased authority (or at least haggled over it).

It must be said at the outset that stark differences between English and Native American exchange norms did develop over time. In many cases, the end of this process for native groups was an increasing dependence on European goods that they could not manufacture and repaired with great difficulty if at all. Further, after generations of increasing reliance on European goods, native knowledge of how to make weapons, cookware, clothing, and tools was gradually lost. The fact of dependency and its importance is not in dispute here. Once Indian groups became reliant on European trade goods and once Europeans recognized the scope of this dependency, the negotiations inherent in early exchanges were over and Europeans were able to dictate increasingly unfavorable terms to their Indian counterparts. By the time this point had been reached, exchanges were clearly governed by European norms: prices were tied to supply and available markets, not the strength of social relationships.

But there is a danger in constructing the narrative of early exchanges with this endpoint in mind, imagining that the motivations that underpinned later exchanges were latent in the earliest. Such a narrative assumes that the cultural differences so obvious in European attitudes toward native groups in the eighteenth and even nineteenth centuries were there all along, even in the halting, fearful exchanges on the shores of the Atlantic in the sixteenth and seventeenth centuries. It is equally misleading to assume that Indian motivations in these early encounters were antithetical to those of their English counterparts.

*   *   *

In 1612, John Guy, the governor of the English settlement at Cupid's Cove, Newfoundland, led a group of settlers on an exploratory voyage. While ashore, the English noticed a fire nearby, which may have been meant as a signal. They scrambled into their boats, rowed offshore, and waited. "Presentlie," Guy wrote in his journal, "two canoaes appeared" and landed a man on the shore. This man approached the English "with a flag in his hand of a wolfe skinne, shaking yt, & making a lowde noice, which we tooke to be for a parlie, wheareupon a white flag was put out."[3]

The encounter between these two groups, strangers to each other until this point, illustrates several important features of early exchanges in general. The first of these is that from the outset, Guy conducted himself in accordance with what he thought were Indian norms. In fact, the Beothuks were following trading customs learned over generations of contact with Europeans. As Dionyse Settle, who accompanied Martin Frobisher on an expedition to the Arctic, remarked of nearby Indian groups as early as 1577, "It seemeth they have bene used to this trade or traffique, with some other people adjoyning, or not farre distant from their Countrie." George Best wrote of the same voyage that the Inuits encountered by Frobisher had no problems acquiring iron.[4]

Thirty-five years later, when Guy arrived, the Beothuks were even more familiar with Europeans, their desires, and their goods. As they approached waving a pelt on a pole, this small group of Indians were following a long-standing custom: indicating their desire for exchange and the items (furs) they had to offer. Watching them approach, Guy understood only part of this message, mistakenly assuming that the fur was a common European symbol—a white flag of truce. Guy's misunderstanding suggests the looseness of these exchanges, the fact that it was not necessary for every sign presented by each side to be precisely received for the encounter to proceed peacefully and profitably.[5]

After his first misunderstanding, Guy made his first misstep. Trying to reciprocate the Beothuk gesture, he moved his two vessels toward the Indians, who retreated. By landing only one man, they expected the English to reciprocate with a small party, and Guy soon got the message. The English vessels anchored and set "master [George] Whittington" on shore "with the flag of truce, who went towardes them." Two men approached Whittington, who took his cues from them. Holding the "white skinne," one of the Beothuks approached Whittington, "made a loude speeche, & shaked the skinne." These gestures were "awnsweared by master Whittington in like manner." And "as the savage drew neere he threw downe the white skinne into the grownde.

The like was don by master Whittington." Although the English interpreted the Beothuk sign as a flag of truce, Whittington's actions clearly demonstrate that he followed the lead of his Indian counterparts. Flags of truce were not customarily shaken vigorously or flung to the ground between parties of Europeans. Nor were they exchanged, but when the two groups parted, the Indian leader "tooke the white skinne, that they hayled us with, & gave yt to master Whittington, & presentlie after they did take our white flag with them in the Canoa."[6]

Guy's signal of reciprocity was clear to the Beothuks, and the English party's peaceful intentions in leaving Whittington alone on shore were also clear. Guy wrote that after shaking the pelt, "both the savages passed over a little water streame towardes master Whittington daunsing leaping, & singing." One presented Whittington with "a chaine of leather full of small perwincle shelles, a spilting knife [or splitting knife, used in the cod fishery], & a feather that stucke in his heare." The other Beothuk gave Whittington "ane arrow without a head." For his part, Whittington gave the first "a linnen cap, & a hand towell," and the Indian "presentlie [put] the linnen cap upon his head." After Whittington gave the second Indian a knife, "hand in hand they all three did sing, & daunce." Then Fraunces Tipton joined the shore party and was given "a chaine such as is before spoaken of," for which he returned "a knife, & a small peece of brasse." Then the group "togeather daunced, laughing, & makeing signes of joy, & gladnes, [the Beothuks] sometimes strikeing the breastes of our companie & sometymes theyre owne."[7]

Dancing, noted by many travelers to the region as a common element of initial encounters with the Beothuks and Inuits, clearly indicates the flexibility of early encounters and the fact that English leaders were willing to accommodate themselves to the Indian norms that often governed them. Dionyse Settle recorded Inuits "leaping and dauncing, with straunge shrikes and cryes" on his 1577 voyage. Subsequent travelers to the region prepared accordingly. Edward Hayes wrote of Humphrey Gilbert's 1583 voyage that "for solace of our people, and allurement of the Savages," the English brought along "Morris dancers" and other "Maylike conceits to delight the Savage people." John Davis's voyage to Greenland in 1585 showed a similar degree of preparation: "When [the Indians] came unto us, we caused our Musicians to play, our selves dancing, and making many signes of friendship." Although his men were not similarly prepared for this encounter, just as Whittington had followed his counterpart's lead in shaking and throwing down their tokens, Guy's settlers participated in these dances.[8]

Encounters like this one are as familiar in the sources that describe early encounters as they are in secondary accounts that interpret them. The objects exchanged—in this case shells, knives, caps, towels, gloves, arrows, and other items—are often at the center of these interpretations and the focus of a broad disagreement over the motivations of both sides. Taking the Indian side first, one scholar has written that the "most heated controversies" over native motivations "take the form of a confrontation between rationalist-materialist and idealist-cultural relativist interpretations of human behavior."[9] Both sides of the debate agree that, long before contact with Europeans, the diverse and dispersed groups of eastern North America participated in what Daniel Richter calls "small-scale long-distance" exchange networks that extended from the Atlantic seaboard deep into the interior. These networks were dominated by certain materials—copper and shells were especially important—and specific colors, especially red and black, whose importance derived from their symbolic associations and ritual significance.[10]

Since European goods were immediately incorporated into these exchange networks alongside more traditional exchange items, the rationalist view argues that Indians wanted European goods because they filled basic needs better than the tools and materials otherwise available. This view stresses the basic similarities between Indians and Europeans, both in their views of an object's practical utility and in their common need for sharp objects to cut and chop with, metal pans to cook in, and so on. The idealist, or romantic, view takes Indian desires for copper objects and colored beads as evidence that Indian groups fitted European trade objects into traditional uses. The most compelling evidence for this view is provided by copper kettles, an object with seemingly "rational" appeal that was used in a variety of ways by Indian groups, who among other uses cut up kettles and fashioned the pieces into gorgets, pendants, and other jewelry, as Granganimeo did with the tin dish offered him by Barlowe.[11]

Guy's account suggests that efforts to infer motivations from items by categorizing them as rationalist or idealist obscure the fact that the items in question conveyed more than one meaning simultaneously. For example, the Beothuks clearly initiated the encounter with Guy's party, and by bringing along a pelt on a pole they clearly did so with an eye toward gaining European goods. Their possession of knives is clear evidence that they had done so in the past. But by offering knives to the English, which signaled their familiarity with European goods and their understanding of their utilitarian value, the

Beothuks exchanged utilitarian items for items whose value was less obviously rational or utilitarian: hand towels and linen caps.

Although the Beothuks carried a bona fide commodity (the pelt) and initiated an exchange similar to those they had presumably conducted in the past, they offered shells and feathers—decorative objects, not utilitarian ones—alongside knives. Even more revealing, there were two offerings of headless arrows, an interesting object that itself blurs a distinction between items with utilitarian and symbolic value. These might have been a signal of friendship and peaceful intentions, or more likely a half-finished utilitarian object, needing only a bone or stone point. Or perhaps the Indians were signaling a desire for iron arrow points.[12]

The point is that what made an object valuable was very subjective, and Jamestown offers an especially rich example. In his *True Discourse* (1615), Ralph Hamor described a visit to the man the English knew as Powhatan, the leader of nearly all the Algonquian groups in the Chesapeake. At the end of their meeting, Powhatan, who was called by his name Wahunsenacawh among his own people, requested a long list of very specific items from Hamor, including a shaving knife, fish hooks, a "cat, and a dogge," and two "bone combes" (Powhatan pointed out that "the wodden ones his own men can make"). Powhatan promised to return furs for these items when they were delivered, and he asked Hamor to record the terms of their agreement "in such a Table book as he shewed me." Hamor, noting that the "Table book," a sort of ledger, "was a very fair one, I desired him, it being of no use to him, to give it mee." From Hamor's perspective, a ledger could be of no use to an illiterate man, who could neither record transactions in it nor decipher the records others had left. But for Powhatan, the book had a very different sort of utility: "he tolde me, it did him much good to shew it to strangers which came unto him."[13]

Powhatan requested specific objects of Hamor for specific reasons. Bone combs, for example, were finer, more durable, and more beautiful than "the wodden ones his own men can make." More plainly than any of the other objects, the bone combs combine the levels of functional and symbolic value. To account for Powhatan's request for a razor, a cat, and a dog as stemming from purely functional needs on the one hand or symbolic desires on the other is a similarly blinkered interpretation. But the table book suggests the most expansive view of an object's value, one that combines symbolic and utilitarian meanings. For Powhatan to possess and display such an item was to associate himself with writing even though he himself was illiterate. Hamor completely

missed this more expansive view of an object's utility, but Powhatan's Algonquian visitors evidently did not.

John Guy and the Beothuks intended their meeting in part to solidify
peaceful relations between the two groups and to suggest mutual respect between the leaders, and in pursuit of this end it was conduct, not the specific
items exchanged, that was most important. Other English leaders acknowledged this point outright. Sir Ferdinando Gorges, for example, praised New
England Algonquians because "in all their carriages [they] manifest shewes of
great civility farre from the rudenesse of our common people." Christopher
Levett warned English travelers not to be too "familiar" with Indians, since in
that case "they will not respect them: therefore it is to be wished that all such
persons should be wise in their Carriage."[14] Given the importance their own
culture placed on a leader's conduct in public, the English no less than the
Beothuks were highly attuned to the meanings of these interactions. Neither
side was wholly a prisoner of culture, bound by a static, culturally determined
set of responses. Instead, each party in early encounters like the one between
Guy and the Beothuks chose from a range of possible responses and counterre-
sponses derived from their own cultural norms of exchange, prior experiences,
and their observations of the other party's conduct during the encounter.[15]

English travelers quickly recognized that exchanges conferred an obligation to reciprocate. As Father Andrew White summed it up, "they are generally so noble, as you can doe them noe favour, but they will returne it." The
Carolina Algonquian man Arthur Barlowe invited aboard the English ship and
offered gifts immediately "fell to fishing" in order to requite these gifts. Recognizing that exchanges conferred an obligation (and that their counterparts
understood and intended this), English leaders tried to conduct themselves
in ways that ensured the obligation lay on the Indian side of the exchange.[16]

To guide their conduct, English leaders drew on their own cultural norms
of gift giving, in which subtle differences in conduct could convey very different meanings. At the Elizabethan court, for example, the monarch's courtiers
competed with each other for royal favor by giving the queen extravagant New
Year's gifts. For her part, Queen Elizabeth carefully marked the relative status
of her courtiers with the value of the gifts she offered in return. The relationship between gifts and status in these exchanges was dynamic: by giving an especially welcome gift a courtier might gain in favor, which would be signaled
by the value of the return gift.[17]

Humbler figures sought the patronage of their social superiors through
gifts as well, although in this case the meaning depended on the fact that

these gifts were not reciprocated. Once a patron-client relationship was established, clients were expected continually to magnify their patrons' importance
and continually to give gifts. By doing so a lesser figure kept himself in his
patron's eye and, he hoped, enhanced his chances of success in the contest
for patronage. In this case, by accepting a client's gift, a patron signaled that
it represented a return for his own patronage and favor, which could not be
returned in kind.[18]

In one case, gifts from inferiors to superiors were reciprocated; in the
other they were not. The meanings of these exchanges are found not in the
objects but in the conduct of the various participants, which was based on
well-rehearsed cultural expectations of giving and receiving gifts. A client
must never insult his patron with an inexpensive gift, for example, but neither should he overstep his social station by presuming to give the sort of
gifts associated with the patron's peers. By doing so, a lesser figure staked a
claim to social equality with his social superiors, or else suggested that the
ties of patronage had been repaid, that the client was no longer dependent
and indebted to his patron. In different circumstances, it would have been
considered a privilege to give gifts to one's social superiors. At the Elizabethan
court, a lesser group of courtiers was given gifts but was not allowed to enter
the privileged circle that could return gifts to the monarch. The acceptance of
one's gift by the monarch was a more accurate reflection of royal favor than the
fact of receiving a royal gift that could never be returned. The monarch alone
could give without receiving.[19]

The importance of all this to the Atlantic world lay in the fact that exchanges in England could manifest either relations of dependency, reciprocity,
or superiority, and which of these meanings was conveyed depended on a
complex set of cultural assumptions. In some cases—for example, a queen's
unrequited gift to her courtiers—unequal exchanges signaled power; in
others—for example, a client's gift to a patron—such exchanges signaled dependency. The meanings lay in the status of giver and recipient, precisely what
was given, and the context of the exchange. This complexity allowed for a
great deal of fluidity and improvisation.

In their conduct during exchanges with native leaders, English travelers tried to present themselves in accordance with these expectations and to
describe their experiences in the same light. It was common for written accounts to mention that English leaders spurned any notion of equivalence
in exchange as beneath the liberality expected of a leader. John Davis in one
instance signaled that the gifts he offered his Indian counterparts in the Arctic

"were not solde, but given them of courtesie." Sir George Peckham, an associate of Humphrey Gilbert who intended to settle in Newfoundland, made the same point: "there must be presented unto them gratis, some kindes of our prittie merchaundizes and trifles." Finally, John Winthrop, a careful steward of his status and reputation, made a similar point when the Massachusett sachem Chickatabut "came to the Governor & desired to buye some Englishe clothes for him selfe." Winthrop "tould him, that Englishe Sagamores did not use to trucke," and proceeded to have a suit of clothes made for his Massachusett counterpart.[20]

When Captain Christopher Levett staked a claim to status by means of liberal giving, his Algonquian counterparts understood the symbolic meanings he intended to convey and accepted his claim. Presented with furs "which they would have let me had for nothing," Levett wrote, he "would not take them so, but gave them more then usually I did by way of Trucke." His Indian counterparts then, Levett claimed, "began to applaude or rather flatter me, saying I was so bigge a *Sagamore*, yea foure fathom, which were the best words they could use to express their minds."[21]

Liberality and authority were also linked in the ways items passed from one group to another, not simply what or how much they were. Arthur Barlowe, at his first encounter with Granganimeo, "presented [him] . . . with such things as we thought he liked." Then, Barlowe wrote, "we likewise gave somewhat to the other[s] that sate with him on the matte: but presently he arose, and tooke all from them, and put it into his owne basket, making signes and tokens, that all things ought to be delivered unto him, and the rest were but his servants, and followers." Leaders expected to distribute valuable items among their own people. For the English to play that role on this occasion, cutting Granganimeo out of the distribution of these status items, could not be tolerated. Barlowe well understood that by insisting these items were his to distribute, Granganimeo was making a statement about authority, that "the rest were but his servants."[22]

Carefully studying their hosts' expectations, many English leaders tried to give gifts that their counterparts would perceive as especially valuable and tried to enhance their status further by freely offering these gifts. To take one example, English travelers quickly learned that the color red was significant to many Indian groups, and they used this knowledge to their advantage. Arthur Barlowe noted that in the Carolina Sounds "redde peeces of copper" worn on the head or around the neck marked "the difference betweene the Noble men, and Governours of Countries, and the meaner sort." In 1605, James Rosier encountered an Indian in what would later be called New England wearing "a kinde of coronet about his head . . . of a substance like stiffe haire coloured red," which, Rosier wrote, seemed to be "some ensigne of his superioritie." Rosier also suggests that the English party tried to get this man to trade his crown, which he refused. George Percy described a werowance wearing a "Crown of Deares haire colloured red" and noted further that this werowance's "body was painted all with Crimson." When the werowance of Arrohattoc gave Captain Christopher Newport "his Crowne . . . of Deares hayre dyed redl [red]," Newport reciprocated with "a redd wastcote," which seems to have been a commensurate sign of status, allowing this werowance, unlike the sagamore encountered by Rosier to the north, to relinquish a badge of status. Red coats were also given to Massasoit by the Plymouth planters and to the Chickahominies by Sir Thomas Dale, in both cases after the conclusion of a treaty. Because of the significance of this color, George Percy wrote to his brother, the Earl of Northumberland, requesting that a large quantity of "incarnadyne velvet" be sent to Jamestown. By itself, this bright red cloth would have been a very valuable exchange item. If made into clothing worn by Percy it would have presented him to the Chesapeake Algonquians as a man of obvious authority.[23]

In some ways, foods were like all other objects. An offer of something to eat, for example, could not be refused. Captain John Smith described the Chesapeake Algonquians' "generall custome, that what they give, not to take againe, but you must either eate it, give it away, or carry it with you." But foods were in many ways unique exchange items with meanings not shared by other objects. Foods were the most significant of all items exchanged in early encounters: not only was it a clear affront to refuse them, but in many encounters an offering of food signaled that early, tentative efforts to establish bonds of friendship, or at least peace, had succeeded.[24]

Returning to John Guy's journal, after the preliminary exchanges, Guy wrote that "signes was made . . . that bread, & drinke should be brought ashoare." The Beothuks "made likewise signes that they had in their canoaes meate also to eate." The mutual offers of food were the decisive gesture that brought the leaders of both sides to join the group. When he stepped ashore, Guy offered the Beothuks "a shirte, two table napkins & a hand towell." In addition, he presented them with "bread, butter & reasons [raisins] of the sun to eate, & beere, & aquavitae to drink." The Indian leader then joined Guy and the rest. "After they had all eaten, & drunke," Guy wrote, one of the Indians "broughte us deeres fleshe dryed in the smoake, or wind, and drawing his knife . . . he cut every man a peece, & yt savoured very well."[25]

Across the Atlantic world, offers of food like this, or the game, fish, and fruit Granganimeo offered Arthur Barlowe, signaled friendship and peace. On John Davis's third voyage in search of a Northwest Passage, in 1587, he was welcomed by Inuits offering "fishes dryed, Salmon, Salmon peale, Cod, Cap-lin, Lumpe, Stone-base and such like, besides divers kinds of birds, as Partrige, Fesant, Guls, Sea birds and other kindes of flesh." Robert Harcourt recounted gifts received from Indians in Guiana: "they brought with them such dainties as their country yeeldeth; as hennes, fish, pinas, platanaes, potatoes, bread of *Cassavi*, and such like cates [treats, dainties] which were heartily welcome to my hungry company." Finally, when the Jamestown settlers arrived in the James River, Indians appeared "in all places kindely intreating us, daunsing and feasting us with strawberries, Mulberies, Bread, Fish, and other their Countrie provisions wherof we had plenty."[26]

In addition to the symbolic meanings of these offers, an intention to es-tablish peaceful ties, the English interpreted them as a sign of the abundance and easy availability of New World foods. Descriptions like these would have eased the fears of investors and promoters regarding the cost of supplying their settlements, by demonstrating both the range of edible plants and animals available to prospective settlers and the Indians' willingness to share them. For ordinary settlers fishing through cloudy barrels of brine for the last pieces of salt pork, or else gnawing on chunks of moldy, worm-riddled biscuit, the food offered by Indians—all of it fresh, tasty, and ready to eat—resonated with popular fantasies of abundance achieved without labor, like the Land of Cockaigne. As we have seen, both motivations underlay Barlowe's descriptions of Carolina, and as was true in Barlowe's case as well, later writers blamed optimistic early accounts for the persistent supply troubles of many settle-ments and the waves of hungry, undersupplied new arrivals expecting to feast without labor.

Both Indians and English regarded food as an especially important and significant exchange item. Beyond this similarity lay a shared understanding that the meanings of specific foods were rooted in the highly gendered labor they embodied. English travelers and writers understood that there were gen-dered meanings associated with foods even when they did not fully understand those meanings. Maize, for example, was identified by most native groups of North America with the women who planted, tended, and harvested it, as were foods like berries that were gathered exclusively by women. Venison was identified in a similar and similarly broad way with the men who left their vil-lages to hunt. According to an Iroquois creation myth, the original union of a

HINDIANE

Figure 12. This painting, from the late sixteenth-century Drake Manuscript (fol. 86) held in the Morgan Library, depicts an Indian woman pounding corn, underscoring the association of this food with femininity. The text that accompanies the painting reads, in translation: "This woman beats the wheat kernel in a wooden mortar and produces a very white flour from which they make very good and very nourishing bread." *The Drake Manuscript in the Pierpont Morgan Library: Histoire Naturelle des Indes*, trans. Ruth S. Kraemer, (London: André Deutsch, 1996), 264. Courtesy The Pierpont Morgan Library, New York.

man and a woman was mediated and reflected in food. A figure known as Sky Woman brought to her future husband bread baked with berries, a distinctly feminine food, which he requited by the quintessential masculine food, a gift of venison.[27]

William Strachey's account of Indians' conception of the afterlife speaks directly to the feminine associations of certain foods and the labor of preparing food in general. Strachey's informants were Patawomekes, Algonquians of the Chesapeake region. Strachey's source for the story was the group's leader, or werowance, Iopassus, who recounted his people's creation myth and beliefs concerning the afterlife to Henry Spelman. According to this account, after death, on their way to the house of "the great hare," their principal deity, the Patawomekes expected to "come to a howse, where a woman goddesse doth dwell, who hath alwaies her doores open for hospitality and hath at all tymes ready drest greene *Uskatahomen* and *Pokahichary* (which is greene Corne bruysed and boyld, and walnutts beatten smale, then washed from the Shells, with a quantety of water, which makes a kynd of Milke and which they esteeme an extraordinary dainty dish) togither with all manner of pleasant fruicts in a readines to entertayne all such as do travell to the great hares howse."[28]

Assuming the *uskatahomen* and *pokahichary* were served together, the dish Strachey described was similar to frumenty, a common and popular English dish of (usually) wheat cooked in milk. The same dishes Strachey described to his readers—pounded, boiled grain and a "kynd of Milke" made from walnuts—were also described by Smith, who gave their names as *ustatahamen* and *pawcohiccora*. The latter would have been familiar to English readers on its own, since almond milk, prepared in a very similar way, had been esteemed a "dainty dish" in England and elsewhere in Europe for centuries. The main point that emerges from Strachey's account is that *uskatahomen* and *pokahichary* were foods clearly identified with women. They were derived from nuts and grain, foods gathered and cultivated exclusively by women, who also performed the considerable labor required to pound and prepare the maize and walnuts. The "pleasant fruicts" in Strachey's account, like the "Strawberries, and other things" that Paspahegh women offered George Percy in 1607, were likewise identified with the women who located, gathered, and prepared them.[29]

English writers understood these connections even when the translation was a bad one. William Morrell, a minister sent by the New England Company to evaluate the state of the New England plantations in 1625, wrote a verse account of (among other things) Indian norms of marriage. Although Morrell was clearly not in favor of polygamy, he recognized the connections between gender and food among the New England Algonquians. After noting that multiple wives afforded a man more children (whose value for Morrell included properly mourning their father), Morrell described the advantages of women's labor:

A second profit which by many wives
They have, is Corne, the staffe of all their lives.
All are great eaters, he's most rich whose bed
Affords him children, profit, pleasure, bread.[30]

Grain becomes bread in the space of two lines, a rhetorical sleight of hand that effaces the arduous labor required to pound maize into meal in wooden mortars and prepare bread. Morrell's lines also signal that the gendered significance of grain was lost in translation, as it usually was. English writers understood grain as a product of male labor and therefore misunderstood much of its gendered significance to the Indians they encountered, but the two sides shared an association of food preparation and female labor. English accounts therefore often described foods associated with women as cooked, preserved, or otherwise prepared: as bread, not grain, to match with English understandings.

When Captain John Smith requisitioned Chesapeake Algonquian corn supplies, he reported that the women of one village wept as he departed, which indicated the strength of their connection with the food stores. These women wept for the loss of the grain that manifested their contribution to the survival of their families and that signaled their own centrality to the subsistence patterns of their people. They realized that responsibility for making up for this loss of food was theirs, meaning a long season of foraging for tuckahoe and other wild foods. But also, given paleobotanical evidence of the severe drought in the Chesapeake during these same years, they mourned the fact that a harvest that had fallen well short of the usual yield had been lost.[31]

The masculine counterpart to grain and bread was venison (which in the early modern usage referred to the flesh of any game animal). In exchanges of venison, English and Indian leaders employed a resonant symbol of masculinity and authority that, like grain and bread, was derived from its production. Unlike bread, the cultural meanings of venison were homologous.

According to English writers, certain North American game animals—

especially deer and moose—were especially prized by Algonquians, and certain parts of game animals were said by some writers to be particularly prized. For native groups across the Americas, venison with the hunting skills it demonstrated was a food that embodied masculine virtues. One writer claimed that among the New England Algonquians, men would not work the land, "for it would compromise their dignity too much, unless they are very old and cannot follow the chase." Further, this writer noted that these highly gendered roles were instilled at a very young age.[32]

Like the Algonquians, the English believed that the consumption of some foods was an indication of masculinity and status. The symbolic power of these animals derived partly from their scarcity or size: "Porposes, Seales, and such like royall fish" were also considered status foods. But the meaning of venison derived primarily from the fact that serving it at table demonstrated that a man had sufficient landholdings to support a population of these animals, the arms with which to hunt them, and the right (often granted by law) to eat them. William Harrison summed up a fact that would remain true throughout this period: merchants and nobles both "will seldom regard anything that the butcher usually killeth."[33]

To preserve the connections between landed property, the right to bear arms (to hunt, as well as to fight), and the right to possess venison, game laws in England strictly enforced its circulation as a sumptuary item. Venison was never to be sold: its circulation was limited to gifts exchanged between people of relatively equal social station, or else distributed slightly down the social scale as a valued mark of favor. Adam Winthrop, father of the Massachusetts Bay governor, noted in his journal receiving several gifts of venison, recording not a meal but a reflection of the fact that men of status held him in high regard.[34]

In a flamboyant bid for favor, Virginia governor Sir George Yeardley presented King James with a gift of deer from Virginia in 1619. His gift was accompanied by a request for royal patronage: Yeardley suggested establishing a royal game park in Virginia with himself in the prominent and lucrative role of royal gamekeeper. But more than simply a request for patronage, Yeardley's gift was intended to enhance his status through gift exchanges of this especially symbolic food. There is no record of whether King James accepted Yeardley's gift, but to have done so would have acknowledged Yeardley's position and enacted a tie with the monarch in a way even more direct than the New Year's gifts between Queen Elizabeth and her courtiers.[35]

There are indications that among the many unrealistic expectations settlers

Figure 13. In this image from the Drake Manuscript (fol. 114), masculinity is as closely associated with game, especially venison, as femininity was with grain and bread: a man carries game to the home of a woman he hopes to marry. Courtesy The Pierpont Morgan Library, New York.

brought with them to the New World was the idea that venison would be a common part of their diet. High-ranking settlers like Thomas Dudley, a leader and sometime governor of the Massachusetts Bay colony, reported that "as for foule and venison, they are dainties here as well as in England," suggesting that he and his correspondent had believed otherwise. Richard Frethorne's pleading letter to his parents also mentioned the scarcity of venison. Because of its cultural associations with wealth, status, and masculine virtue, venison was in great demand. It was not the taste of the meat that Dudley, Frethorne, and others were anticipating—some status foods, like bear, were reported tasty; others, swans and peacocks for example, are reportedly nauseating. Instead, access to venison was by long habit thought to be synonymous with a life of leisure.[36]

Because of the symbolic importance of venison, Guy's experience eating it with his Beothuk counterpart as part of their initial encounter was shared by many other English leaders. Indian gifts of venison were nearly always presented at relatively formal occasions, when leaders or leading men of both sides were present. It was the only food treated in this way. At the first formal introduction of Wahunsenacawh's people to the English, Wowinchopunck, werowance of the Paspaheghs, was preceded by emissaries. These men informed the Jamestown settlers that the werowance himself would soon arrive with a "fat Deare" to "be merry" with the English. Edward Maria Wingfield received deer as gifts from Wahunsenacawh, as did George Percy, gifts that befitted their station as governors of the Jamestown settlement. In the same way William Bradford received venison when he visited nearby sachems.[37]

Another clear indication of the close association between venison, masculinity, status, and political authority is the demand of deerskins and venison as tribute by Algonquian leaders from the Chesapeake to New England. In New England, tribute was owed to the sachem of the territory on which a deer was killed: according to Edward Winslow, a forequarter if the deer was killed on land and the hide if killed in water. For this reason, when Niantics killed five deer in water, they asked the Massachusetts Bay magistrates what to do with the hides, recognizing English sovereignty in the region and in essence asking whether the English leader intended to assume the role of sachem. John Winthrop was angry when a sachem of the region demanded tribute from the same group, a clear challenge to Massachusetts Bay authority in the Algonquian language of tribute the English had learned and adopted. A similar episode concerned the Narragansett sachem Miantonomi, whose receipt of deerskins in tribute proved his control of subordinate groups. Miantonomi confirmed the connections between tribute and authority in a speech related to Lion

Gardiner. According to Gardiner, Miantonomi told a Long Island sachem to "give no more wampum to the English," for the simple reason that "they are no Sachems, nor none of their children Shall be in their place if they die." As proof, Miantonomi told the Montauk sachem Wyandanch, "they have no tribute given them" and each English leader was subordinate to the monarch's authority, which Algonquian sachems were not.[38]

In short, native leaders intended to convey complex messages about gender and status when they offered venison to English travelers, and the English received and recorded both foods and what they understood to be their meanings. Two final examples make this clear. The first is from early Jamestown, where Gabriel Archer, on the first voyage of discovery up the James River, encountered the werowance of Arrohattoc. During this initial encounter, the werowance gave the English party "a Deare roasted; which according to their Custome they seethed againe." Although it was clearly not the werowance doing the roasting or the seething, Archer perceived and reported that the deer was the leader's gift, recognizing the connections between masculine authority and gifts of venison. Other foods were offered during this encounter as well. Archer reported that the werowance "caused his weomen to bring us vittailes, mulberyes, strawberryes &c." and "caused his weomen to make Cakes for us." Arrohattoc was not directly associated in Archer's eyes with these feminine foods and female labor, as he had been in the case of venison. Instead, his authority was manifest in his ability to control the labor of others. The meanings from the other side may well have been different. Although Archer's account stated that Arrohattoc "caused" these foods to be prepared and presented, the women whose labor created this meal may have seen their participation in it as a demonstration of their importance to Chesapeake Algonquian society, however obscured such possible meanings were in Archer's account.[39]

The second example, the 1621 "first Thanksgiving" at Plymouth, neatly sums up this discussion of exchange norms and the semantics of food in the early English Atlantic world, especially its possibilities as a medium of symbolic communication. The very brief passage describing the "first Thanksgiving" begins with Plymouth's leaders' decision to hold a harvest feast: "our harvest being gotten in, our Governour sent foure men on fowling, that so we might after a more speciall manner rejoyce together, after we had gathered the fruit of our labours." As many writers remarked, fall was the season of huge waterfowl migrations, making this a prime opportunity for hunting. In one day, Plymouth's four fowlers "killed as much fowle, as with a little helpe beside, served the Company almost a weeke."[40]

The next phrase is key to the meaning of the encounter: "at which time amongst other Recreations, we exercised our Armes, many of the *Indians* coming amongst us." The decision of Plymouth's leaders to drill the militia was, like the decision to hold a harvest feast, in itself unremarkable. Militia musters were a not uncommon festive occasion during which the authority of leaders was demonstrated by their adornment and command. The loyalty of militia soldiers was customarily reciprocated by leaders' distribution of copious amounts of alcohol (although there is no mention of this at Plymouth). What is unusual about this description is the implied connection with the arrival of a huge, unannounced party of Wampanoags that included "their greatest King *Massasoyt*, with some nintie men." Roughly half the original one hundred or so planters at Plymouth had died during the first winter, meaning that this party of Wampanoags, all able-bodied, armed men, was almost double the population of Plymouth including the elderly, infirm, women, and children. The arrival of Massasoit's men, no matter how friendly the earlier relations between the two groups, would have been ample cause for unease, and demonstrating their coordination and weaponry was likely meant in part as a demonstration of strength. Massasoit responded to the abundant food present at Plymouth and the fusillade that greeted his men by departing briefly and returning with "five Deere," which he "brought to the Plantation and bestowed on our Governour, and upon the Captaine, and others."[41]

The specific meanings of this encounter are most clear when compared to others between the same men. At their very first meeting with Massasoit in 1621, only months after their arrival, Captain Miles Standish, Plymouth's military leader, advanced to meet him with a guard of "halfe a dosen Musketiers." After what the account described as salutes on both sides, Standish "conducted [Massasoit] to an house then in building, where we placed a greene Rugge, and three or foure Cushions, then instantly came our Governour with Drumme and Trumpet after him, and some few Musketiers. After salutations, our Governour kissing his hand, the King kissed him, and so they sat downe." Afterward, Bradford and Massasoit shared meat and alcohol. Here, as on so many other occasions, the leaders of both groups clearly saw their status on display and conducted themselves accordingly. The careful conduct of Plymouth's leaders, and their equally careful description, suggests that after living in close proximity with the Wampanoags for less than two months, Plymouth's planters conducted themselves more fluently in the symbolic language of exchange than Guy did. But the language remained substantially the same in both cases.[42]

Returning to the "first Thanksgiving" with this earlier encounter in mind, it is clear that Massasoit's conduct during the later encounter was intended to convey additional messages. The first of these stemmed from the fact that Massasoit had not been notified of the feast beforehand. If he had been invited, Massasoit presumably would not have arrived empty-handed, and therefore his abrupt departure and prompt return bearing a liberal gift of venison conveyed meanings on many levels. First was to demonstrate his friendship toward the English. By bestowing gifts of venison on each of Plymouth's leading men, Massasoit suggested that he regarded them as men of status commensurate with his own. Each of these reassuring and flattering meanings was clearly received (and recorded) by the Plymouth planters, whose own conduct sought to make corresponding claims.

But these meanings were parallel to others that conveyed a less rosy picture of the overall relationship between English and Wampanoags. For one thing, Massasoit did not present his gift to his counterpart, William Bradford, but to each of Plymouth's leading men separately. This signaled that they should look to him for such status gifts and not to their own governor. Massasoit's gift of venison also asserted a clear claim to control of the region in that the deer were killed (and the gift presented) by a formidable group of armed men.

In their own way, the Plymouth planters sent corresponding messages. Their decision to fire weapons at Massasoit's arrival was similarly rich in meanings, combining the honoring of a guest (as on the first meeting between the two groups) with a demonstration of their own combined strength. Although they were celebrating a season of rare abundance at the time, the Plymouth planters were not far removed from the hunger of their first winter. The deeper meaning of Massasoit's food gifts—his own ability to provide or withhold food—was never far from the surface, and this message of their own dependency was difficult for English leaders to swallow.

Chapter 4

"Would Rather Want Then Borrow, or Starve Then Not Pay": Refiguring English Dependency

English leaders like William Bradford consistently sought signs that their Indian counterparts had understood and accepted their claims to (at least) commensurate status. Since exchanges were so frequent and conveyed such rich meanings, they were one of the most important sites for such negotiations in the early period. And since both sides recognized that the relationship between English and Indians was not only represented but subtly reshaped in the shared language of exchange, leading figures on both sides struggled to make often contradictory claims.

As part of these struggles, exchanges of food could convey many meanings, even conflicting meanings, simultaneously. Massasoit's five deer expressed his desire for peaceful relations and acknowledged horizontal bonds of status between him and Plymouth's leaders, both gratifying messages. But equally significant were the signals of dominance embodied in the number of deer and the speed with which Massasoit's warriors had killed them. Much to their discomfort, English leaders knew that only their Indian counterparts had the ability to offer venison, along with all the meanings it embodied. Since gifts of food could not be refused without insult, English leaders were forced to accept both welcome and unwelcome meanings.

Not surprisingly, when they wrote about their experiences these men often chose to describe them in ways that muted this message of dependency. Unrequited gifts from Indian leaders could be described as tribute, for instance, offerings by a client or vassal to secure favor from a superior. Unrequited gifts from English leaders, on the other hand, were always described as the liberal giving of a magnanimous ruler or patron. Describing unequal exchanges in terms of trade encouraged readers to believe that both sides had received what they saw as equal value in the exchange, not that the English were stingy trading partners. In these ways, English settlers avoided describing their negotiations with Indians in terms that underscored their own weakness.

Shifting attention to the unflattering meanings of exchanges, whether to English leaders or to those who read written accounts of their experiences, introduces a new dimension of early encounters. In addition to the efforts of men like John Guy and William Bradford to conduct themselves in accordance with the image of a leader, English writers were engaged in a rhetorical effort to portray the English experience in the Americas in a way phrased to appeal to metropolitan officials and investors. Few of the early English settlements had sufficient supplies of money and men to draw on. Most were engaged in a nearly continual search for investment, and written accounts were a vital part of this search.

This complex effort to describe exchanges in a positive light, to refigure dependency in more flattering terms, is most clearly seen in the case of theft. When Indians stole items from the English, these incidents were always regarded as an intolerable affront, a plain and direct declaration of hostility often attributed to Indian leaders. But ordinary English men and women sent the same messages in the other direction when they stole food. When English stole from Indians, the uncomfortable message was that English leaders could neither adequately feed nor effectively control their settlers, and to avoid acknowledging this, English accounts studiously avoided using the term "theft" in reference to their own people. In especially clear terms, theft encapsulated the struggle between English and native groups on the ground in the Americas and the struggle to represent those encounters favorably in writing. Food was at the heart of both.[1]

To begin with an example, a 1614 gift of venison at Jamestown signaled many of the same meanings as the venison gifts that marked the "first Thanksgiving," and in both cases English leaders had no choice but to accept them. The marriage of Pocahontas and John Rolfe in that year concluded five years of fighting in the Chesapeake and suggested that the region's future might be marked by closer ties between the English settlers and Wahunsenacawh. This was likely welcome news for most Chesapeake Algonquians, not to mention the inhabitants of Jamestown, but not for the leaders of the Chickahominies, the only group in the region that had not submitted to Powhatan. Wahun-senacawh's most recent marriage alliance, this time with the English, posed a threat: with their combined strength, Wahunsenacawh could easily crush the Chickahominies and absorb them as another tributary group, as he had done to several other groups in the region within recent memory.

But the English also posed an opportunity for the Chickahominies to maintain their independence through an alliance of their own. To protect themselves from attack by Wahunsenacawh, the Chickahominies needed to convince the Jamestown settlers of their peaceful intentions and their willing-ness to submit to the English. But to maintain their status as the only autono-mous group in the region, the Chickahominies needed to make sure they did not exchange one unwelcome overlord for another.

The Chickahominies settled on a way to communicate their subtle dip-lomatic goals through carefully calibrated exchanges. First, emissaries ap-proached the English with "two fat Bucks" as a signal of their desire for an alliance. The Chickahominies promised to submit to King James—not to Jamestown's governor, Sir Thomas Dale—and to change their names to Tas-santasses, or "Englishmen." They would continue to govern themselves sepa-rately from both Jamestown and Powhatan and would continue to choose the eight members of their ruling council. As a mark of their agreement, James-town's governor would give each of these men a red coat and copper badge of office. The Chickahominies also promised to pay a tribute in corn to James-town. Chickahominy diplomats seemed to have succeeded: giving up only the promise of future corn payments and the promise to use a new name, they had secured a guarantee of their independence and markers of a special relation-ship with the English.

Red coats and copper badges are a perfect example of the flexibility of symbols in the early period, the ability of signs like these to embody very dif-ferent understandings that nevertheless accommodated the goals of both sides. Ralph Hamor described the coats and copper as markers of submission, but given the well-documented desire of native groups for precisely these items, the Chickahominy council doubtless viewed them as emblems of status. After seven years of interaction during which both the color red and items made from copper were especially prized trade goods, it is difficult to imagine a well-informed metropolitan reader like Captain John Smith accepting Hamor's interpretation of these items' meaning, but it is likely that other readers did.

As we have seen, food did not allow for creative misunderstanding to the same degree. A tribute of corn would have manifested Dale's and Hamor's vision of what had happened during these negotiations, if it had ever arrived. Annual deliveries of grain would surely have been grandly received and requited with some sort of small token, just enough to suggest a leader's regard for those dependent on him but not enough to mark the Chickahominies as holding equivalent status in the region. But the corn tribute never arrived, at least not on the regular basis necessary to convey these meanings. What did change hands was venison, and after concluding the terms of this treaty, Sir Thomas Dale offered the Chickahominies "copper for their venison, which they refused to take." Dale's inability to requite the gift clearly encapsulated his settlement's dependence on Indian hunters for their status meals of game, but rejecting the Chickahominies' offer of venison in order to avoid these signs was unthinkable, an overt declaration of hostility. Instead, Dale tried to reverse the implications of the Chickahominies' gift, erasing a momentary imbalance in the relationship between the two groups. By offering copper, he tried to signal that what had happened was not an unrequited gift exchange but a reciprocal exchange, or even a magnanimous return by Dale of more valuable for less valuable items. Recognizing Dale's efforts to drain their gift of its meaning (or suggest a different meaning), the Chickahominy leaders refused.[2]

Placing this example alongside those in the previous chapter, it is clear that English leaders conducted themselves in exchanges in ways calculated to assert a dominant position. Hamor's account of these events suggests a further dimension. When they wrote about these encounters, the English tried subtly to refigure them, reassuring their superiors and backers at home that they were living up to the standards expected of a leader. But there were limits to this effort, as Hamor's account again makes clear. Unlike red coats and copper, the meanings of venison were shared closely enough that Hamor could not simply claim that this exchange meant something it did not.

Another dimension of this exchange highlights the difficulty English leaders faced in making corresponding claims to masculine authority, which were ultimately rooted in household government. The Chickahominies presented Dale with two dead animals, not a status meal. The women's labor required to transform the former into the latter was in scarce supply at Jamestown during this period. Helen Rountree has suggested that gifts of venison like this one may have been accompanied by cookware and women to prepare the meal, underscoring the connections between any meal and the gendered labor required to prepare it. But it is equally important that English sources are unanimously silent on this point. Whether or not Rountree's inference is correct,

English men were demonstrably poor hunters, and in many cases could not even command the labor of English women to dress, butcher, and prepare deer carcasses handed to them. Their limitations brilliantly illuminated on occasions like this one, English leaders could not make a corresponding claim in what was clearly a shared language of masculine authority.[3]

When, as was often the case, English travelers or settlers depended on Indians for food, even for part of the year, the meanings of food exchanges became if anything even more difficult for the English to accept. Wahunsenacawh well understood the symbolic meanings his counterparts among the English tried to convey, and he responded to English displays of liberality with messages intended to manifest his own claims to eminence. Wahunsenacawh knew that the English at Jamestown could not simply abandon exchanges, since the settlement depended for survival on the corn produced by Wahunsenacawh's people. Bound together by English need, the two sides struggled in the early years to determine who would prevail in the Chesapeake.[4]

Although there were a series of official leaders of the Jamestown settlement—Edward Maria Wingfield and John Ratcliffe in the first year alone—and a collection of men like George Percy who energetically displayed their status, there were only two men whom Wahunsenacawh seems to have recognized as his counterparts among the English before 1609. Until his departure in that year, Captain John Smith was the only regular visitor in native villages and the main conduit for English supplies. Before taking over as the settlement's third president in September 1608, Smith was the Virginia Company's cape merchant, an official in charge of accounting for the trade goods supplied by the Virginia Company and conducting the settlement's official trading relations. The second man, Captain Christopher Newport, was a sporadic presence in the Chesapeake, periodically arriving on supply missions, but he played an unmistakably important role in the English settlement that was quickly recognized by the Chesapeake Algonquians. Although changes in the conduct of exchanges and the meanings each side derived from them had many causes, these three men (Wahunsenacawh, Smith, and Newport) had a decisive role in shaping encounters.

Although Smith and Newport were unaware of the fact, their division of responsibility—one man who conducted relations with other groups and a second man, the more eminent of the two, who remained at home—fit precisely with the "dual sachemship" practiced by many eastern Algonquians (though not in the Chesapeake). Smith supported this conclusion by referring to Newport as his "father" and the leading figure among the English when talking to Powhatan. This was a tactical move by Smith, who hoped to gain some freedom from responsibility for his actions by claiming that ultimate authority lay with the (often absent) Newport rather than with Smith himself or where it more accurately lay, with the settlement's president.[5]

Accordingly, Smith never tried to display majesty or magnificence before Powhatan, to assert any sort of position commensurate with that of the man he described as "emperor." This inequality played to Smith's advantage, excusing his inability to give liberally and perpetuating a relationship between Wahunsenacawh and Smith characterized by liberality and greatness on only one side. By doing so, Smith could secure supplies for Jamestown, but not without consequences. Through these exchanges, Wahunsenacawh intended to convey a meaning with a precise analogue in English society: that the Jamestown settlement was a tributary of the emperor Powhatan. Smith refused to acknowledge, in his actions or his writing, that by accepting Wahunsenacawh's magnanimity he had accepted the role of a vassal. Instead, Smith presented himself as a soldier, the agent of a power superior to Powhatan, a fearsome enemy with the authority and ability to pursue his enemies implacably, and yet without the power to reward his friends through liberal gifts.

For several reasons Newport was a perfect foil for Smith, far superior to the duly elected presidents and the appointed councillors resident in the Chesapeake. An experienced sailor and veteran of many privateering voyages, Newport had been named to the Virginia council by the Virginia Company, and his judgments regarding the affairs of the settlement were highly regarded. A regular visitor in both Jamestown and London, Newport carried news to the Virginia Company and instructions to the settlement, but this role meant that Newport was rarely present in the Chesapeake. Therefore however much Smith claimed to Wahunsenacawh that his own abilities were limited, that ultimate authority lay with his "father," Newport, Smith avoided the (to him) unpleasant need to acknowledge inferiority, a subordinate role to Newport that he clearly did not accept. Newport, on the other hand, was eager to put himself forward as a leading figure in exchanges. By offering liberal gifts Newport asserted his priority over Smith and enraged him by devaluing the goods Smith offered in exchanges.

Clearly recognizing their rivalry and his opportunity, Wahunsenacawh played the two men off each other. According to Smith, at a meeting attended by all three men, Wahunsenacawh seemed "to despise the nature of a Merchant, [and] did scorne to sell." In the *Generall Historie,* Wahunsenacawh is reported to have said to Newport that "it is not agreeable to my greatnesse, in

this pedling manner to trade for trifles; and I esteeme you also a great Werowance. Therefore lay me downe all your commodities together; what I like I
will take, and in recompence give you what I thinke fitting their value." In the
language of liberal giving, Wahunsenacawh suggested to Smith and Newport
that the Jamestown settlers "freely should give him, and he liberally would
require us."[6]

The heart of the problem lay in the fact that the English wanted food above
all else. Wahunsenacawh was used to exchanging status goods with counterparts, and his specific requests for firearms and other English technology were in
keeping with this experience. But because the English settlement at Jamestown
could not supply itself with food, and because food was the only thing they
asked of Powhatan, the settlement's leaders were placing themselves under his
authority whatever the written accounts of these exchanges claimed. And Wahunsenacawh, an astute observer of the English and a man with a keen eye for
the protocol of exchange, made this point clearly. Wahunsenacawh is reported
to have said that he regarded "a Basket of Corne [as] more precious then a Basket of Copper; saying he could eate his Corne, but not the Copper." Under the
circumstances, the items the English offered were in no way commensurate, and
Wahunsenacawh punctured English efforts to assert a different meaning: despite
Newport's efforts at liberal giving, English dependency made it impossible to
avoid the meanings Wahunsenacawh intended to convey.[7]

As Wahunsenacawh well knew, food is never simply a commodity or a
status item to hungry people. Despite their efforts to present the items they
offered as valuable, the English depended on these exchanges for survival.
Under these circumstances settlers across the English Atlantic world regarded
their Indian neighbors as obligated to continue feeding them. John Nicholl,
for example, reported of English experience on the Caribbean island of Saint
Lucia that when the Caribs "did not come unto us with victuals as they had
wont," their actions made the English "suspect that they were at the slaughter
of our men." This reaction, connecting an abandonment of food exchanges
with hostile intentions, was not far from the truth in Nicholl's case. In other
examples as well, native groups who sustained early settlements during their
first hungry years withdrew that support as a sign of hostility. At Roanoke, Algonquian leaders cut off supplies to force the English out, just as Wahunsenacawh's people did at Jamestown. In the latter case especially, the Chesapeake's
severe drought was also a major factor. But in addition, English dependency
required settlers either to submit to the authority of native leaders or else to
withdraw, a choice Wahunsenacawh presented very clearly.[8]

English leaders submitted to the authority of native leaders only in the most desperate and extreme circumstances. As careful as they were to record the symbolic meanings of exchanges when favorable to English claims, they were extremely careful to avoid signaling such submission in their conduct and to avoid describing it in the written accounts of their experiences. These dimensions of early encounters are most clear in the case of theft.

When English leaders gave liberally, for example, they expected that this demonstration of their own status and favorable disposition toward their Indian hosts would be received appropriately, and it often was. Because theft sent the opposite message, it received equally close attention. English accounts described Algonquians as habitual thieves who made off with anything and everything they could when they visited the English. "[S]eeing iron," one English man wrote, the Indians "could in no wise forbeare stealing." Gabriel Archer was equally definitive: "The people," he wrote, "steale any thing comes neare them." Captain John Smith tried to suggest that such statements were true only of some Chesapeake Algonquian groups: "their custome is to take any thing they can ceaze off, onely the people of Pamunke, wee have not found stealing: but what others can steale, their King receiveth." For Smith, the Pamunkeys were the exception that proved the rule.[9]

These statements are especially noteworthy because English writers agreed that Indians rarely stole from each other. The author of the *Relation of Maryland* claimed that "it is never heard of, that those of a Nation will rob or steale one from another," and Captain John Smith reported that "they seldome steale one from another, least their conjurers should reveale it, and so they be pursued and punished." Nevertheless, in one instance, Henry Spelman witnessed what he was told was the execution of a thief. Descriptions like these suggest that Indians conducted relationships with each other in terms of a shared set of norms, even laws. Therefore the fact that they stole from the English could not be explained as evidence of lawless savagery.[10]

English accusations that Indians were habitual thieves have received a great deal of scholarly attention. For the most part, the scholarly literature has attempted to excuse or explain the supposed eagerness of Algonquians to steal from the English in their midst, accepting the fact of theft but disputing the conclusions drawn by contemporary writers, which were that Indians were innately untrustworthy, deceitful, and dishonest. Some secondary accounts deny that Indians had any conception of theft, pointing to the essentially communal conception of property among most Indian groups as proof that things that were not being used were common property and subject to being used by another. But strong leaders like

Wahunsenacawh ended up in control of stolen English items, as Smith pointed out. And unless they demanded their return, the English never encountered their tools, weapons, or cookware lying around unattended for them to use. To deny that Indians were habitual thieves, it is not necessary to suggest that Indian societies were purely egalitarian, innocent, and communal.

Another way the secondary literature has explained Indians' theft from the English is by arguing that Indians were acting to enforce their own norms of exchange through stealing. Expecting to receive goods equal in value to those they offered the English, many Indian groups made up the (often substantial) difference by simply taking things they wanted. It is possible that such a misunderstanding could have characterized some early exchanges, but given the depth of English feeling about theft, it is hard to imagine innocent misunderstanding lasting for very long. Also, theft did not always occur within the context of an exchange, a fact that weakens this case somewhat. But this argument suggests an important point: if Indians stole in order to even out unfavorable exchanges, then Indian intentions were to issue a challenge, or at least a clear signal that the English were not conducting themselves in accordance with Indian norms. In one especially dramatic case, Uncas, sachem of the Mohegans, reacted strongly to the Connecticut decision in 1646 to settle on disputed lands and forge an alliance with a rival, the Pequot Robin Cassacinamon. Uncas displayed his scorn for the Pequots and those that presumed to protect them by plundering their goods, beating and humiliating both Pequot and English residents of Nameag, and then proclaiming (in English, a rare recorded instance of him speaking that language): "I am the victor."[11]

The important question is not why Indians stole from the English—there are a number of possible answers, including simple greed—but what it meant to both sides. Most English leaders were very clear in their response to Indian thefts, often suddenly and disproportionately violent. In 1585, English explorers in the Roanoke region sent an emissary to the nearby village of "Aquascococke" "to demaunde a silver cup which one of the Savages had stolen from us, and not receiving it according to his promise, we burnt, and spoyled their corne, and Towne, all the people beeing fledde." Disproportionate reprisals were not limited to occasions like this when the English enjoyed favorable odds. In Jamestown, theft and a violent English response marred the very first formal meeting between the settlers and the Paspaheghs, in whose territory they had settled. Wowinchopunck, the werowance of the village of Paspahegh, arrived at the Jamestown peninsula only days after the English fleet began unloading its provisions and settlers. The werowance, along with one hundred armed men, was allowed to enter "the Fort," such as it was. The English had been instructed "not to offend" the Indians, and for this reason fortification was minimal. Also, most of the settlement's arms remained packed, and the settlers were unskilled in their use. According to George Percy, Wowinchopunck then "made signes that he would give us as much land as we would desire to take." The Jamestown settlers responded to what they interpreted as a quite generous offer with violence. In spite of their orders and the unfavorable odds, when one colonist noticed a Paspahegh man taking a hatchet, he took it away from the Paspahegh man and beat him. Both sides seized arms, and the Indians withdrew "in great anger."[12]

In one light these responses are puzzling, wildly out of proportion and directly contrary to the central concerns of early settlers, namely maintaining friendly relations with powerful nearby groups that might supply a settlement with food, among other things. With so much at stake, the value of a single hatchet was clearly negligible, but theft embodied meanings beyond the loss of goods. From the English perspective theft provided a way to evaluate the disposition of Indian groups toward the English and the effectiveness of Indian leaders in controlling the men supposedly under their authority. When, for example, Jamestown's settlers wrote that everything stolen from them ended up in Wahunsenacawh's hands, this signaled that these items, however small, had been stolen either at Wahunsenacawh's direction or with his tacit acceptance. Indians need not even have done the actual stealing: accounts of early Jamestown are rich with reports of settlers plundering the stores and conducting illicit exchanges with Indians. But when the English demanded the return of stolen items, they were evaluating the authority of native leaders and assessing whether their intentions were peaceful or hostile.[13]

An example from early New England illustrates these connections. On a 1602 voyage, the Reverend John Brereton described an encounter with several groups of Algonquians along the coasts of Cape Cod and the islands to its south. The English received gifts of "their fish readie boiled" and tobacco and returned gifts of "certeine trifles, as knives, points, and such like." Then the English began fortifying a settlement on "Elizabeth's Isle," where they were approached by a party of Indians. The leader of this party offered the English a beaver skin, and the English leader, Bartholomew Gosnold, returned "certaine trifles" for the pelt and then offered his Indian guests a meal. According to Brereton, "While we were thus mery, one of them had conveied a target [a small shield] of ours into one of their canowes." The English "suffered" this theft "onely to trie whether they were in subjection to this Lord." The English party "made signes" to the Indian leader "by shewing him another of the same likenesse, and pointing to the canow." The Indian leader spoke "angerly to one about him (as we perceived by his countenance)" and "caused it presently to be brought backe againe."[14]

Like Jamestown, Elizabeth's Isle was supposed to be a permanent settlement, and this was the first substantive meeting between the English settlers and the Indians of the region. At least two members of the Gosnold expedition—Gosnold himself and Gabriel Archer—were later among the Jamestown settlers who responded so violently during their first encounter with Wowinchopunck, werowance of the Paspaheghs, when one of his men stole a hatchet from the English. Archer may have applied the lesson learned from this encounter to his subsequent experiences at Jamestown. In addition to the encounter with the Paspaheghs, Archer recounted another example from the initial voyage of exploration up the James River. On this voyage, Chesapeake Algonquians stole "two bullet-bagges which had shot and Dyvers trucking toyes in them." After the English demanded their return to the werowances present, they "instantly caused them all to be restored, not wanting any thing." Captain Newport went on to lecture the Indians present that "the Custome of England" was "Death for such offences" before returning everything stolen to those who had taken them (except the bullets). Similar demands were made by the Plymouth planters in their settlement's early years.[15]

Archer summed up the meanings of these encounters from the English perspective. Writing of the Chesapeake werowances, Archer claimed that each was "potent as a prince in his owne territory," and as an indication of their authority Archer noted that they "have their Subjectes at so quick Comaund, as a beck brings obedience, even to the resticucion of stolne goodes which by their naturall inclinacion they are loth to leave." Theft was a challenge, and return of stolen items signaled both a strong leader and his respect for the English.[16]

English assumptions regarding leaders' authority over their men cut both ways when it came to theft, which English travelers and settlers routinely committed. If Algonquians had left written accounts of their experiences during this period, they would certainly have described the English settlers as habitual thieves as well, probably noting that instead of iron, the English could not forbear stealing food. In written accounts, unpleasant truths like these had to be represented in more palatable ways for a metropolitan audience. It was difficult for English leaders and the writers who described their experiences to admit the fact that they were unable to supply enough food, that their hungry settlers stole from the Indians, and that they were unable to control their settlers in the way they expected Indian leaders to control those supposedly under their authority. Hunger and the resort to desperate measures to survive were indictments of a leader's authority, and for this reason English writers resisted holding themselves to the same set of understandings regarding theft, refiguring through their written accounts the imbalance of power in early America by insisting that their own conduct in exchanges fell under traditional norms.

English accounts never described theft by English settlers as a challenge or an insult to Indian leaders, even though nearly every case of theft by an Indian was interpreted in these terms. In one case, where the Massachusetts Bay leadership demanded that the Narragansetts pay recompense for killing a cow, the Narragansett leaders pointed out the double standard this represented. Roger Williams wrote that they did not "believe that the English Magistrates doe so practice, and therefore they hope that what is Righteous amongst ourselves we will accept of from them." In another example, George Percy recorded that a canoe stolen from the Rapahannocks was returned when requested, signaling precisely the sort of connections he hoped Indian leaders would make. But Percy's example was a rare one.[17]

Dionyse Settle signaled that the English intended to send a message to the Inuits encountered on Frobisher's 1577 voyage. Settle wrote that after learning firsthand of the Indians' "fiercenese and crueltie, and perceiving that fayre meanes, as yet, is not able to allure them to familiaritie, we disposed our selves, contrarie to our inclination, something to be cruel, returned to their tentes, and made a spoyle of the same." Theft in this case represented a form of cruelty, a deliberate reprisal on the part of the English that was, Settle carefully pointed out, contrary to their nature.[18]

Food was usually eaten, of course, and could not be returned, so English writers excused their settlers' propensity to steal by finding other names with which to describe theft, for example, "borrowing." In their first winter on Cape Cod, the Plymouth settlers raided Indian corn stores to survive. William Bradford and Edward Winslow returned to this episode repeatedly in their writings, insisting that "so soone as we could meete with any of the Inhabitants of that place," they would be certain "to make them large satisfaction." Unattended supplies might be legitimately described as "abandoned" and therefore free for the taking, especially since the corn supplies the Plymouth planters raided were buried by Algonquians decimated by a recent epidemic. Still, the repeated mentions of this episode suggest that Bradford and Winslow understood it to reflect poorly on their own abilities as leaders as well as their conduct as Christians.[19]

Hunger presented a political problem to English leaders other than those of the Plymouth settlement, who found other ways to excuse or explain their own need and their willingness to steal. Exceptions to the prohibition on theft could be found in military examples. Thomas Dermer, for example, described seizing an Algonquian sagamore and holding him for ransom, in this case, "a Canoas lading of Corne." During wartime, many otherwise forbidden actions were permitted, for example, pillaging stored food. Another example was Captain John Smith's coerced trade with the Chesapeake Algonquians. When Wahunsenacawh began backing away from the liberal exchanges that marked an early period in his relations with the English settlement, he ordered the groups of the region to refuse exchanges with the English as well. Smith's response was to compel "trade": he took the food he needed and left what he decided was a fair amount in exchange. This sort of exchange was in keeping with neither side's norms, more akin to an army's requisitioning of supplies than any other relationship.[20]

But even here, Smith tried to portray outright theft in the same way Settle had, as something "contrarie to our inclination." When Smith visited a Chesapeake Algonquian village on an expedition to secure food supplies by any means necessary, he found the men of the village absent. The women claimed that they were not permitted to trade the corn stores under their effective control. Smith wrote, "Truck they durst not, corne they had plenty, and to spoile I had no commission," and he left the village's food supplies untouched. Helen Rountree has argued that these women were deceiving Smith, shielding the product of their labor from the English by falsely claiming that as women, they had no control over it and could not conduct exchanges. Perhaps the men of the village fled before Smith's arrival, knowing that he might compel trade from men but hoping he would not take that step with women. It is also possible that these women had legitimate cause to be afraid, less from their gender than their status as subjects of Powhatan, who had restricted Jamestown's supplies during this period. In at least one documented case, Powhatan punished unauthorized trade with the English with death, clearly asserting his exclusive right to negotiate relationships with other groups. But it is certain that Smith's description of his own actions was intended to signal that even with Jamestown facing hunger, he "would rather want then borrow, or starve then not pay."[21]

Because theft reflected badly on their own abilities, when they could catch thieves, English leaders punished them, often making an example for others. One well-documented case from Massachusetts Bay concerned a man named Josias Plaistowe and two servants, who in 1631 stole four baskets of corn from nearby Indians. For this crime, Plaistowe was "degraded from the title of a gentleman," forced to pay double the amount of corn in restitution, and fined. The servants were whipped. Plaistowe's extraordinary public disgrace— Thomas Morton pointed out that the Massachusetts Bay magistrates had no authority to take such a step—and the whipping of the servants were intended to show that English leaders controlled their men in the way the English expected of the Indians.[22]

To take a final example, hunger drove English settlers at Wessagusset, near Plymouth, to depend on the Massachusetts for food, as many settlements did. But in Wessagusset's case, dependency led to subjection, the inevitable conclusion so many English leaders struggled to avoid, or at least to avoid acknowledging. Wessagusset's disgrace culminated in a case of theft, in which the Massachusetts demanded punishment for an English thief and received it. Perhaps the most singular aspect of Wessagusset's case was the fact that Plymouth's leaders refused in the end to help their English neighbors, leaving them without food and without the option of abandoning their settlement to join with Plymouth. More, in their accounts of Wessagusset's decline and dissolution, Plymouth's leaders painted a deliberately negative portrait of their English neighbors as a way of solidifying their own claim to the region. Theft and dependency were relatively common; a negative account of an English settlement was not.[23]

In 1622, roughly sixty men unexpectedly arrived in Plymouth. They had been sent by one of Plymouth's principal backers in England, Thomas Weston, to found a competing colony that Weston hoped would recoup his investment. Weston asked William Bradford to feed his colonists while they searched for a place to settle, planted corn, and harvested their first crop. Weston promised to repay Plymouth for the expense of supporting his colonists, but in the meantime, Plymouth would be their main source of support.[24]

Weston's men were unwelcome for a number of reasons. They threatened to drain Plymouth's scarce stores of food, and their new settlement, once established, would restrict the Pilgrims' access to furs and therefore reduce Plymouth's chances to retire its debts. But further, nearly all accounts describe them as a shiftless and dissolute bunch who stole corn from Plymouth's fields and stores. Plymouth's leaders were finally able to convince Weston's men to strike out on their own after dividing their food supplies with the new arrivals, and the new colony was established at Wessagusset, just north of Plymouth.

The new settlement got off to a very bad start, after a disappointing harvest and with meager support from England. The two settlements joined forces in several trading expeditions to nearby Indian groups in order to secure corn supplies for winter, but the Wessagusset colonists were unable to make their provisions last. By the winter of 1622 Weston's colony was in serious trouble. The colonists continued to steal food, this time from their new neighbors, the Massachusetts, and as the colony began to starve, the Wessagusset colonists tried to feed themselves in any way they could. Some sold their clothes to the Indians; some sold their labor, building boats and carrying burdens for corn. Finally, unable to survive within the walls of their fort, many of the settlers dispersed into the woods to forage, abandoning their houses, property, and weapons.[25]

In his book *Good Newes from New England*, Edward Winslow connected the Wessagusset settlers' hunger and dependency with subjection to Massachusett authority, arguing that when Weston's men abandoned their houses and land, sold their clothing, and agreed to work for Massachusetts in exchange for food, they also abandoned most of the norms that governed early modern English society. Not only did the Wessagusset settlers' claim to their land ultimately rest on "improvement," on the very houses and fields they had abandoned, but by entering Indian households as laborers, they had accepted a servant's position under the "government" of Indians. This strikingly negative portrait was intended in large part to undermine Plymouth's rivals in the fur trade. By focusing on precisely those instances when the conduct of Wessagusset's leaders and settlers violated English social and political norms, Winslow's account aimed to publicize English subjection and not (as was more common) to efface it.

The execution of one of its settlers for theft underscored the extent of Wessagusset's submission. A survivor of the colony, Phineas Pratt, wrote that one Wessagusset settler was repeatedly caught stealing Indian corn. The Massachusetts demanded justice from the settlement's leaders, who punished the man repeatedly without effect. In an effort to appease the Massachusetts, Wessagusset's leaders offered to turn the thief over to the Indians for punishment: "We give him unto you to doe with him what you please." But the Massachusetts believed that punishment was the responsibility of the guilty man's sachem, and they therefore refused to punish the Wessagusset man. According to Pratt, the Massachusetts claimed that "All Sachams do Justis by thayr own men. If not we say they ar all Agreed & then we ffite [fight], & now I say you all steele my Corne."²⁶

The Massachusett demands reflected precisely the same argument used by many English leaders who demanded the return of stolen items. All parties viewed unpunished theft as part of a coordinated approach, if not centrally directed then at least condoned by leaders. The only other explanation was weak leadership, which was the lesson drawn by Edward Winslow. Winslow placed the blame on the fact that Wessagusset's "overseers were not of more fitness and ability for their places." Because of incompetence or inability, Winslow argued, Wessagusset's leader, John Sanders, had allowed the settlement to deteriorate to the point where the Massachusetts in effect ruled its settlers.²⁷

The problem was not the execution itself. Plymouth executed three men for murdering a Narragansett man in 1638 under English law and, as Bradford put it, with "all due means" and "after due trial." As Gates showed on Bermuda in 1609, executions, or last-minute reprieves, were a vital and accepted component of what William Strachey called a leader's "art of authority."²⁸ John Sanders's case was very different from Sir Thomas Gates's. By asking the Indians to judge and punish an English man according to their own customs and then by proceeding with capital charges against the English thief when the Massachusetts refused, Sanders showed that he accepted Indian authority over the lives of his subordinates. Instead of augmenting an English leader's authority as in the Bermuda case, the hanging of this man signaled its dissolution. Wessagusset's settlers, dispersed and living among the Indians, one and perhaps more of whom had "turned salvage" in Winslow's eyes, likely saw this demonstrative death as proof of Native American strength if it seemed to serve any purpose at all.²⁹

It is not necessary to rely solely on Winslow's admittedly partisan account. Phineas Pratt provides a perspective from within the Wessagusset settlement itself, and Thomas Morton, another neighbor of Plymouth, supported some of Winslow's central contentions. Morton led a small settlement, which he named Ma-re Mount, located near Plymouth. He quarreled continuously with Plymouth Plantation and later with the Massachusetts Bay settlers, who accused him of various crimes including trading arms to the Indians, sheltering runaway servants, and hosting vaguely pagan celebrations in mixed company fueled by plenty of liquor. For his part, Morton made the modest and most likely more accurate claim that first Plymouth and then the Massachusetts Bay magistrates wanted him removed from his legitimate claim to Ma-re Mount for trading with the Indians for furs so successfully that Plymouth stood to lose its own profitable fur trade. Morton's *New English Canaan* was a counter to the contemporary histories of the other colonies' earliest years, and one of its chief aims was to discredit Winslow's accounts of early Plymouth. Morton disagreed with almost everything Bradford and Winslow said and did, and yet his own account of Wessagusset describes this execution in terms similar to Winslow's, taking place according to the English law of felony theft. Morton concluded his discussion of the episode as follows: "For I know that this falls out infallibly where two nations meet: one must rule, and the other be ruled, before a peace can be hoped for. And for a Christian to submit to the rule of a Salvage, you will say, is both shame and dishonor: at least, it is my opinion, and my practice was accordingly." The flow of food from one group to another had in effect carved out new social relationships over time, and the fragile Wessagusset settlement slipped from dependency to subjection.[30]

In most cases, the written accounts of early exchanges tried to mask English weakness and dependency by finding other words for theft and unrequited giving. English leaders knew that their actions and the accounts that described them were of interest at home. They knew their ability to remain as leaders and the ability of their settlement to attract investors, men, money, and provisions depended on the judgments of a metropolitan audience. So they searched for ways to present their actions in a light that corresponded with the assumptions and expectations of that audience. But Plymouth's intentions were to highlight, not efface, the disgraceful submission of English men to Indian leaders as a way of asserting its exclusive rights to the region and its furs. Although they condemned Wessagusset's leaders, Plymouth's leading men were quite willing to raid buried corn stores and refer to their theft as "borrowing."

The importance of these accounts lies not only in their effect on metropolitan readers but also in the light they shed on the language of exchange in early America. Governor Dale's treaty negotiation with the Chickahominies shows that there were few opportunities to misunderstand or misrepresent the meanings inherent in an exchange of food. Therefore some of the interpretive problems facing students of the early period derive from the difficulty English leaders faced in demonstrating their own importance in ways Indians not only understood but accepted. The refiguration of exchanges in the way Dale attempted continued on the pages that described them, as English writers stressed the reciprocity of exchanges and used the term "trade" to describe them, a category of exchange whose most central symbolic meaning is that it is drained of symbolic meaning. Trades leave no residue of obligation, and their central premise is that each side receives what it believes to be an equivalent return or else refuses the exchange.

When efforts at liberality failed, when their need for food drove its price well above the exchange value of copper and beads, English writers could describe their exchanges as trade and present an image of both sides approaching each other as equals, voluntarily entering a relationship that either could abandon without damaging their relationship, and when it was completed, both sides believed they had benefited. But as Dale found in his effort to, in effect, pay the Chickahominies for their venison, the meanings of food could not be so easily blurred in this way. When food passed from one group to another, it carried with it powerful messages regarding dependency and subjection, as Wahunsenacawh knew and the Wessagusset example shows most clearly. English efforts to refigure these exchanges, no matter how subtle, could not mask these unpleasant meanings.

Chapter 5

"A Continuall and Dayly Table for Gentlemen of Fashion": Eating Like a Governor

In 1611, George Percy, the son of a nobleman and sometime deputy governor of the Jamestown settlement, wrote a letter asking his brother, the ninth Earl of Northumberland, to send food. Claiming that "the place which I hold in this Colonie . . . cannot be defraied with smale expence," Percy wrote that his reputation depended on his ability "to keep a continuall and dayly Table for Gentlemen of fashion aboute me." It is a striking comment to make barely a year after the end of Jamestown's "starving time," when by Percy's own account English settlers resorted to cannibalism to survive. Presenting the jarring image of "Gentlemen of fashion" sharing Percy's abundant table, the letter speaks volumes about the expectations English leaders had regarding the links between hospitality, status, and authority.[1]

To examine these expectations requires shifting focus from occasions when food was exchanged between English and Indians to occasions when it was shared and eaten by English men. This narrower focus reveals that at meals, the stakes were even higher. English officials struggled as much with each other over offers of hospitality as they did in exchanges with Indian leaders, for many of the same reasons. Hospitality presented unusually rich opportunities to display status and gender distinctions, to stake a claim to superiority, or to challenge such claims. Hosts and guests paid minute attention to their treatment at meals, especially when those who shared their table also shared their cultural assumptions.

When Percy remarked to his brother that he felt obligated "to keep a continuall and *dayly* Table," he signaled a unique feature of meals, one that separated them from other forms of exchange. Facing a formal encounter with Indian leaders, an English official could prepare himself, could assemble what resources he had in order to stage an appropriate demonstration of what he felt to be his own status. Assuming they had food, leaders could not avoid eating, and it was impossible to lower the stakes at mealtime. An invitation could neither be refused nor withheld without giving offense, meaning that English leaders were often forced to *extend* an invitation, even when doing so threatened to undermine their claims to status and precedence.

Last, as they navigated the challenge of presenting themselves on daily occasions as men suited to wield the authority of office, leading figures conducted themselves and described their conduct with reference to quite different models of a leader. Some men, like George Percy, sought to maintain a patriarchal connection between display, conduct, and status. Others, like Captain John Smith, phrased their claims in the language of humanism and military leadership. These languages both paid careful attention to how a leader conducted himself, especially at his daily meals. This opens up a further dimension of the struggle between English men for status and authority in the Atlantic world, a rhetorical struggle over what sort of leader was best suited for the early settlements. Alongside struggles for precedence in the settlements themselves, these rhetorical struggles to describe the image of an appropriate leader involved not only English settlers but also metropolitan investors and officials.

As Felicity Heal has shown, the early modern English approached hospitality with a set of assumptions unique to that time, place, and people. Heal's work draws on a considerable body of printed literature, from sermons to royal pronouncements, that described hospitality as key to the political stability and social health of the English nation. One contemporary definition of hospitality captures its most important facets: "a Liberal Entertainment of all sorts of Men, at ones House, whether Neighbours or Strangers, with kindness, especially with Meat, Drink and Lodgings." Caleb Dalechamp, in a 1632 sermon, defined hospitality as encompassing "all the works of charity and mercy and courteous kindenesse." One might expect such concerns to emerge in the course of a sermon, but Dalechamp focused especially on "the feasting of mean neighbours, the relieving of the poore, and the entertaining of honest guests and travellers of the same countrey."[2]

Most of these writers described elite households and large, inclusive, formal meals. Therefore, these descriptions stressed that hospitality must encapsulate hierarchy as well as reciprocity, the patriarchal relationships that underpinned the English social order. Social distinctions were manifested by means of a range of symbols and practices: guests were arranged, served, and offered utensils according to their status. Even the freshness and quality of bread might decrease with distance from the head table: from the small white manchet loaves of finely bolted wheat flour to loaves containing more and more bran and a higher proportion of other grains.[3]

However important the distinctions between host and guests were, it was equally important to the political meaning of large formal meals to demonstrate reciprocity as well as degrees of eminence. Everyone was served the same dishes and everyone ate together: these were vital elements of hospitality. To a modern eye, it is more accurate to say that at such meals everyone ate in the same room at the same time, and that everyone was served from the same dishes, but as they made their way down the tables, the choicest morsels were soon taken. Those at the lowest reaches of the table could expect to eat venison, for example, but it would be in the form of "umble pie," a dish made of the umbles, or internal organs, of the animals whose rarer and tastier parts had been eaten by those at the upper reaches of the table. In this way, the status of certain foods was signaled by their absence. Those not invited to share the meal waited outside the gates of the manor house and received whatever was left. Their presence and their incorporation into the hospitality offered by the host reflected the patriarchal obligations of landed elites and, to early modern writers on the subject, the proper functioning of England's social order. Those participating in large meals as the guests or dependents of a high-status man would never expect to return the invitation. Since subordinates could not return hospitality in kind, they were expected to reciprocate the invitations of their superiors with loyalty and deference.[4]

The literature of hospitality stressed its importance as a guarantee of social stability. But at the turn of the seventeenth century, a time of profound social and economic uncertainty, the context for these discussions was troubling. English writers described an alarming tendency to abandon hospitality and simple rural generosity on the part of landed elites. Hospitality was such a key symbol of properly functioning social relationships that many viewed it as a way to restore stability or mend a social fabric that seemed dangerously frayed. Others pushed this connection further, finding the roots of social instability in elites' abandonment of rural hospitality. In 1616, King James argued that social disturbances required the gentry to leave London for the localities, in part to serve as administrators of royal policy. But the monarch also expected that rural elites' hospitality would provide direct relief in times of famine. As he put it, "the poore want relief for fault of the Gentlemens hospitalitie at home." Clearly (and unsurprisingly) evoking the patriarchal obligations of elites to relieve hunger, King James's proclamation underscores the fact that the social distinctions and ties of patronage manifested at meals were only part of the meaning of hospitality. Its importance was also defined in times of scarcity by elites' provision of the necessities of life, however clear it might seem from a modern perspective that leftovers could not possibly make up for a failed harvest.[5]

James I's anger at local elites' absence from their rural estates was a common theme in the early modern literature of hospitality. According to Richard Brathwaite, "the reason why this defect of noble Hospitalitie hath so generally possessed this Realme, is [the gentry's] love to the Court." The court and London more broadly drew aspiring officeholders to the seat of power and the source of patronage, and London's urbane manners were a stark contrast to the simple rural living praised by Tusser and others. Rural denunciations of city life and culture were not new to this period; neither were calls to return to a lost time of rural simplicity and virtue. During this period, though, the flight of gentry from their country seats to London dominated many discussions of hospitality. Brathwaite contrasted the gentry of his day with "Their ancient Predecessours, whose chiefest glory it was to releeve the hungrie, refresh the thirstie, and give quiet repose to the weary." For the "sweet-sented Humorists" of London, these honorable forebears appeared "men of rusticke condition, meere home-spun fellowes."[6]

Writers like Brathwaite believed rural hospitality to be a defining characteristic of the English as a nation, one that distinguished the English above all other people. According to James I, "it was wont to be the honour and reputation of the English Nobility and Gentry, to live in the Countrey, and keep hospitalitie; for which we were famous above all the Countreys in the World." In his book *The Elements of Architecture* (1624), Henry Wotton argued that owing to "the naturall Hospitalitie of England, the Buttrie must be more visible" than in Italian-style houses. Even the shape of rural English houses must be singular, Wotton argued, to accommodate the "naturall Hospitalitie" found there and nowhere else. In his *Description of England*, William Harrison took the unusual rhetorical step of disagreeing with ancient authorities, writing that the English are not "so hard to strangers as Horace would seem to make us." Another author, Sir Thomas Palmer, tried to have it both ways. He

Figure 14. This image, found in a collection of seventeenth-century ballads, depicts "Mock-begger Hall," an elite household with its door (and ample supplies of food) barred to travelers. Images like this one called attention to what many English men and women of the time saw as a decay in the norms of rural hospitality. *The Roxburghe Ballads*, vol. 2 (Hertford: Stephen Austin and Sons for the Ballad Society, 1874), 132.

claimed that whereas the "Commons" of England showed a lack of hospitality to strangers, its nobility and gentry were exemplary in this respect.[7]

Criticism and nostalgia for a lost time of rural hospitality was also sparked by the gentry's retreat into increasingly exclusive settings. Even if they remained in the countryside, elite English men and women began during this period to associate with a small group of social peers. Thomas Cooper, in his work *The Art of Giving*, asked his contemporaries to return to the virtues sketched by Brathwaite, Dalechamp, and others: "Is not our friendship turned into flattery, our hospitality to stately houses, and gay cloathes?" Cooper identified the material components of hospitality—houses, furniture, dishes, utensils, and so on—and contrasted true hospitality with vain display. In similar terms, Michael Sparke wrote: "And how may I complaine therewith of the decay of Hospitality in our Land, whereby many poore soules are deprived of that releeft which they have had heeretofore. The time hath bene, that men have hunted after Worshippe and Credite by good House-keeping, and therein spent great part of their Revennewes: but now commonly, the greater part of their Livings, is too little to maintaine us and our Children in the pompe of Pride." Caleb Dalechamp distinguished true hospitality from "good fellow-ship or some such like thing," which he saw as taking the place and assuming the name of Christian and English hospitality. "Hospitalitie falsly so called," Dalechamp insisted, "is the keeping of a good table; at which seldome or never any other are entertained then kinsfolks, friends, and able neighbours, merry companions, parasites, jesters, and tellers of news."[8]

The concern these authors expressed regarding the gentry's abandonment of their role in the localities had some basis in fact. The trend toward more exclusive displays of status and consumption was irresistible, and it began to be reflected, as Wotton might have predicted, in the shape of English houses themselves. Wistful writers evoked the grand feasts of medieval lords, which took place in the hall of the manor house and included the lord himself and nearly all his tenants, servants, and dependents. As gentry and noble families began withdrawing at mealtime from the head table in the hall to more exclusive settings, the shape of English houses changed as well. Although some aspects of the medieval pageantry of dining were at first retained—servants paraded the meal through the hall and into the more exclusive and private areas reserved for elite dining, then returned with the leftovers—these practices were gradually abandoned for increasingly separate meals. Material culture also intensified in importance in the private settings in which elites shared meals, as Cooper suggested. The physical separation of leaders and ordinary diners was certainly a telling sign: not just of social distinction, which was also reflected in the separation of diners in the medieval lord's hall, but of social separation. If, as Wotton argued, a man's "Mansion House and Home" was "the Theater of his Hospitality, the Seate of Selfe-fruition . . . a kinde of private Princedome; Nay, to the Possessors thereof, an Epitomie of the whole World," the world it reflected and the performances it hosted must include an audience of strangers.[9]

Exclusivity was antithetical to the ideal of inclusive rural hospitality because it restricted the theater of hospitality to social peers of the host, or "able neighbors," in Dalechamp's phrasing. Such guests were expected, for the most part, to return the invitation, which profoundly changed the meanings of hospitality, removing vertical ties of patronage, obligation, and charity to stress horizontal ties between a homogeneous group of mostly male elites. These guests were not expected to reciprocate with loyalty and obedience, and therefore a central political meaning was lost. Dalechamp, for one, opposed exclusivity and refinement for just this reason: hospitality to those that have the ability to return it, he argued, is not true hospitality. Cooper expanded on this point by connecting giving with ownership and noting that subjects—a category that included women and servants—could not give anything, strictly speaking, because they could not own property. Since people of this sort must be included in the exercise of hospitality, he argued, hospitality by definition must not presuppose an equivalent return in kind. Instead, in the eyes of these men and many of their contemporaries, hospitality was meant to be a demonstration of the English social order's legitimacy and solidity.[10]

When they left home English travelers tailored their norms of hospitality to suit new circumstances. Aboard the *Arbella* bound for Massachusetts Bay, Captain Peter Milborne invited "the masters of the other 2: shippes, & mr Pincheon" to dinner aboard the flagship. The men, John Winthrop wrote, "dined with us. in the rounde howse, for the Lady & gentle women dyned in the great Cabbin." In this case, social status and gender were clearly marked: Lady Arbella Johnson, sister of the Earl of Lincoln, clearly outranked the rest of the passengers. Lady Arbella ate with the other women separately but in the better room, the captain's great cabin. Aboard a ship, subtle grades of precedence, deference, and reciprocity were part of the intricate hierarchy of space, and in this case Captain Milborne did his best to fit the social hierarchy of his guests into the spatial hierarchy of his ship, to improvise a proper degree of respect to Lady Arbella (and, although it isn't mentioned by Winthrop, to himself: Milborne almost certainly hosted the meal in the "rounde howse" and sat at the head of the table).[11]

Examples abound in the English travel literature of passing ships' captains being invited to a meal, even between enemies (of sufficient rank) during wartime. In 1591, Sir Richard Grenville, commander of the *Revenge*, fought a furious battle against a much larger force of Spanish ships. After Grenville was mortally wounded and struck his colors, he was taken aboard the Spanish flagship. The Spanish officers offered Grenville food and drink, as was expected between European men of status, and Grenville signaled his spite by chewing up and swallowing the wine glasses offered him at meals.[12]

Sir Humphrey Gilbert offers an especially rich example of hospitality's role in supporting, or undermining, claims to authority. Gilbert could not avoid the responsibility of hosting formal meals even when doing so risked disaster. He had no choice but to preside over what Percy called a "continuall and dayly Table," and as a result meals were the focus of conflict between Gilbert and those he hoped to lead. In 1578, Gilbert organized a sizable fleet of ships for a transatlantic voyage under his command. The precise intentions, and even the destination, of this voyage remain unclear. Settlement may have been one of Gilbert's goals, although it was likely secondary to the privateering campaign that Gilbert outlined in his 1577 "Discourse how her Majesty may annoy the King of Spain."[13]

Assembling a fleet of the size Gilbert was commissioned to command—ten ships in all, along with men, arms, ammunition, and over a year's worth of provisions—was an enormously expensive undertaking. To achieve it, Gilbert depended on the ships, money, and men of private adventurers as well as Queen Elizabeth's legal and financial support. His own financial resources were completely inadequate for such an undertaking. Like many in the Elizabethan period, Gilbert's 1578 voyage therefore comprised "a very mixed brood" of sailors and commanders, "many of them pirates." This coalition of diverse parties and interests was united under Gilbert's authority, delegated to him from Queen Elizabeth via royal patent. Gilbert's success depended on his ability to unify these diverse interests in pursuit of his plan.[14]

There were many obstacles to Gilbert's success, but the decisive one proved to be his principal associate, Henry Knollys. Knollys was the son of Sir Francis Knollys, whose personal connection with Queen Elizabeth and family ties to many noble households gave him considerable influence. A well-connected man like Sir Francis was in a good position to forward Gilbert's career. He supported Gilbert's plan for a colony in Ireland and invested in Gilbert's 1583 expedition. Henry, his eldest son, may have been included in the 1578 expedition as a representative of court interests, of the financial interests of his father and wealthy, well-connected friends, or both.[15]

For his part, Gilbert was also a well-placed courtier of a prominent West Country family, though not of Sir Francis Knollys's stature. His own career at court was helped by his younger half brother Walter Ralegh, and Gilbert's court connections had secured him leading roles in military expeditions on the Continent and in Ireland. He was knighted for his service in Ireland in 1570. These connections and Gilbert's sustained interest in the New World, both in a possible Northwest Passage and in settlement, had led to his commission as

admiral of the 1578 fleet; Henry Knollys's social position and family connections had secured him a place, but although he was only five years younger
than Gilbert, Knollys could claim only the title of captain of the *Elephant*.[16]

In a letter he wrote to Elizabeth I's secretary of state Sir Francis Walsingham in November 1578, Gilbert described the gradual disintegration of his
fleet. As the ships lay near Plymouth, delayed by contrary winds, Gilbert's relationship with Knollys went from bad to worse. According to Gilbert, Knollys tried at one point to leave the voyage, only to be persuaded by Gilbert's
brother Sir John Gilbert to remain. Despite the resolution of this crisis, Gilbert wrote that "noe curtesie or patience of my parte could possiblie cause Mr
Knoles to thinke me either mete to direct or advise hym." Gilbert claimed
that "without eny accasion" Knollys "often and openly persuaded my company and gentlemen to my disgrace howe much he embased and subjected
himself to serve under me." According to Gilbert, Knollys, who had not been
knighted, accounted "him self as he often and openlie saied equal in degree
to the best knightes and better then the most in Englande." And furthermore,
Knollys claimed that he "often tymes had refused that degree [i.e., knight-
hood] as a callinge he estemed not of."[17]

The tension between Gilbert and Knollys reached a peak in connection
with a meal Gilbert hosted, presumably aboard his flagship, the *Anne Aucher.*
Knollys was among those invited, and faced with a difficult choice—joining
Gilbert's table as his inferior or spurning the invitation of his admiral—Knollys
chose the latter. According to Gilbert's account, Knollys's public rejection of
his invitation challenged Gilbert's social standing and his authority as admiral
of the fleet. As Gilbert recounted it, "in open presence of gentlemen of all
sortes to my grete disgrace when I entretid him unto my table he answered me
that he had money to paie for his dynner as well as I, and that he would leve
my trencher for those beggers that were not able to paie for theire meles."[18]

Knollys clearly understood that to accept Gilbert's offer of a meal, at the
admiral's table in the great cabin of the flagship, was to accept his inferior
position. Backed into a corner, Knollys seemingly rejected the notion of hospitality altogether, equating Gilbert's guests with the poor waiting "outside the
gates," not Gilbert's social equals. In Knollys's presentation of the incident,
Gilbert's guests were there because they could not otherwise afford a meal, not
because the admiral of the fleet had honored them with an invitation.[19]

Knollys's conduct ultimately led to the dissolution of Gilbert's fleet and
the abandonment of his planned voyage, and later events suggest that this may
have been Knollys's intention. Knollys's extreme conduct may have stemmed

from his desire to pursue a different goal from Gilbert's (probable) plan for a West Indian voyage. After leaving Gilbert's fleet, Knollys sailed off with three ships on a series of privateering raids in European waters. It is possible that Knollys, who needed the monarch's permission to leave England with ships and men, used the Gilbert expedition as a means to this end. After trying once to leave the voyage and being persuaded to return, Knollys may have insulted Gilbert and refused to submit to his authority as a way to be dismissed from the voyage and pursue his original plan to cruise for prizes in European waters. But whatever the root of the disagreement, these explanations cannot wholly account for Knollys's acrimony toward Gilbert, which continued after Knollys abandoned the voyage. Knollys may have used this meal as a means to extricate himself from Gilbert's authority, but it is clear to say the least that there was genuine reluctance on Knollys's part to serve under a man he viewed as his social inferior.[20]

The difficulties between the two men were deeply rooted, and they did not suddenly appear at this one meal. In fact, it is likely that Gilbert used the occasion of a meal to challenge Knollys to submit, to be seated below Gilbert at a meal in his cabin, and by doing so to solidify his own claim to lead the voyage. When Knollys did not, Gilbert made one more effort toward the same end, hoping by enlisting other elites to shame Knollys into retracting his inexcusable remarks and returning to his place in Gilbert's voyage (and at his table).[21]

It is no accident that Gilbert's difficulties were encapsulated at a meal, the most symbolically charged setting of everyday life. The daily need to eat meant that there was no way for Gilbert to avoid the situation, and hospitality, it must be remembered, was expected of a leader. The assumptions that governed the interactions between Gilbert and Knollys were shared by officeholders of considerably humbler origins, who were nevertheless equally prone to clash over shared meals. John Winthrop, the near-perennial governor of the Massachusetts Bay settlement, is an excellent example. Winthrop was painfully aware that his social position (the only son of a middling landowner) did not match his powerful office, a fact that presented him with continual difficulties.

Winthrop's extensive journal, although not intended to circulate in print, was clearly written and revised with an eye to presenting Winthrop's actions during the early years of the Massachusetts Bay settlement in a positive light. Winthrop was acutely attentive to the symbolic aspects of his claim to authority in the settlement, and he carefully noted many instances on which he felt his authority had been challenged. A number of these dealt directly with food and meals. For example, Thomas Graves, a ship's captain and veteran of many voyages from London to Boston, refused to visit Governor Winthrop on a 1633 trip to Massachusetts Bay. Graves claimed that "he was not well entertained the first tyme he came hether," and therefore "except he were invited he would not goe see him." Graves's was a serious charge: it suggested at bottom that Winthrop's claim to office was not supported by the conduct expected of a man in that position. As we have seen, Winthrop made a point of setting a table appropriate to his station, incurring significant expense in doing so. In making this charge, Graves hoped to transform the obligatory deferential visit of any traveler to the region into an invitation to share the governor's table. Claiming to have been disappointed by his initial reception, he would only attend the governor if personally invited, which would suggest a more equal relationship. Winthrop would not hear of it. Rejecting Graves's claim that he was poorly received, Winthrop pointed out that Graves's first visit took place "at their first Cominge, before they were housed &c." and claimed that Graves had rudely imposed himself and his friends on the governor at "suche an unseasonable tyme." Moving to Graves's second point, his insistence on a personal invitation, Winthrop wrote that to have "invited him standinge upon these termes" would have "blemished his [Winthrop's] reputation." It is telling of the weight of invitations and proper hospitality that Winthrop felt his reputation to be on the line in this case. As was usual in such symbolic clashes, Winthrop reported in his journal that he prevailed.[22]

On a more serious occasion, Henry Vane rejected Winthrop's hospitality during what Michael Winship calls the "free grace controversy" in 1636. Vane, a relatively young man of twenty-two with strong puritan leanings, was a prominent figure in Massachusetts from the moment he arrived. His own family connections were strengthened by the patronage of the puritan noblemen Lord Saye and Sele and Lord Brooke, who enlisted Vane as an agent for their plans to settle in what would become Connecticut. Vane arrived in Massachusetts in 1635. He was welcomed at first by the settlement's elite as the sort of well-connected puritan ally the colony needed in its dealings with England, and he quickly rose to prominence. At the first opportunity, in May 1636, he was elected governor at age twenty-three, replacing Winthrop.[23]

Vane's quick ascent to the top of Massachusetts's social hierarchy proceeded alongside his embrace of Massachusetts's "antinomian" or "free grace" faction, whose most famous members were Anne Hutchinson and John Wheelwright. This group opposed the "orthodox" faction, whose most important secular figure was none other than Winthrop. Vane has always been identified as a supporter of the antinomians, and the transfer of the governor's duties from Winthrop to Vane in 1636 and back to Winthrop in 1637 has been taken as the political reflection of larger struggles within the settlement. Vane's final departure from New England in August 1637 likewise signaled the waning influence of Hutchinson and Wheelwright. But in his overview of the controversy, Michael Winship argues that Vane's role was far more central than historians had previously thought. Winthrop's opponents pinned their hopes for taking control of Massachusetts on Vane; his departure was not just a signal of the declining fortunes of the free grace faction but a decisive end to their plans, one they were unwilling to accept. Vane loomed in the minds of many in the years after 1637 as a potential claimant to authority in Massachusetts. Because of Vane's ongoing influence, Winship argues, it was necessary for the orthodox faction to defeat their opponents without casting blame on a man whose power and influence were expected to grow enormously once he left New England. Others were publicly blamed for fomenting the troubles that led to the rancor of 1636, but Vane was notably not among them.[24]

Within this complex and dense context, Winthrop and Vane limited their public clashes, as befit leading men. But on one occasion, an invitation to a meal brought the conflict and the underlying issues of status and office to the surface. Soon after Vane had been replaced by Winthrop as governor, Winthrop invited him to a dinner intended to honor a visiting nobleman, James Ley, who became the third Earl of Marlborough in 1638.[25] But Vane, Winthrop wrote, "refused to come (alleging by letter that his conscience withheld him)." And far worse, Vane compounded the insult by convincing Lord Ley to dine with him elsewhere. More than an insult, it was a serious challenge to Winthrop's authority as governor. Vane's invitation to Lord Ley forced the nobleman to choose which invitation to honor. Ley's decision to dine with Vane demonstrated Vane's social status and strengthened his claim to authority in Massachusetts Bay. At the same time, Ley's decision dramatized Winthrop's middling social status and weakened his position atop the political hierarchy of Massachusetts. As Winship suggests, Winthrop could not confront Vane publicly, however grievous the insult, without alienating a powerful man. Winthrop's delicate position is plainly seen in the manuscript of his journal, where Winthrop struck out the contention that Vane had taken Lord Ley elsewhere for dinner, perhaps attempting to mute Vane's role in the "free grace controversy."[26]

To place this episode in perspective, it was not the pivotal moment in the controversy, nor was it a defining moment in Vane's struggle with Winthrop. Vane's stay in Massachusetts was brief: Winthrop prevailed in the contest with Vane despite this embarrassment, and he went on to solidify his hold on authority in the colony, maintaining a leading role until his death. Vane's public insult is therefore in one sense only a sidelight to the larger story of the clash between the orthodox and free grace factions in Massachusetts in the mid-1630s. In another light, though, the incident, like Gilbert's invitation, demonstrates some of the ways political authority was constituted, legitimated, and challenged in the English Atlantic world. Winthrop's social standing was clearly inferior to Vane's, and yet as long as he held office as governor, Winthrop was Vane's superior.

Ordinary men like Winthrop were placed in positions of authority across the English Atlantic world, and their effectiveness as leaders demanded that they be treated as extraordinary men. Winthrop was particularly insistent on this point. When he lost his honor guard as a result of the controversy with Vane and his followers, Winthrop paid for a new ceremonial guard of halberdiers himself. Halberds, a combination spear and battle-ax mounted on a long shaft, had no military value in America, but their symbolic power was significant. Winthrop's processions through the muddy streets of Boston accompanied by his leased halberdiers did not have the full meaning of those provided for him by the General Court, but Winthrop clearly felt their form essential to his station and reputation. A leader like Winthrop might carefully stage-manage rare and ceremonial occasions like these, in order to present himself in just the way desired. Meals, on the other hand, could not be avoided and their meanings could not be ignored. At his own table, an English officeholder sometimes had to put his authority on the line no matter what the stakes.[27]

Early Jamestown provides an especially rich example of this point. Jamestown's early struggles provoked considerable debate over what sort of leader was best suited to ensure stability and prosperity in the Chesapeake. Three of Jamestown's first leaders—George Percy, Captain John Smith, and Edward Maria Wingfield—each struggled in the settlement's early years to establish a solid claim to authority. As part of this effort, each man wrote in praise of his own experience and ability and in condemnation of his rivals' claims, and each employed a different language of leadership and authority in making these claims.[28]

The situation at Jamestown was especially fraught because its investors were pouring men and money into the Chesapeake to replace Jamestown's staggering losses. Ultimate authority lay with the highly placed members of the Virginia Company, who named the settlement's leaders and arbitrated its many disputes. Offices at Jamestown as elsewhere were a form of patronage, and certain qualifications were clearly appealing to the members of the Virginia Company. The Virginia Company was most likely to choose men with experience as navigators, commanders of overseas forces in the Low Countries and Ireland, and those who had traveled, especially those who had traveled to North America. But it was not simply experience that mattered. The key for a would-be officeholder was his ability to persuade the members of the Virginia Company that his experiences had given him skills and knowledge applicable more generally to the situation in the Chesapeake. Since no one could claim a record of success governing an English settlement, this was a rhetorical struggle to claim what Eric Ash has called "expertise."[29]

Making their situation more complicated, each man had to appeal not just to the metropolitan audience of the Virginia Company in writing but to the hungry settlers at Jamestown through their conduct in office. There was more than one set of images and references available to Jamestown's leading figures in their efforts to present themselves to these very different audiences as effective leaders. The patriarchal vision, best exemplified by George Percy, had its roots in history, the English social hierarchy, and the landscape itself. It rested on the fundamental elements of political authority: control of land, labor, and the foods they produced. Percy, brother of the Earl of Northumberland, saw his role at Jamestown as representing hierarchy through his appearance and daily conduct, and he expected that others would share these assumptions. Among other things, Percy expected that the way he made use of his own private stores would reflect his status and legitimate his claim to preeminence.

Humanism offered a very different image of the leader, best exemplified at Jamestown by Captain John Smith. Smith presented himself as a soldier and scholar whose claim to leadership rested on his active pursuit of the common good. He was famously scornful of Jamestown's "gentlemen of fashion," to use Percy's term, and of the displays of leadership and status they favored. Drawing from classical examples a model of conduct that distrusted luxury as a sign of political corruption, Smith shrewdly made use of the image of the leader as distributor of food in times of scarcity. Rather than displaying his own eminence, asserting his right as leader to the rarest and choicest, Smith presented himself as a leader who, in the eyes of one subordinate "never allowed more for himselfe, then his souldiers with him; that upon no danger would send them where he would not lead them himselfe; that would never see us want, what he either had, or could by any meanes get us."[30]

Both languages placed special emphasis on hospitality as a reflection of a leader's legitimate claim to his position. Both languages also agreed that when a leader failed to conduct himself properly at meals he undermined those claims. Accusations that a leading man excluded others from his table or strove for luxury and refinement to an unseemly degree carried slightly different connotations in each language but the same basic meaning, namely that a leader had abandoned his responsibility for those subject to his authority. A leader's table and his use of the common stores were especially important at Jamestown, where supplies were few and disagreements many. For these reasons, food was a common thread in the political vocabularies of these three very different men.

In many ways Edward Maria Wingfield is the logical place to begin, since his effort to navigate these waters was a spectacular failure, and an instructive one. To all appearances, Wingfield had plenty to recommend him for a leading position in the Chesapeake. He came from a reasonably prominent family, had received some education at the Inns of Court, and had a distinguished career as a soldier in Ireland and the Low Countries, including experience with a colonizing project in Ireland. His family relation to Bartholomew Gosnold, who played a pivotal role in the organization of the original Virginia voyage, was an added factor in Wingfield's favor. In fact, most of the recruiting for the voyage was done by these two men, who took the further step of volunteering to travel to the Chesapeake with the initial voyage. Wingfield was by no means the most exalted figure behind the formation of the Virginia Company, or even among those on the initial voyage. Nevertheless, his efforts, connections, and qualifications led the London backers of settlement in the Chesapeake to place Wingfield's name on the 1606 royal patent. As far as his own motivations, Wingfield had few prospects in England and doubtless hoped that playing a leading role in Virginia would be a means to advancement.[31]

As the only royal patent holder among the original settlers, there was no question that Wingfield would be chosen a member of the council appointed to govern the settlement. For the same reason, his election by the rest of the council to serve as its president was a formality. Wingfield was joined on the council by several men whose social standing was clearly beneath his but whose connections or skills nevertheless qualified them for a leading role in the venture. Most notable among these was Captain John Smith, whose military service across Europe and his association with influential families compensated for his yeoman origins. Other members of the council owed their appointment to specific skills—Captain Christopher Newport had long experience as a navigator and privateer in American waters—or connections based in family and patronage.

The most prominent man by birth among those on the original voyage, George Percy, was not even granted a seat on the council. In part, Percy's recent family history discouraged the Virginia Company from placing him in a leading role. Two of George's brothers had participated in the Earl of Essex's futile rebellion in 1601; more serious, a distant relative had joined in the Gunpowder Plot. For their family associations, Henry Percy, the ninth Earl of Northumberland, and two of George's other brothers were imprisoned in the Tower of London afterward, Henry for sixteen years. In their efforts to secure a royal charter, the Virginia Company would naturally keep the Percy family name off both their documents and the governing council. But there may have been other, more personal reasons for Percy's exclusion. Percy had been sickly as a child and suffered from epilepsy, which might have dissuaded some from placing him in a position of authority. When he did hold office, he could hardly be called an unqualified success, which might have made Percy, however prominent, at best a stopgap officer. His birth made his right to rule unquestioned, though his ability to rule remained doubtful.[32]

In the eyes of the Virginia Company's influential investors and backers Wingfield was clearly suited to lead the new settlement, but the councillors resident in Virginia soon came to feel very differently. In September 1607, after only four months ashore at Jamestown, the remaining councillors summoned Wingfield to appear before them and charged him with corruption, mismanagement, incompetence, and slander. Then, after a brief deliberation for the sake of appearances, the Virginia council removed Wingfield from office and fined him the enormous sum of three hundred pounds.[33]

Hoping to restore his reputation, Wingfield returned to England at the first opportunity, eager to appeal his conviction before his peers in London. Soon after his arrival in May 1608, Wingfield completed a written defense, known as the "Discourse," and presented it to the Virginia Company. Wingfield intended the "Discourse" to circulate privately, in manuscript, among the members of the council, in part to spare himself the embarrassment of airing the details of his dispute with his social inferiors. But further, in the written words of his manuscript, Wingfield made a personal appeal to his friends and peers and was personally present in his text in a way the author of a printed work would not have been. In this way, the "Discourse" represented an effort to reestablish patronage ties by demonstrating the existing bonds between the men of status who made up the Virginia Company. The tone and rhetorical stance of the "Discourse" presented Wingfield as a gentleman, sharing the social status and patriarchal assumptions of his elite readers, while his accusers appear as both politically corrupt and socially unfit for their positions running the settlement. In its depictions of luxury as the counterpoint to virtue, it also plainly drew on humanist assumptions.[34]

According to the "Discourse," the charges against Wingfield fell under two broad headings. The first was that Wingfield had "Combyned with the Spanniards to the distruction of the Collony." This was a potentially serious charge: George Kendall, one of the original councillors, had been shot for his supposed participation in just such a plot. Nevertheless, the charge of treason was backed by slender evidence, and Wingfield dismissed it with few words. Most of the "Discourse" focused, in extensive detail, on the second set of charges: that Wingfield had "affected a Kin[g]dome" and hidden "the Comon provision in the ground." Wingfield took the latter accusation very seriously. The procurement and distribution of food amounted to the most significant exercise of political authority in early Jamestown. The charges describe the common stores as sufficiently well stocked that the settlement expected to survive from them. Wingfield was accused not of incompetence in supplying the settlement—he seems to have assumed that was the responsibility of the Virginia Company—but of improperly and unjustly distributing its supplies.[35]

In Captain John Smith's *True Relation* (1608), the first published account of Jamestown, Smith claimed that Wingfield had kept the stores (particularly "the Sack, Aquavitie, and other preservatives for our health") for himself and his associates. This was a public charge, unlike the comments by Percy and Wingfield, which had been more narrowly and decorously shared with an elite audience. Wingfield expanded on Smith's charge in his defense, reporting that John Ratcliffe, elected president after Wingfield was deposed, claimed that Wingfield "denyed him . . . a Chickyn, [and] a spoonfull of beere, and served him with foule Corne." Wingfield also reported John Martin's claims that Wingfield neglected the colony to "tend [his] pott, spitt, and oven" and further that Wingfield had also denied Martin's son, who was sick and soon to die, "a spoonefull of beere." In his defense, Wingfield wrote that he had not "carryed any favorite over with me, or intertayned any thear" and that he "did allwayes give every man his allowance faithfully." In short, Wingfield hoped to head off the charges against him by pointing out that he had "always . . . equally devided [the stores] amongst the Collonye" according to the ration set by the same men who deposed him. Smith provided a possible explanation of this disagreement in the *Generall Historie* (1624), where he elaborated on the charges, accusing Wingfield of "ingrossing to his private, Oatmeale, Sacke, Oyle, Aquavitae, Beefe, Egges, or what not," but allowed that "the Kettell; that indeed he [Wingfield] allowed equally to be distributed." In short, Smith's accusation was that Wingfield had taken the choicest foods for his own table and left only meager rations of porridge in the "Kettell."[36]

The pose Wingfield struck in his rebuttal was one of rigid ethics and total impartiality and, in a rhetorical move typical of the entire "Discourse," he tried to turn his rivals' charges back upon them. It was his rivals who, hoping for "some better allowance for themselves and some few [of] the sick their privates," had tried to enlist Wingfield in a scheme to increase their rations, with (Wingfield claimed) no success. Refusing to dignify with an explicit denial the accusation that he had, in effect, stolen from the common stores, Wingfield presented the other councillors as guilty of favoritism in their efforts to secure an extra ration for "their privates." And yet it was vitally important to the patriarchal conception of Wingfield's readers that a leader demonstrate the reciprocity of the social order in his or her distribution of food. Martin's charge that Wingfield denied his son a spoonful of beer before his death suggested another dimension to the criticism of Wingfield, that he had ignored the sick and needy. Accordingly, the deposed president wrote in his defense that he had "caused half a pinte of pease to be sodden, with a peese of porke of my owne provision for a poore old man, which in a sicknes (whereof he died) he much desired." Wingfield intended this anecdote to demonstrate his understanding that "Curtesey and Civility became a governor"; in other words that charity and liberality, qualities expected of a leader, eased this man's final moments and, equally important, did so without depleting "the Comon pott," as Wingfield's rivals had attempted.[37]

The fact that Wingfield controlled private supplies was not held against him. As president and patentee Wingfield was expected to maintain private stores of choice foods, which in the Jamestown setting meant for the most part pork and beer. For one thing, Wingfield's private stores gave him the ability to distribute food to the sick and needy in the way expected of English leaders. And, as Wingfield himself carefully pointed out, by handing out food from his own stores he could do this without reducing others' rations. But more broadly, a man of Wingfield's status and office was expected to command supplies beyond the reach of ordinary settlers, in quality and quantity, simply because meals were an inescapable and daily marker of status and office.

Jamestown's president and a patentee of the Virginia Company could not be expected to eat like a servant any more than he could appear in public wearing a servant's clothes. Wingfield therefore made two central claims in his "Discourse" that plainly rested on patriarchal assumptions: a claim to elite status by virtue of the foods he ate and a claim to leadership by virtue of the way he distributed his supplies.

But no matter how effectively Wingfield defended himself, the fact remains that his actions while at Jamestown failed to secure the loyalty of either his fellow councillors or other settlers. One way to understand his failure lies in the way Wingfield and Smith used the term "private." When Smith accused Wingfield of "ingrossing to his privat" the choicest foods, he was claiming that Wingfield was improperly using the common stores to support his claims to status. By sharing the best foods with, presumably, Jamestown's leading figures, Wingfield in Smith's eyes was guilty of corruption. But when Wingfield defended himself, he took the word "private" to be synonymous with "favorite," and stressed his impartiality, as we have seen. Elites in Wingfield's eyes had exclusive claim to the choicest foods, with the possible exception of their obligation to be charitable to those in need. Smith and Wingfield differed in the way they understood the term "private," but they shared the understanding that it connoted corruption. Wingfield's very traditional assumptions in this regard were that food was, in essence, simply a sumptuary item. What Wingfield failed to recognize was that Smith's understanding of the term was closer to that of ordinary settlers and sailors, and therefore the charge of corruption stuck against Wingfield for reasons that had everything to do with the heightened importance of distributing and consuming food in early Jamestown.

Wingfield was hardly alone in his assumptions. George Percy also made sure to demonstrate his office and station in food and clothing. During his brief career at Jamestown, Percy spent a shocking amount on clothes and furnishings, displaying his status with a gilded sword, gold buttons and thread, gold trimmings for his hats, and a brass bed with feather mattress. All of this was located in a house built for him in Virginia by workmen paid by his brother, the Earl of Northumberland, who also supplied Percy regularly with biscuits, cheese, butter, and valuable trade goods. In 1608 the Northumberland accounts show an expenditure of £53 8s. 9d. on Percy's supplies, of which £32 14s. 7d. was for clothing. That number only increased, to £58 14s. 8d. in 1610, with an additional £76 18s. 10d. in other expenses. The enormity of these sums is clear when one considers that £5–6 would pay for passage to the New World, in exchange for which servants would sign indentures agreeing to work for terms of five years and sometimes more. Nevertheless, Percy sent a letter to his brother in the summer of 1611 asking for still more. In it, Percy acknowledged that "this last yere hath not bin a little Chardgable unto your Honnor," but hoped his brother would "not think any thing prodigally by me wasted or spent which tendeth to my no little Advancement." To advance in Jamestown required fine clothing and, equally important, ample private supply: "True it is the place which I hold in this Colonie (the store affording no other meanes then a pound of meale a day and a little Oatemeale) cannot be defraied with smale expence, it standing upon my reputation (being Governour of James Towne) to keep a continuall and dayly Table for Gentlemen of fashion aboute me." Percy viewed setting a fine table as part of his office, just as a gilded sword was appropriate for the son and brother of an earl, and his words suggest that his social peers at Jamestown understood Percy's claims to status and office to rest on this basis.[38]

It was also important that Percy's hospitality be "continuall and dayly." Like Gilbert and Winthrop, Percy understood that the image of a leader he sought to present was not to be reserved for ceremonial occasions. And like Wingfield, Percy appealed to traditional assumptions: that although leadership involved among other things procuring and providing food to inferiors in times of sickness or scarcity, the social order itself was predicated on essential distinctions that were reflected and sustained in the performance of specific social roles. For Percy, this meant setting a comparatively lavish table for "gentlemen of fashion," a term that suggests that each of Percy's supper guests also displayed what they believed to be their own status in daily interactions at Jamestown. In the eyes of this select group, Percy's table was a necessary site for a mutual display of "fashion" and social distinction at Jamestown, a theater where social distinctions were manifested and ties of loyalty and patronage consolidated. Although Percy governed Jamestown during its most desperate period, his efforts to connect private stores with status and office in no way involved Jamestown's ordinary settlers. It may have been that Percy's family connections made his use of private stores difficult to criticize, however much his displays of wealth may have rankled and appalled. The son and brother of an earl may have been immunized at birth from the sort of criticism Wingfield endured, and Percy's insistence on demonstrating his status did not cost him his office. But Percy's two appointments to leading positions at Jamestown were temporary. In no case was he named to a leading position in his own right, and his tin ear for the nuances of a leader's role may have combined with his family's questionable reputation to deny him a more prominent position.

Wingfield shared many of Percy's assumptions, but his position was slightly more complex. Like Percy he looked to tradition to support his claim to authority, and like Percy Wingfield had to accomplish this delicate negotiation in the difficult circumstances of early Jamestown. But since Wingfield's presidency did not last until the first supply arrived from England, he could not rely on the material supports that Percy did. One passage from the "Discourse" encapsulates Wingfield's difficulty more plainly than any other: "It is further said I did much banquit, and Ryot: I never had but one Squirell roasted, whereof I gave part to Mr Ratcliff then sick."[39]

This rich statement embodies several claims, chief among them Wingfield's frugality. We know from Wingfield's own account that he ate venison while at Jamestown, and yet he chose to describe a meal of squirrel to demonstrate his qualifications as a leader. The first possibility is that he was not referring to the familiar rodent at all but using the term to refer to an animal in a slighting or derogatory way, in this connection as thin or stringy or otherwise contemptible. Assuming it was in fact a squirrel that Wingfield was referring to, he was notably frugal in allowing himself only one (and only part of a squirrel at that). Several sources claim that Virginia's squirrels—gray squirrels, not the smaller red squirrels native to Europe—were very tasty, and Wingfield would have been tempted to eat more than one for this reason alone, making his forbearance in the face of his suffering subordinates especially praiseworthy. The point of all this was to insist that, in the difficult conditions of early Jamestown, Wingfield was not living a luxurious life but had sacrificed along with the settlers he had been charged with governing, a claim to virtuous leadership clearly phrased in the vocabulary of humanism.[40]

As had his other meals, Wingfield's roast squirrel echoed the patriarchal social vision of Percy and others. By giving "part" of the squirrel "to Mr Ratcliff then sick," Wingfield intended to make a point, just as he had when giving pork and peas to a dying man (and then writing about it). In the latter case, the recipient was dying and may have asked for familiar English foods whose status at Jamestown derived from their scarcity. In Ratcliffe's case, when Wingfield carved a haunch or saddle of squirrel for his dinner guest, or had it delivered to Ratcliffe's sickbed by a servant, he delivered food from his own table, perhaps even his own plate, to another member of the settlement's elite. The two examples suggest that not only did Wingfield demonstrate the reciprocity of the social order by distributing food to the sick, but the way in which he did so could mark either the relationship of president and ordinary settler or the relationship between the settlement's president and one of its leading men.[41]

Wingfield made this same twofold point in another way, by contrasting his own abstemious and rarefied meal of roast squirrel with the meals of the president and council that succeeded him. According to Wingfield, those men (including Smith) were of inferior social status and did not understand the need to demonstrate the fine nuances of hierarchy and reciprocity at meals; instead, the hunger of the "triumvirate" that deposed Wingfield was manifested as greed and gluttony, shading into tyranny. Wingfield wrote that the "Presidentes and the Councellors spittes haue night & daie bene endangered to break their backes so laden with swanns, geese, duckes, &c" and "many tymes their flesh pottes haue swelled." Wingfield's carefully chosen words here were vital to his meaning. The councillors were portrayed gorging themselves on one of the quintessential status foods. By eating swans, they clearly overstepped their social station, since swans were reserved for the very highest reaches of the social order. But more, the reference to the "triumvirate" plainly referred to classical writers and in particular Cicero, who wrote about the fall of the Roman Republic after the seizure of power by Julius Caesar and the Triumvirate. Here again, humanist conceptions of the leader intersect with the distribution of food, though this time in a negative sense intended to denigrate Wingfield's rivals.[42]

But even worse than these demonstrations of greed, gluttony, and social presumption, Wingfield continued, was the fact that "many hungry eies did behold [these feasts] to their great longing." In this image, the audience to the councillors' display of social standing and political authority was starving, making the council's claims to legitimacy hollow if not cruel. Wingfield recognized the weight of the charge against him and again turned the argument back on his accusers in this passage, suggesting that they were devoid of charity and virtue. A strikingly similar accusation was made by Nathaniel Butler, an early governor of Bermuda. Bermuda's first governor, Richard Moore, departed in 1615 and left the settlement in the hands of a group of six men, a number that soon dwindled to two. According to Butler, these men, having squandered the supply, shared "the liquor and best necessaryes" among themselves. The "weake and sick people, women with child and such like . . . fell quickly into many distresses and miserable wants," Butler wrote. In a phrase echoing Wingfield, he added that "the Governour and his gourmandizeing minions, dayly and hourely wallowed in their swineish excesses," a period Butler sarcastically termed a "perpetuall Christmas." Smith himself presented similar charges against Wingfield's successors, claiming that John Ratcliffe, who was elected president in Wingfield's place, "riotously consumed the store."

The similarity in these accusations suggests that such accounts were a potent charge against a leader. Feasting oneself while the sick and weak starve was tyranny in its plainest form.[43]

It is very revealing that this was the only occasion on which Jamestown's lower orders played any role in Wingfield's account: as passive "hungry eies" whose mute condemnation underscored the illegitimacy of his rivals. On this point he and Smith differed profoundly. For Smith, ordinary people played an active and central role in legitimating his claim to authority. In fact, Smith understood that at Jamestown a leader must appeal to that audience, though in different terms than when addressing a patron. Since Smith's claim to authority could not rest on his own relatively humble birth, he based it on his experience as a soldier and, at Jamestown, his ability to provide food when others could not. Smith was likely chosen to serve on the resident council because he had managed to convince the leading figures behind the Virginia enterprise that his experience amounted to the sort of expertise they needed. After arriving in the Chesapeake, Smith based his claim that he alone could direct the Virginia settlement to stability and prosperity on his ability to provide food. Just as the patriarchal language had different emphases depending on whether it was aimed at superiors in writing or inferiors in conduct, so too did Smith's humanist vocabulary.

According to the Virginia Company's "Instructions given by way of advice," Jamestown's leaders were to "Endeavour to Store yourselves of the Country Corn" in order "to avoid the Danger of famine." Warning of the dangers of unrestricted trade, the "Instructions" directed the president and council to maintain tight control of trading privileges. But each of Jamestown's leaders interpreted these instructions differently. Wingfield seems not to have left the confines of Jamestown, reporting that "the Salvages brought to the Towne such Corne and flesh as they could spare" in the first months. It was Smith alone among the settlement's leaders who understood that trading with the Chesapeake Algonquians for food was the president's most pressing responsibility, apart from defending the settlement itself. Wingfield wrote that after he was deposed, "the Councellors (Master Smyth especially) traded up and downe the River with the Indyans for Corn, which releved the Collony well." For the year following Wingfield's deposition, Smith served as Jamestown's cape merchant, charged with managing the colony's trade. From September 1608 until he was forced to leave Jamestown roughly a year later, Smith served as president. During this two-year period, Smith's voyages throughout the Chesapeake were the settlement's lifeline and the basis of Smith's authority.[44]

One might account for the different approaches of Smith and Wingfield in several ways. Wingfield was able while remaining at Jamestown to collect gifts of food from Wahunsenacawh and the several subordinate werowances of the region surrounding the settlement. Gifts of food were a common feature of the very first contacts between English and native groups, as we have seen. But they were not a long-term solution to the colony's supply problems, in part because even if Wahunsenacawh had been willing to continue supplying Jamestown with food, the region's severe drought would have made this very difficult. For this and other reasons, as time went on gifts became fewer and the terms of exchange less favorable to the English. By the time Smith took over as cape merchant, with sole and exclusive responsibility for the colony's trade, he was forced to find more distant sources of supply. Underlying these complex factors is a larger point. By "adventuring abroad to make them provision," Smith saved the lives of everyone at Jamestown. And since the Chesapeake Algonquians played such a key role in providing food for the settlement, Smith understood that they were a crucial element of his own claim to authority. Until Jamestown could survive on its own it could not afford a war, and therefore Smith had to account for Indian expectations as well as the various English constituencies at Jamestown and in London.[45]

The sources are silent on the effect on ordinary settlers, who could only have viewed Smith's return from each voyage, his barge loaded with food, as a deliverance from hunger. Smith therefore was first to understand and exploit the connection between providing food and assuming command, but he was not alone. Recognizing that Smith's authority had its roots in his relationship with Wahunsenacawh and other native leaders, his rivals tried to undermine these claims by replacing Smith at the head of Jamestown's trading voyages. There was no practical reason to do this, since Smith was more familiar than anyone else at Jamestown with the landscape and waterways of the Chesapeake; the location, disposition, and allegiances of Algonquian villages that might have corn; the language, customs, and expectations of the inhabitants; and in every other conceivable qualification. The only reason for another to assume command was to supplant Smith as Jamestown's provider of food and by doing so undermine the basis of his authority. Smith understood this very well, writing that "some so envied his good successe, that they rather desired to hazzard a starving then his paines should prove so much more effectuall then theirs."[46]

Smith's rivals, of course, disagreed. These men saw theirs as the legitimate claim and Smith's the usurpation, and as was true of the successful effort to depose Wingfield, consumption of food played a role in the attacks on Smith and in his defense. When the bulk of the 1609 supply fleet reached James-town bringing neither the new charter nor the officials named in it, Smith was dismayed to find some of his old adversaries among the new arrivals, and these men quickly tried to depose him. Gabriel Archer, one of the original settlers and a principal rival of Smith's, wrote that in order "to strengthen his authority, [Smith] accorded with the Mariners, and gave not any due respect to many worthy Gentlemen, that came in our Ships." George Percy, who was elected president in Smith's place, described Smith's methods in similar terms: "feareinge . . . thatt the seamen and thatt factyon mighte growe too stronge and be a meanes to depose him of his govermentt," Smith "Jugled with them by the way of feasteinges Expense of mutche powder and other unnecessary Tryumphes." In other words, Percy accused Smith of squandering the com-mon stores in order "to Insinewate with his Reconcyled enemyes and for his owne vayne glory for the which we all after suffred." At the heart of this ac-cusation are two charges: Smith's misuse of the stores and his appeal to the lower orders at Jamestown at the expense of the "worthy Gentlemen." Word reached England that the disagreement stemmed from "dissention . . . about the distributing of the Vittles," but to Archer and Percy, Smith's crime was broader and more fundamental. Bypassing their claims to authority and their judgment of who was fit to rule, Smith appealed to the lower orders at James-town, who upheld his claim to authority.[47]

In Wingfield's eyes it was his peers who legitimated a claim to authority, not ordinary settlers, and in fact a true leader should learn, as he claimed to have, "to dispise the populer verdict of the vulgar." Defending himself from the charge that he "did much banquit, and Ryot," Wingfield focused in his "Discourse" on stressing that he had been evenhanded and moderate in dis-tributing the stores, insisting that he had not feasted himself and his favorites while others went without. The accusation against Smith was at bottom the same: he had squandered the stores in an effort to support his claim to lead-ership. The difference lay in who participated in the feasting, and therefore whether the accusation was a misappropriation of the common stores to "pri-vate" or demagogic ends.[48]

However his rivals tried to portray him to an elite audience in London, Smith's appeals resonated with the audience he addressed. Like Wingfield, Smith made use of his private supplies, but in a way aimed to confirm his standing among Jamestown's lower orders. In the spring of 1609, after rats had devoured the common stores and before the Chesapeake Algonquians' harvest was ready, Jamestown's settlers were desperate, ready to trade all they had for food, when Smith announced to the hungry and fearful Jamestown settlers that "all my English extraordinary provision that I have, you shall see me divide it amongst the sick." For those well enough to work, "he that gathereth not every day as much as I doe," Smith warned, would be banished from the settlement. Reserving nothing for himself, neither provisions nor the right to live from others' labor, Smith was able to encourage his settlers to plant, gather, and preserve food. The circumstances demanded that he renounce any claim to a private store or an inner, select circle, which in this speech Smith ostentatiously did. Similarly, on one of the exploratory voyages Smith took up the Chesapeake, his men were afraid their stores would run out and begged him to return. Smith continued the voyage by promising to share all their hardship: "for what is to come, of lodging, dyet, or whatsoever, I am contented you allot the worst part to my selfe." The difference from Wingfield's peas and salted pork or his haunch of squirrel, both displays marked by an equal degree of ceremony and self-congratulation, could not be more stark. For Percy and Wingfield, private stores represented the ability to assert exclusivity and gentility, a social separation that gave Wingfield's efforts at charity their meaning. Smith's use of his private stores was exactly the reverse, giving them away as a means of erasing the social distinctions between leaders and led. Smith's intention was to establish a different basis for his claim to authority.[49]

The Jamestown example illuminates several connections between food and political authority in the English Atlantic world. First, to accuse a leader of misusing the food supply was a potent charge, one that portrayed him as corrupt and tyrannical. But the potency of this accusation grew from the fact that misusing the stores was more than a metaphor for tyranny: it questioned a man's fitness to govern at the most basic level. For the early modern English, the bonds of reciprocal obligation that underpinned political relationships were rooted in food—finding, hunting, or growing it; distributing it to subordinates, guests, and dependents; and consuming it—more than in any other realm of social life.

Second, the example shows that the symbolic weight of food—the way social and political relationships were, as Percy noted, encapsulated in meals—was a feature of everyday life. Unlike other means of asserting and legitimating authority, meals were (ideally) ubiquitous, which for Wingfield meant that his clumsy manipulation of the symbolic connections between eating and authority was both unavoidable and vitally important. The same inescapable, daily nature of meals and of a leader's need to conduct them in a way that reflected his station required Gilbert to extend an invitation to Knollys and Winthrop to Vane. This combination brings into focus the contingency and negotiation that characterized the political culture of the early modern English Atlantic world, but it also captures the role of ordinary men and women in the legitimation of political authority on a formal level, a point Smith understood better than anyone.

In these ways food embodied and supported the political relationships of the early modern English Atlantic world, representing to contemporaries the most basic human necessity and a rich site of symbolic meanings. One need look no further than Wingfield's roast squirrel for evidence of these points. And no matter how important the symbolic overtones of food and meals were, food always had a simpler and more direct meaning, especially to hungry settlers and travelers. This fact—food's importance as sustenance—has the added effect of grounding interpretations of theatrical displays like Percy's or textual claims to authority like Wingfield's. No matter how well-dressed, well-fed, or wellborn a leader might be, his claims to authority ultimately rested on the staff of life.

Chapter 6

"To Manifest the Greater State": English and Indians at Table

Formal meals are, as one scholar of the subject has called them, "a fundamental instrument and theater of political relations," but the distinction between playwright, players, and audience in this particular theater was not always clear. English leaders like Sir Humphrey Gilbert, John Winthrop, and Edward Maria Wingfield recognized that they could not always hope to stage a successful performance at meals even when they hosted their own countrymen. To offer a meal was the most direct way to express rich meanings, whether distinctions of status and precedence or a desire for peaceful relations with an important visitor. But one could not avoid conveying these meanings by failing to offer a meal, by failing to mark the meal as an important occasion, or worst of all by failing to include a visitor in a meal.[1]

Formal meals were even more fraught with tension when they included Indian and English leaders, occasions that return the spotlight to where we began: the hospitality offered by Granganimeo's wife to Arthur Barlowe and the rest of his party. A narrow focus on the fine details of dining—seating arrangements, furniture, clothing, tableware, hand washing, manners, the foods served, and the manner and order of serving them—draws on food's many layers of meaning to examine the most subtle and nuanced of all encounters. English and Indians closely examined every feature of the meals they shared, knowing that they carried messages. Both sides soon became familiar enough with the symbolic language of meals to convey the meanings they wanted, and as they learned about each other, both sides used this knowledge not only to avoid offense but to assert superiority.

English writers paid special attention to wedding feasts, occasions when gender and status distinctions were marked with special care. This signaled their interest (and their readers' interest) in how social relationships were staged at formal meals. An even more striking example of the significance of meals is false hospitality. Time and again, English and Indians invited each other to a meal with the intention of violent betrayal, and with puzzling regularity these invitations were accepted. These occasions underscore the fact that invitations could not be ignored without making a powerfully negative statement. They also remind us that the early period was marked as much by violence as by peaceful alliances. Food lay at the heart of all these encounters.

At home and abroad, the English placed a high importance on hospitality, and the accounts of English travelers and settlers in the Americas often remarked that Algonquians held hospitality in similarly high regard. Many writers recounted evidence of unstinting generosity among Indians even when food was scarce. William Wood was one of these approving observers: "they are as willing to part with their Mite in poverty, as treasure in plenty. As he that kills a Deere, sends for his friends, and eates it merrily: So he that receives but a piece of bread from an English hand, parts it equally betweene himselfe and his comerades, and eates it lovingly." Sharing food when it was available was expected even when "they be sometimes scanted," Wood claimed. Thomas Morton made a similar point regarding the generosity of New England Algonquians: "A bisket cake given to one, that one breaks it equally into so many parts as there be persons in his company, and distributes it. Plato's Commonwealth is so much practiced by these people." James Rosier similarly mentioned that New England Algonquians were "so kinde, as if you give any thing to one of them, he will distribute part of [it to] every one of the rest." And Roger Williams wrote of the same groups that "If any provision of fish or flesh come in, they make their neighbours partakers with them." Williams summed up New England Algonquian liberality in the following verses:

> Sometimes God gives them Fish or Flesh,
> Yet they're content without;
> And what comes in, they part to friends
> and strangers round about.[2]

Accounts like these praised Indians' generosity but also their customs of hospitality in the specific sense used by the English: a meal shared with strangers in one's home. Thomas Shepard noted that it was "a common practise" among the New England Algonquians "freely to entertain travailers and strangers." Thomas Dermer, in a letter to Samuel Purchas, indicated that he had read earlier accounts, perhaps including those compiled by Purchas and Richard Hakluyt. Dermer wrote that two "kings" "gave mee content in whatsoever I demanded, where I found that former relations were true." And later, Dermer's party "had good quarter with the Savages, who likewise confirmed former reports." Thomas Morton wrote of the hospitality of New England Algonquians, who, he claimed, always had a pot on the fire and welcomed strangers into their homes. According to Morton, it was common for a host to prepare a bed "if anyone shall come into their houses," and "if he sleep until their meat be dished up, they will set a wooden bowl of meat by him that sleepeth, and wake him, saying Cattup keene Meckin: that is, If you be hungry, there is meat for you, where if you will eat, you may. Such is their Humanity."[3]

According to Roger Williams, New England Algonquians would if necessary take hospitality to extreme lengths. If their house was too full to shelter English visitors for the night, the host would sleep outdoors and give his place to a visitor. William Wood also claimed that New England Algonquians were "very hospitable," noting that "they have entertained [the English] into their houses, quartered them by themselves in the best rooms, providing the best victuals they could." Even after "a fortnight's or three weeks' tarrying," a period when one might expect any guest to have overstayed his welcome, Wood wrote, his hosts tried "to provide accommodation correspondent to their English custom." More important, they did so without "grumbling." Wood directly linked Indian and English customs of hospitality, even suggesting that the English might have something to learn from their Algonquian hosts. Roger Williams made this point more directly: "It is a strange truth, that a man shall generally finde more free entertainment and refreshing amongst these Barbarians, then amongst thousands that call themselves Christians." Thomas Morton echoed Williams: "I have found the Massachusetts Indians more full of humanity than the Christians, and have had much better quarter with them."[4]

Another fact frequently remarked upon by English observers was that Indians did not lock their doors. In the English literature of hospitality, an open door was a metaphor for generous rural hospitality, while a closed door signified its reverse. For some of those who denounced the decline in rural hospitality, a locked gate and darkened house signified everything that was wrong with the gentry's retreat into exclusive company and their migration to London. Again, when English writers noted, as William Strachey did of the

Algonquians of the Chesapeake Bay region, that their "doores be hung with matts, never locked nor bolted," they signaled to their readers that the Indians shared some cultural values with the English, and perhaps even held them more tightly. Roger Williams made a similar observation of the Algonquians of the Narragansett Bay region: "Commonly they never shut their doores, day nor night."[5]

Only a few pages after this passage, Williams described the efforts of some Algonquians to make sturdier doors, out of boards and bolts procured from the English or, failing that, out of bark, "which they make fast with a cord in the night time, or when they go out of town." Williams's apparent contradiction speaks to the metaphorical connection between an open door and generous hospitality. Even though doors were in fact often fastened, they were "open" to travelers and strangers. Another demonstration of the metaphorical meaning of an open door is the impossibility of locking a wigwam or *yihakan*, built as many observers noted of rows of saplings bent into a half-barrel or dome shape and then covered with woven mats or bark. The "door" of such a structure was nothing more than an opening covered by a mat that could be moved aside or propped open to let light and air into these smoky dwellings. It is also interesting that Williams's Algonquian neighbors seem not to have thought of locking their doors until after contact with Europeans. Some of this impulse may have stemmed from an interest in English houses and technology. Wahunsenacawh, for example, asked the Jamestown settlers to build him a house, and according to Edward Waterhouse, Opechancanough was fascinated with a lock and key he received as a gift, locking and unlocking it repeatedly. But it is also likely that theft only became a widespread problem after the arrival of hungry English settlers, and perhaps the trade goods they introduced into native communities.[6]

Often by praising Indian hospitality writers meant to make a negative comparison with English settlers. Although hospitality is a basic Christian virtue, Thomas Morton pointed out that few of his puritan neighbors in New England practiced it strictly. By this observation Morton hoped to undermine puritan claims to have founded a godly commonwealth and to dilute the criticisms of John Winthrop, William Bradford, and other New England puritan leaders of his own conduct with New England Algonquians. Contemporaries with a humanist education would have understood specific references in these accounts. The implicit (and, as in Morton's reference to Plato, occasionally explicit) references to classical models offered a way to describe the peoples the English encountered in the New World with reference to familiar examples. But these descriptions were also a commentary on England itself. If, as many authorities suggested, England was taking the place of Rome in colonizing and civilizing the New World as Britain had itself been colonized and civilized, the comparison was not necessarily an entirely positive one. The Romans' treatment of colonized peoples, as described by Tacitus, was a clear indication of the empire's descent into tyranny and luxury. Critical writers like Morton suggested that English settlers ignored this comparison at great risk.[7]

Offers of food and shared meals demonstrated more to early modern English travelers than just a laudable commitment to generous hospitality on the part of ordinary Indian households. These offers were also a way for Indian leaders to assert their superiority in a variety of ways. Many English writers interpreted Algonquian leaders' offers of hospitality in the same terms they did of English elite hospitality: it reflected the control of food that legitimated elite claims to authority. William Wood, for example, wrote of his New England Algonquian hosts that they were "as free as Emperours" with food and lodging, "both to their Country-men and English, be he stranger, or neare acquaintance." George Percy used similar language in declaring one Chesapeake werowance to be "a Prince of civil government" because he had entertained the English "in good humanitie." Wood and Percy were not, in these quotations, defining their hosts as emperors or princes based on their liberality, but they were assuming a connection between magnificence, control of food stores, and authority and recognizing that their hosts intended to make just that connection.[8]

Edward Winslow noted that among the Algonquians of eastern New England, it was customary for the sachem of a village to offer hospitality to unfamiliar travelers or visitors of high status, as it was the custom among the leading men of rural communities in England. These offers ultimately relied on the labor of a man's household, the properly ordered relationships of gender and status that were reflected in a shared meal. This meant that even when a leading man was not at home, his household would expect to offer hospitality in his stead. As Winslow described, on one occasion when the Wampanoag sachem Corbatant was not at home, his wife "gave us friendly entertainment" in her husband's absence.[9]

Arthur Barlowe's account of the lavish meal offered by Granganimeo's wife to the English party exploring Roanoke Island underscores this point. The men of the village were excluded from this offer of hospitality because the English party was clearly afraid of ambush: they were noticeably nervous when armed men approached the structure where they were eating. Their hostess,

seeing their anxiety, ordered the men to withdraw, a clear signal of her peaceful intentions, but possibly not enough to allay English fears. Despite the fact
that, as Barlowe wrote, he and his companions "were entertained with all love,
and kindnes, and with as much bountie, after their manner, as they could possibly devise," the English party rejected their hostess's offer of a place to sleep,
despite the fact that it was raining and they had nowhere else to go.[10]

Barlowe and his companions risked a breach by rejecting this offer. English writers noted that their Indian counterparts understood the rejection
of hospitality in the same way they did, as a serious affront. William Wood
claimed that the Algonquians of New England "count[ed] it a great discour-
tesie, not to eate of their high-conceited delicates, and sup of their un-oat-
meal'd broth." Wood continued: "as they are love-linked thus in common
courtesy, so are they no way sooner disjointed than by ingratitude." The author of *New Englands First Fruits* recounted approvingly the story of an Indian
whose newfound Christianity demanded that he reject the hospitality of an
English couple. Their arguments offended the Algonquian man's sense of a
Christian marriage enough that he demonstratively walked out of their home
when offered a meal. The Algonquian man meant this as an insult, and it was
likely received as such.[11]

Feeling themselves at risk, the English party decided to return to their
open boats to sleep offshore. As they did so, Granganimeo's wife sent further
gifts of food and mats with which to cover themselves from the rain as they
slept. Their hostess may have been trying to maintain her offer of hospitality
even though the suspicious English men had rejected her offer of lodgings by
providing them with food and a temporary roof. Wahunsenacawh himself
made a similar offer when Captain John Smith and an English party that included Captain Christopher Newport refused his offer of a place to sleep and
like the Roanoke party chose the discomfort and security of their boats. An
offer of hospitality was rejected only in extreme circumstances, and in these
cases the extension of hospitality amounted to an effort to prevent a breach.[12]

Not all of a meal's meanings were as broad and plain as an invitation to join
an important man at his table. Although English writers described meals as
an especially direct form of communication, English travelers knew that some
nuances of conduct might escape their attention. To guide their conduct when
abroad, Sir Thomas Palmer's *Essay of the Meanes how to make our Travailes, into
forraine Countries, the more profitable and honourable* encouraged travelers in
all parts of the world to observe and record specific features of foreign cultures.

In this way, Palmer wrote, travelers could contribute their own observations in terms congruent with those of other travelers and therefore valuable to a range of possible readers. As Palmer put it, gaining knowledge of "the tongue, the Nature of the people, the Countrey, the Customes; the Government of the State; & the secrets of the same" were "the utensils, and materialls of States men, concerning forraine matters." And firsthand reports were especially valuable, since travelers have an advantage over "a home States man, which is fed by advertisements only, and is ledde by other mens eyes."[13]

Along with useful knowledge regarding ports, rivers, commodities, and similar qualities of foreign places, careful study of manners was important for two reasons, Palmer argued. The first was to ensure that a traveler would not give offense. The "customes of other nations, where a man liveth, are to be followed," instructed Palmer, except "in the case of God, or of a mans own conscience." In "every State" a traveler should observe customs of "Diet, Apparell, Gesture, Curtesie, and such like, which in some places are precisely to be observed. But as concerning that other branch, let men avoid to sacrifice or do reverence to any Idole or Hobgoblin." Unless doing so constituted blasphemy or heresy, Palmer counseled, a traveler should follow the customs of his host.[14]

Another reason for the kind of careful study Palmer encouraged was to describe foreign manners and customs, especially those of elites, as accurately as possible. As Palmer wrote, "the customes and prerogatives of the Nobilitie of a nation" rest on "their superioritie and preheminence in sitting, going, talking, eating, washing," and similar public occasions. It was important for English leaders in the New World to recognize when their Indian counterparts were claiming "preheminence" in each of these areas and to make their own claims in similar terms. Since all parties tried to present themselves in a way calculated to secure the respect of their counterparts, it was vital that English leaders recognize whether their claims had been accepted.[15]

By "sitting," Palmer meant to encapsulate a range of customs connecting status and precedence to both seating arrangements and to seats themselves. One of the most common remarks English writers made about Indian meals was to note how the participants were arranged while eating. Not surprisingly, in light of its importance to both the English and Indians, gender was a primary concern in seating arrangements. Henry Spelman, who lived among the Chesapeake Algonquians as a boy, wrote that although Wahunsenacawh himself shared his table with two English boys (Spelman and Thomas Savage), werowances did not share meals with women. In a rich description of "The setting at meat," Spelman wrote: "They sett on matts round about the howse the men by them selves and the weomen by ther selves the weomen bringe to every one a dish of meat . . . if any leaft the weomen gather it up & ether keeps it till the next meall, or gives it to the porer sort, if any be ther."[16]

Men and women were segregated at meals when they included leaders of high rank, and women did the work of cooking, serving, and clearing. William Wood, discussing New England Algonquians, described a more stark separation at meals. Wood claimed that "they all meet friends at the kettle, saving their wives that dance a spaniel-like attendance at their backs for their bony fragments." Women, Wood wrote, gather, dress, and prepare food but "see it eaten over their shoulders" by men and then "scramble for their scraps."[17]

There is some evidence to counter these observations. John White's watercolor inscribed "Theire sitting at meate," painted during his stay at Roanoke in 1585, shows an Algonquian man and woman eating together, out of the same dish. One way to explain the discrepancy between White's and Spelman's observations is to recognize that Spelman was living in and observing a very high-status household, where everyday meals may have had a significance not shared by most others, including the simple meal painted by White. In general, when English were present at a meal in an Indian home, the meal's importance was elevated. Drawing a conclusion about Indian food habits based on these meals therefore almost certainly overstates the segregation of women. A similar observation could be made of England: gentry women as a rule ate with their husbands, but formal occasions called for a more overt demonstration of gender and status distinctions. On these occasions, only high-status women would be present, and therefore to dine at a formal meal with one's wife was a mark of special significance among the English. Similarly for a great leader like Wahunsenacawh, the number of his wives present at a formal meal (although not at the table) was another indication of his status.[18]

Another way to explain the discrepancy between Spelman's and White's observations is to note that English writers frequently misunderstood or misrepresented the nature of Indian gender roles. The image of the "female drudge" was a staple of English ethnographies, but it was largely based on a misunderstanding. Noting that women did all the field work, a male role in England, writers denounced Indian men as lazy and idle; the fact that men's responsibility hinged on hunting, an elite pastime in England, only made this point more clear to contemporary writers, who saw similar drudgery in other forms of women's work. William Wood, for example, claimed that Algonquian women's "subjection" required them "to sit on the lower hand and to carry water and the like drudgery." Since English women were treated with more respect, according to Wood, this proved the superiority of English culture. Wood included in his account a description of English women sheltering Indian women from their spouses, and even driving Indian men away. Wood's intention, which was also true of other writers on the "female drudge," was to underscore the illegitimate household government of Indian men, whose supposed insistence on strict gender separation smacked of tyranny. As Wood's example suggests, some writers assumed that Indian women preferred English gender roles to those of their own culture.[19]

Although the misunderstandings upon which Wood and others based their accounts of Indian gender roles were substantial, Kathleen Bragdon has pointed out the dangers in overcompensating for the negative assumptions evident in English accounts of Indian gender roles. Indian societies were not egalitarian, at least not in all aspects, and Bragdon has cautioned historians not to presume commensality, communalism, and gender equality, an image just as misleading as the "female Indian drudge." Proper household government as the English settlers understood it rested on gender inequality, and similar assumptions of gender distinctions structured Indian societies as well.[20]

For example, George Percy's account of a meal that followed a ceremonial occasion clearly shows the way English travelers drew inferences about gender relations from what Palmer summed up as "sitting": "When they had ended their Ceremonies, they went into their houses and brought out mats and laid upon the ground, the chiefest of them sate all in a rank: the meanest sort brought us such dainties as they had, & of their bread which they make of their Maiz or Gennea wheat, they would not suffer us to eate unlesse we sate down, which we did on a Mat right against them." In England and clearly in Percy's mind, status determined who served the meal. For a woman to serve in such a context was a sign of her subordinate status, and although Percy does not specify the gender of the "meanest sort" that served this meal, they were certainly women. For the Algonquians of the region, there was clearly a hierarchy embodied in these meals, but the meaning of women serving food may have been quite different from what Percy assumed based on his experience as the son of the Earl of Northumberland. Women's control of many common food supplies, especially the corn crop, may have been the social relationship on display on these occasions. The key point for an Indian audience may have been that women alone produced, prepared, and provided the (only) food for the prominent men at such feasts. Their exclusion from the table, in this light, was less important.[21]

Meals shared between English and Indian leaders, like those between English leaders, were especially fraught. Unsurprisingly, two of the proudest and most powerful figures in early New England—John Winthrop and Miantonomi, sachem of the Narragansetts—clashed openly at the dinner table. At the time the English arrived in the region, the Narragansetts were the largest and most powerful Algonquian group in southern New England. Over the course of the 1630s, their influence began to wane, in part because of the maneuverings of Uncas, leader of the Mohegans. Although both groups formed alliances with the English during the Pequot War, Uncas quickly established himself as an unswervingly loyal ally of the English. In the aftermath of the war Uncas played on his loyalty to gain significant autonomy in the region at the Narragansetts' expense despite the limited numbers and territory under his control. For their part, English officials in the Massachusetts and Connecticut colonies consistently supported Uncas's ambitions at Miantonomi's expense. Massachusetts officials hoped for a counterweight to the powerful Narragansetts and to undercut the Rhode Island settlers by undermining the power of their Indian neighbors and allies. The conflict between Uncas and Miantonomi continued for years after the Pequot War, with various English officials and envoys firmly in the middle. On several occasions, English magistrates summoned Miantonomi and Uncas in efforts to broker a truce between the two, and on other occasions Narragansett envoys implored the Boston magistrates to allow them to make war on Uncas. But the English settlements refused to allow this, and when fighting finally did break out, the English ensured Uncas's survival and condoned his execution of his rival Miantonomi.[22]

One episode can serve to encapsulate these complex relationships and to underscore the importance of meals as a stage upon which social relationships were negotiated and contested. At a meeting held at Hartford in September 1638, Uncas, Miantonomi, and English officials of the Connecticut colony tried to resolve the simmering conflict between the Mohegan and Narragansett leaders, which had flared over the spoils of the Pequot War as well as their competition for influence in southern New England. "At last," wrote Roger Williams to John Winthrop, "we drew them to shake hands" in order to formalize the proposed agreement. After shaking hands, "Miantunnomu invited (twice earnestly) Okace to sup and dine with him, he and all his company (his men having killed some venison)." Although Williams and the other English officials present tried to persuade him to accept, Williams wrote that Uncas "would not yield."[23]

By encouraging the two sachems to shake hands, the Connecticut magistrates and Williams believed they were encouraging a demonstration of mutual respect and reciprocity that bound both men to the terms of the treaty they had just negotiated. What Uncas (and to a lesser extent Miantonomi) believed that their participation in this handshake signified is unclear, in light of the spurned invitation that followed. Perhaps the sachems did not fully understand the meaning of a handshake, but this is extremely unlikely given each man's extensive experience negotiating with the English. It is more likely that Uncas did not feel that his participation conveyed the meaning Williams and other English men invested in it, that shaking hands had a sufficiently flexible meaning to encompass the very different understandings of Uncas, Miantonomi, and Williams. It was a shrewd calculation by a man whose life was filled with shrewd calculations. Shaking hands before a (doubtless) beaming English audience, Uncas signaled in a foreign symbolic vocabulary that his difficulties with Miantonomi were over, when of course they were not.

A meal, on the other hand, was plainly understood by all parties and could not be strategically employed by Uncas the way a handshake could. Although its symbolic meaning also had roots in English culture, Algonquian norms of hospitality were similar enough to make the meaning of this incident clear to both sides. By accepting Miantonomi's invitation, Uncas would have demonstrated his acceptance of a truce. But accepting the invitation would also have required Uncas to play the subordinate role of guest. Miantonomi's invitation was a bid not only for peace but for the upper hand in the relationship, and the venison he offered only amplified this message of masculine status and dominance. Miantonomi certainly realized that Uncas would be unlikely to accept venison from his table. An experienced negotiator with the English, his invitation may even have had the same motivations as Sir Humphrey Gilbert's to Henry Knollys. Either Uncas would sit at Miantonomi's table and eat his venison or he would refuse the invitation. In the latter case, a churlish refusal would support Miantonomi's claims that Uncas was unwilling to make peace and that Miantonomi was a more attractive ally for the English. Whatever the intentions of both men, it is clear that an offer of hospitality was understood by all parties to be a potent occasion to demonstrate relations of reciprocity, superiority, and inferiority.

In this light, it is not surprising that Miantonomi was minutely attentive to the meanings conveyed by his own participation in meals shared with English leaders. On several occasions, the Boston magistrates demanded that the Narragansett sachem appear before them to demonstrate his loyalty or answer complaints, occasions that surely galled a man like Miantonomi. Making

the situation worse was the way John Winthrop and the other councillors
of the Massachusetts settlement reflected their ideas of the relationship between them and the Narragansetts in the seating arrangements at meals. In
October 1636, Miantonomi arrived in Boston with another sachem and "near
twenty sanaps" to negotiate an alliance against the Pequots. Relations between
Miantonomi and Winthrop were never better than during this period, when
the sachem bound his powerful group to assist the English by securing their
southern flank. Nevertheless, the Indian party was not invited to share a table
with its English counterparts. Winthrop wrote in his journal that "the sachems
and their council dined by themselves in the same room where the governor
dined, and their sanaps were sent to the inn." Winthrop ensured that social
distinctions *among* the Indians were acknowledged by seating the sachems and
leading men together and separating the rest. The Narragansett leaders ate in
the same room with Winthrop, but separately, suggesting that not even the
sachems were of sufficient status to share a table with the English.[24]

In November 1640, relations were much worse: Miantonomi was sus-
pected of trying to assemble a conspiracy against the English and was called
to answer these charges. After what Winthrop described as a warm welcome
by Governor Thomas Dudley—Miantonomi was saluted with "a guard of
twelve musketeers, and well entertained . . . by the governour"—Miantonomi
disagreed with Dudley's choice of an interpreter. This was hardly a trivial disagreement: Miantonomi recognized the importance of accurate translation
in negotiations with the English, and on this occasion he was determined
that Roger Williams should interpret for him. But since Williams had been
banished from the Bay Colony, the Massachusetts authorities insisted on a
Pequot woman: not just a member of a group hostile to the Narragansetts,
but a woman at that. The sachem left Roxbury, where Dudley lived, "in a rude
manner, without showing any respect or sign of thankfulness to the governour
for his entertainment, whereof the governour informed the general court, and
would shoe him no countenance, nor admit him to dine at our table, as formerly he had done" until Miantonomi confessed his fault. This Miantonomi
did, although he pointed out to Winthrop that "when our men came to him,
they were permitted to use their own fashions, and so he expected the same
liberty with us."[25]

As Winthrop recounted it, Dudley's report suggests that Miantonomi was
invited to dine at the governor's table, perhaps because Dudley was not as careful
as Winthrop to assert his preeminence at meals. In June 1643, two minor sachems of the Narragansetts (subordinate to Miantonomi) were called to Boston

to acknowledge their submission to the Massachusetts Bay Company. According to Winthrop, their visit was intended to publicly acknowledge that they were received not "as confederates but as subjects." "So," Winthrop continued, "they dined in the same room with the governour, but at a table by themselves," as Miantonomi's party had in 1636. Miantonomi's status demanded different treatment, and the sachem made it clear to Winthrop that he expected it. Winthrop wrote of a 1642 meeting: "When we should go to dinner, there was a table provided for the Indians, to dine by themselves, and Miantunnomoh was left to sit with them. This he was discontented at, and would eat nothing, till the governour sent him meat from his table. So at night, and all the time he staid, he sat at the lower end of the magistrate's table."[26]

Winthrop's conduct of meals with Miantonomi had not changed between 1636 and 1642, but Miantonomi's expectations had. This may have been because he was invited to sit with the governor on other occasions, perhaps only during the rare years when Winthrop did not hold that office. Miantonomi may have heard of a very early meeting between Winthrop and Chickatabut, sachem of the Massachusetts, at which "beinge in Englishe Clothes the Governor sett him at his owne table." Also, relations between the two groups had gradually deteriorated, and by 1642 Miantonomi was chafing under the English demands that he overlook Uncas's repeated encroachments and insults. Whatever the precise combination of causes, Miantonomi was unwilling in 1642 to accept the subordinate role at meals he had earlier.[27]

Winthrop's response is revealing. Although Miantonomi asked only that food be sent from the magistrates' table to his, Winthrop responded by seating the Narragansett sachem at "the lower end" of his own table. This was a profound difference. In England, when local elites passed foods from their own table to those occupied by lesser men, they manifested the incorporation of the lower orders in a social structure they dominated. Winthrop's refusal to do this suggests that he held a different view of the meanings of meals and manners, one identified with exclusive settings and the host's social peers. By seating and serving the Narragansetts separately, Winthrop made it clear that he saw no correspondence between the leaders of the two groups, a statement that would have been an unforgivable insult to a visiting English leader. The proud, powerful, and astute Miantonomi immediately recognized the meaning of Winthrop's behavior. Reluctantly, Winthrop asserted that only Miantonomi was of sufficient status to eat with the Massachusetts leaders. The rest of his party remained at a separate table by themselves, sharing neither the governor's table itself nor the foods placed on it.

After Miantonomi was captured and ultimately executed on Uncas's orders in August 1643, his uncle Canonicus remained at the head of the Narragansetts and was joined by Miantonomi's younger brother Pessacus, who replaced Miantonomi as the subordinate sachem responsible for relationships with outside groups. Pessacus proposed revenge on Uncas, and the General Court sent emissaries to the Indian leaders for an explanation. It is tempting to conclude that Canonicus and Pessacus had heard stories of Miantonomi's poor treatment in Boston. They offered the Boston men an unmistakably insulting welcome: "When our messengers came to them, Canonicus would not admit them into his wigwam for two hours, but suffered them to stay in the rain. When he did admit them, he lay along upon his couch, and would not speak to them more than a few froward speeches, but referred them to Pesacus, who, coming after some four hours, carried them into an ordinary wigwam, and there had conference with them most part of the night." The Massachusetts men were no longer, to use Miantonomi's phrase, "permitted to use their own fashions." Instead, it is plain that they were required to submit to Algonquian norms as a condition of gaining an audience with the Narragansett sachems. Canonicus would not admit the English when they arrived, and when he did admit them, Pessacus—who conducted external negotiations—did nearly all the talking.[28]

Edward Johnson may have been a member of an earlier diplomatic mission from Massachusetts to the Narragansetts, to gain their support against the Pequots. Canonicus on this occasion, "hearing of their comming, gathered together his chiefe Counsellors, and a great number of his Subjects to give them entertainment," but decided that Miantonomi "should receive their message, yet in his hearing." As in the later case, Canonicus would not speak himself. After a feast, the Indian leaders gave the English an "Audience, in a State-house." Johnson continues, "In this place sate their Sachim, with very great attendance; the English comming to deliver their Message, to manifest the greater state, the Indian Sachim lay along upon the ground, on a Mat, and his Nobility sate on the ground, with their legs doubled up, their knees touching their chin; with much sober gravity they attend the Interpreters speech." As these occasions suggest, there were a great many ways for Indian and English leaders "to manifest the greater state" through what Palmer summarized as "sitting," signaling respect or its opposite in the way they arranged themselves on ceremonial occasions. All parties to these occasions understood that "sitting" demonstrated and affirmed a person's social position in the presence of his peers, superiors, and inferiors.[29]

In addition to these examples drawn from New England, there are abundant examples of the importance of "sitting" and meals from the Chesapeake. The Algonquians of that region, headed by Powhatan, recognized many levels of status, from the *mamanatowick* himself to his subordinate werowances, and represented these in their feasts and ceremonies of welcome. At an early meeting between Jamestown's settlers and the Powhatans, for example, the werowance of Arrohattoc "satt upon a matt of Reedes, with his people about him," and "caused [a mat] to be layd for Captain Newport," which recognized Newport's commensurate status among the English. Later, with two werowances present, Arrohattoc and Parahunt, the message was the same. The Indian leaders "satt by themselves aparte from all the rest. . . . Many of his company satt on either syde: and the mattes for us were layde right over against the kynges." This image is in stark contrast to Winthrop's clear demarcation between the Massachusetts Bay leaders and the Narragansetts, who were seated separately.[30]

According to Gabriel Archer, the female Indian leader, or *werowansqua,* Opossonoquoske insisted on asserting her own "preheminence": she "would permitt none to stand or sitt neere her." Given the otherwise strict separation of men from women in ceremonial meals, both Indian and European, Opossonoquoske's hauteur may have been necessary to maintain the distinctions appropriate to her station. Nevertheless, her decision not to allow any English men to sit at her side rankled, as Winthrop's decision had with Miantonomi.[31]

Wahunsenacawh himself was extremely conscious of the importance of "sitting." In the *True Relation*, Captain John Smith recorded his first encounter with Powhatan, "proudly lying upon a Bedstead a foote high upon tenne or twelve Mattes, richly hung with manie Chaynes of great Pearles about his necke . . . on each side sitting upon a Matte upon the ground were rounged his chiefe men on each side the fire." The sight, Smith wrote, "drave me into admiration to see such state in a naked Salvage." Wahunsenacawh was similarly regal at his first meeting with Christopher Newport: "Sitting upon his bed of mats, his pillow of leather imbrodered (after their rude manner with pearle and white Beads) his attyre a faire robe of skinnes . . . his chiefest men in . . . order in his arbour-like house." One suggestive fact that emerges from the two descriptions of Wahunsenacawh is the difference in his posture when he met Smith and Newport. When Wahunsenacawh first encountered Smith, Smith was brought before him as a captive. On that occasion, the *mamanatowick* was "proudly lying upon a Bedstead," a position meant by Canonicus to clearly demonstrate his superiority (on the two occasions when Canonicus met English emissaries lying down, the English parties did not include

Massachusetts Bay magistrates). On the other hand, Wahunsenacawh had been told that Newport was Smith's "father," and he chose to meet a higher-ranking English counterpart accordingly, seated.[32]

English sensitivity to the meanings conveyed by "sitting" was clear in another example from early Jamestown. As they traveled up the James River, a party of English men met Powhatan's son Parahunt and believed him to be Wahunsenacawh himself (Parahunt did nothing to correct the English mistake). While the English party was in the company of a group of Chesapeake Algonquians, Parahunt appeared, and the Indians stood and shouted a welcome. Mindful of the fact that their host, "kyng Arahatec," had remained seated, the English travelers did not want by their actions to acknowledge an inferior position. They therefore "saluted [Parahunt] with silence sitting still on our mattes." English travelers were aware that their participation in ceremonies like this had meaning. As Palmer had warned, they were very careful not to convey subservience, even when, as was the case on this occasion, they risked offending their host by doing so, and they were equally careful to record this fact in writing.[33]

Mutual attention to the meanings of "sitting" continued after this incident at a series of shared meals. The English party left Arrohattoc's territory to travel upriver to Parahunt's seat. At a meal there, Parahunt placed the English leaders on mats next to him. Although the English had been treated appropriately in these settings, as honored guests, the role of guest was nearly always inferior to that of host. A meal, Captain Christopher Newport knew, could manifest relations of either superiority or equality. At meals shared between a landlord and his tenants, for example, the gift of food and shelter was never requited, but between two English elites of roughly equal station, a return invitation was expected. Therefore Newport, the leader of the English party, "caused two peeces of porke to be sod a shore with pease; to which he invyted King Pawatah." Agreeing to come, Parahunt indicated to the English that he accepted a rough equality of position between himself and Newport and that he understood the requirements of the role of guest. Gabriel Archer's account of these events goes on to describe how "King Pawatah with some of his people . . . fedd familiarly, without sitting in his state as before," and Parahunt ate "very freshly of our meate, Dranck of our beere, Aquavite, and Sack." Archer's account does not mention how Newport tried to demonstrate his own status vis-à-vis Parahunt. The English were content, it appears, that Parahunt only decline to sit "in his state" when at a meal with the English. Parahunt recognized that he was a guest, and in that role displays of status appropriate to a host would be an insult.[34]

Material culture contributed to the meanings of these occasions. Each of the Chesapeake examples focuses on the mats laid for leaders and honored guests, and Wahunsenacawh's status was indicated during his encounter with Smith by the number of mats upon which he lay. In England during the Stuart period, chairs were becoming increasingly common in wealthy households, but the notion that the host or guest of honor would sit in an easily recognizable chair, often the only chair, was still prevalent. In the New World, the lack of important props in the theater of manners was indicative of the larger problems faced by English leaders attempting to assert and confirm their authority in a fluid context. The Massachusetts Bay governor Thomas Dudley, in a 1631 letter to the Countess of Lincoln, touched on this fact when he noted that he did not have a desk or even a table to write on.[35]

On his 1605 voyage to New England, George Waymouth "had two [Algonquians] at supper with us in his cabbin to see their demeanure, and had them in presence at service: who behaved themselves very civilly, neither laughing nor talking all the time." The author of this account, James Rosier, may have been referring to the Indians' behavior at religious services as much as their behavior at table, but in both cases civil conduct prohibited laughing and talking.[36]

Rosier's description of Waymouth's supper guests illustrates the importance of both "talking" and "eating" to displays of "preheminence." The quotation from Rosier continues with his claim that the Indian guests "at supper fed not like men of rude education, neither would they eat or drinke more than seemed to content nature." At Winthrop's table, "beinge in Englishe Clothes," Chickatabut received perhaps the highest praise Winthrop could bestow on an Algonquian leader: "he behaved him selfe as soberly &c: as an Englishe man." Francis Higginson noted that if Indians visited an English home during a meal, they "will aske or take nothing but what we give them," another indication of careful attention to manners among Indian guests.[37]

As Palmer used the term "eating," he meant to include under this general heading what he elsewhere divided into "diet" and "feeding," in other words, what a people ate and how they ate it. Thomas Morton wrote of New England Algonquians that "they feed continually, and are no niggards of their vittels." William Strachey claimed that the Chesapeake Algonquians "be all of them huge Eaters," and Gabriel Archer wrote of the same group that "they eate often and that liberally." William Wood presented a mixed picture of New England Algonquian eating habits. After writing that the Algonquians did not stop eating "till their full bellies leave nothing but emptie platters," he observed that when Algonquians "visit our English, being invited to eat, they are very moderate, whether it be to show their manners or for shamefacedness I know not."[38]

Other writers suggested that Indians' "temperance in eating and drinking," like their customs of hospitality, could serve as a model for the English. Thomas Tusser urged his middling readers to "Make hunger thy sauce, as a medcen for helth," and travelers in the Americas shared his views on moderation and health. Thomas Harriot wrote that the Algonquians near Roanoke were "verye sober in their eatinge, and trinkinge, and consequently verye longe lived because they doe not oppress nature." Robert Cushman warned English men and women against overindulgence: "Neither must men take so much thought for the flesh, as not to be pleased except they can pamper their bodies with variety of dainties. Nature is content with little, and health is much endangered, by mixtures upon the stomach. The delights of the palate doe often inflame the vitall parts." And Thomas Morton drew from such ideas to make a favorable comparison with New England Algonquians, who "are indeed not served in dishes of plate with variety of sauces to procure appetite, that needs not here." These descriptions resonated with the humanist vocabulary of virtue and luxury, in which the simple foods and modest appetite of the Indians contrasted with the rich foods, sauces, and dainties desired by the English. To these writers, the experience of colonization suggested that the English were dangerously close to overcivilization, decadence, and effeminacy.[39]

A particularly strong example of humanists' connection of virtue, particularly military virtue, with "eating" was the food known to New England Algonquians as "nocake," or parched cornmeal, which was carried in a bag on long voyages and eaten with a mouthful of water. Roger Williams connected this food with warriors, who could carry days of provision with them, and Robert Beverley noted the practice, describing the food as "Rockahomonie, that is, the finest Indian Corn, parched, and beaten to powder." Scottish writers of the early modern period, concerned that foreign influences on the Scottish diet might sap the military virtues of their forebears, held up the example of hardy Highland warriors marching to battle with only a bag of dried oatmeal for provision, a strikingly similar image. Such images carried a historical and cultural meaning separate from the specific grain carried in each case, an image of hardiness, simplicity, and frugality tightly linked to notions of military virtue. The specific reference was to the provisions carried by Roman legions, which also included a bag of meal.[40]

Utensils were important in the theater of manners, just as chairs were. The richness of a host's plate demonstrated his wealth, but the use of that plate on the table conveyed a range of subtler meanings. It was usual in England for two people to share a single trencher, which in the medieval period was a slice of stale bread but by the early Stuart period was a sort of small tray or platter made of wood or metal. Meals were served all at once, with an array of dishes on the table at the same time, which meant that the trencher functioned primarily to hold the small amounts of food taken from the serving dishes but not yet eaten. It was a mark of status to have one's own trencher, and when they saw similar customs among the Indians, English writers were careful to note them. Henry Spelman wrote that among the Chesapeake Algonquians, "the better sort never eates togither in one dish, when he hath eaten what he will, or that which was given him, for he looks for no second corse he setts doune his dish by him and mum[b]leth ceartayne words to himself in maner of givinge thankes." The author of the *Relation of Maryland*, also writing of the Chesapeake Algonquians, described "one of their feasts, when Two hundred of them did meet together; they eate of but one dish at a meale, and every man, although there be never so many, is served in a dish by himselfe." The author of the *Relation of Maryland* follows Spelman in two crucial respects: that each diner had his own dish and that there was only one dish—"no second corse," in Spelman's words—to the meal. At a meal of this size in England, it would have been very unusual for each guest to have a dish of his own, a clear mark of the wealth and status of the host's household.[41]

In England honored guests might be offered the use of a knife, or perhaps a matched set of knife and spoon. Most guests, though, were expected to bring their own knife, and probably their own spoon as well. Forks (for eating, not roasting) were almost unknown in England throughout this period, very slowly making their way northward through Europe from Italy. Queen Elizabeth was given a fork as a gift in 1582, one of the first appearances of the fork in England, but the habit of using them did not penetrate very far down the social order for at least another century (although John Winthrop owned one). Cups were another important utensil and status symbol. Like trenchers, most cups were shared, but honored guests might have one all to themselves. The delicate Chinese wine cup recently unearthed at Jamestown would have been an especially visible display of wealth and status at mealtime. Equally impressive is the silver ear picker found there, which included a loop for wearing around the neck. Both these rare status items required the right sort of audience in order to appreciate the displays of gentility that they required and enabled. In this way, material culture allowed English colonial elites to mark

A pleasant Countrey new Ditty;

Merrily shewing how
To driue the cold Winter away.

To the tune of *When Phœbus did rest, etc.*

All hayle to the dayes
That merite more praise
　　then all the rest of the yeare;
And welcome the nights,
That double delights
　　as well for the poore as the peere :
Good fortune attend
Each merry mans friend
　　that doth but the best that he may,
Forgetting old wrongs,
with Carrols and Songs,
　　to driue the cold winter away.

Figure 15. In an image from a collection of seventeenth-century ballads, four men share a table set with trenchers made of bread and drink from a single cup. Despite the well-laid table and well-dressed diners, the only utensils visible are knives. Forks would remain a novelty for English diners for nearly a century. Charles Hindley, ed., *The Roxburghe Ballads* vol. 1 (London: Reeves and Turner, 1873), 113. Courtesy Rare Book and Manuscript Library, University of Pennsylvania.

their status in their possession and use of items not available to less wealthy settlers or Algonquian leaders.[42]

Although it was more commonly interpreted as evidence of religious life than manners, several writers noted Algonquian customs of saying grace, either before or after meals. The quotation from Henry Spelman above mentions the Chesapeake Algonquians' custom of "givinge thankes." Captain John Smith wrote that "the better sort" cast a bit of food into the fire before eating, "which is all the grace they are known to use." It is unclear from Smith's comment whether he inferred the status of the "better sort" from their manners or was recognizing that these customs were peculiar to high-status Algonquians. William Wood claimed that English visitors who forgot to say grace were sometimes scolded by their Algonquian hosts.[43]

Returning to the example of John Guy and the Beothuk leader, Guy concluded that his counterpart "seemed to have some command over the reste," and, not coincidentally to an early modern English mind, "behaved him selfe civillie. For when meate was ofred him he drew of his mitten from his hand, before he would receive yt." Conduct at meals could signal either civility and authority, as in this case, or the reverse. As described by Sir Anthony Weldon, King James I's rustic manners were indicative of the corruption of his court. According to Weldon, James's "tongue [was] too large for his mouth, which . . . made him drink very uncomely, as if eating his drink, which came out into the cup of each side of his mouth." Although Weldon was a member of James's court, he was a fierce critic of the monarch, his favorites, and many royal policies. Whether or not King James actually drooled when he drank, the connection Weldon hoped to forge with this image between the proper government of the body and proper government of the state is a staple of conduct literature in general. It also suggests the connections drawn by English readers of approving accounts of Algonquian manners, linking mannered conduct, social status, and political authority. By noting examples of Indian table manners, early English writers made a case that Algonquians were civilized, albeit to a lesser degree than the English, and that in paying close attention to what they ate and how they ate it, Algonquians demonstrated a capacity for government in the broadest sense (as James I, in Weldon's view, did not).[44]

Dionyse Settle provided a rare and noteworthy description of barbarous table manners. Writing of the native peoples he encountered on Martin Frobisher's 1577 voyage to the Arctic, Settle declared that they did not cook or prepare their food at all: "They eate their meate all rawe, both fleshe, fishe, and foule, or something perboyled with bloud & a little water, whiche they drinke." And equally upsetting to Settle was the natives' treatment of vegetables: "If they, for necessities sake, stand in neede of . . . such grasse as the countrie yeeldeth they plucke uppe, and eate, not deintily, or salletwise, to allure their stomaches to appetite: but for necessities sake, without either salt, oyles, or washing, like brutish beasts devoure the same." In a marginal note to this passage, Settle's text includes the words "Barbarous behavior," a conclusion his contemporaries would have drawn immediately. Cooking was associated by the early modern English with civility, or even civilization itself, and to eat food raw was a clear indication that a people lacked the discernment to prefer cooked foods or, as Settle's quotation suggests, had animal appetites that must be sated immediately. In 1610 the Virginia Company castigated its settlers for idleness, trying to claim that the failures of Virginia owed to the poor quality of the colonists (rather than, for example, to the poor quality of their leaders). The Virginia Company's *True Declaration* claimed that settlers in the Chesapeake ate their fish raw rather than take the time to cook it, linking them to the type of barbarism noted by Settle. This was an effort to paint the Virginia colonists not simply as lazy but as ungovernable because of the way they approached and performed basic rituals of civil life, chief among them cooking and eating.[45]

In his description of the Inuits, Settle pointed to the lack of furniture and utensils, essential equipment for refined eating in Europe. "They neither use table, stoole, or table cloth for comelinesse," Settle wrote, "but when they are imbrued with bloud, knuckle deepe, and their knives in like sort, they use their tongues as apt instruments to licke them cleane: in doeing whereof, they are assured to loose none of their victuals." The image of Indians licking bloody knives clean was clearly meant to suggest not poor manners but the absence of the internal regulation necessary for manners. The traveler Fynes Moryson wrote a similar description of the Irish: "What do I speak of Tables? since indeede they have no tables, but set their meate upon a bundle of grasse, and use the same Grasse for napkins to wipe their hands." William Wood, whose views of Indian food habits were generally negative, echoed Settle's comments. After preparing "homely cates," a host presents the meal to his guests "in a rude manner, placing it on the verdant carpet of the earth which Nature spreads them, without either trenchers napkins, or knives, upon which their hunger-sawced stomacks impatient of delayes, fals aboard without scrupling at unwashed hands, without bread, salt, or beere." This meal is "rude" not because Indians cannot make or afford utensils but because they either see no need for them or their hunger will not admit any delay in eating. Either way, English writers and readers drew firm conclusions from evidence like this regarding a culture's capacity for government and civility.[46]

George Best, like Dionyse Settle, traveled with Martin Frobisher to the Arctic in the 1570s, and, like Settle, Best had little good to say about Inuit foods. When a group of Inuits came aboard his ship bearing gifts of "Salmon and raw fleshe and fishe," Best wrote, they "greedily devoured the same before our mens faces." The Inuits indicated savagery both in their taste for raw meat and their unwillingness to properly cook their food, which as Best suggested was born of impatience and hunger rather than custom. Best went one step further than Settle in his inference that a taste for raw meat was sure evidence of cannibalism: "considering also their ravennesse and bloudy disposition, in eating anye kinde of rawe fleshe or carrion, howsoever stincking, it is to be thoughte, that they had slaine and devoured our men." Further, the Inuits ate dogs, Best claimed, and fed their babies raw meat, two images that compounded the portrait of savagery. Best summarized with a comparison that hinted at a state even below that. Since the soil in the Arctic "yeeldeth no graine or fruite of sustenaunce for man, or almost for beast to live uppon," Best wrote, the Inuits "will eate grasse and shrubs of the grounde, even as our kine doe."[47]

The comments of Wood, Settle, and Best provide a neat transition to the subject of "washing," which Palmer used in reference to one of the customary elements of ceremonial meals in England: hand washing. Settle's example suggests the connection between cleanliness and refined eating, but the ritualized act of washing one's hands was as important as cleanliness itself. Before and after formal meals, high-status men (and, more rarely, women) were provided by their host with basins and ewers for this purpose. (Very large medieval households even employed a ewerer on such occasions to take charge of the plate and the ceremony. Like many others, this office was beginning to fade during the Elizabethan period.) As was true of most utensils involved in ceremonial meals, these were often expensive and ornate, and honored guests might, like the host, have a separate basin and ewer.[48]

When Wahunsenacawh "dineth or suppeth," Smith wrote, "one of his women before and after meat, bringeth him water in a woden platter to wash his hands. Another waiteth with a bunch of feathers to wipe them instead of a Towell, and the feathers when he hath wiped are dryed again." Recognizing Wahunsenacawh's use of "washing" as a means of manifesting his authority, the Virginia Company sent him, among other gifts, a basin and ewer. In at least one other case, hand washing was a mark of distinction among the Powhatans. The concubine of a deposed werowance named Pepiscunimah, or Pipsco, washed her hands publicly and had an attendant bring her "a bunch or towe of fresh greene ashen leaves, as for a towell to wipe them."[49]

Again according to Sir Anthony Weldon, James I presented a negative example of cleanliness as well as table manners: "His skin was as soft as Taffeta Sarsnet, which felt so, because hee never washt his hands, onely rubb'd his fingers ends slightly with the wet end of a Napkin." James I's aversion to washing is supported by a letter to him from his favorite, the Duke of Buckingham, who closed with the phrase, "And so I kiss your dirty hands." As he had in suggesting that King James drooled when he drank, Weldon intended by these comments to suggest that the monarch's improper government of his own body suggested his incapacity for governing the state, whereas Wahunsenacawh's display of hand washing indicated his status in a similar way. In each of these cases, English writers recognized that manners were a basic feature of civilized life, but with very few exceptions, like Settle's comments on the Inuits or William Wood's disapproving comment that the Algonquians of New England neither used plates nor washed their hands, native manners were not described as barbarous. The humanist emphasis on the virtues of simplicity and moderation and the corresponding anxiety about the destructive effect of luxury and empire meant that Indians' table manners were most likely to be interpreted as virtuous.[50]

Weddings offer a specific case through which to examine these larger themes, a formal, ritualized occasion on which each of Palmer's categories was on display. Weddings conveyed a range of meanings simultaneously, defining the gender distinctions at the core of household government, honoring guests that included the families of the bride and groom, and signaling the important social transition to marriage. In different ways and to different degrees, Indians and English intended weddings to convey each of these meanings, and in all cases weddings centered on food. In both cultures, weddings were accompanied by an especially ceremonial meal, and in the English case by a unique food, the wedding or bridal cake.[51]

The author of the *Relation of Maryland* described an Algonquian wedding ceremony that began with gifts of food and culminated in a shared meal. On the wedding day, this account claims, "all the friends of both parts meet at the mans house that is to have the wife, and each one brings a present of meate, and the woman that is to be married also brings her present." The soon-to-be husband played an interesting role in this ceremony. Although the wedding and the meal took place at his house, he was not the host of this gathering. Rather than providing food to his visitors, his role was more akin to that of an honored guest, who accepted gifts without returning them. After all the guests had arrived, "the man he sits at the upper end of the house, and the womans friends leade her up, and place her by him, then all the company sit down upon mats, on the ground (as their manner is) and the woman riseth and serves dinner, First to her husband, then to all the company."[52]

The man's seating at the "upper end" of the house and the arrangement of guests on mats symbolically below him were familiar signifiers of status. The *Relation of Maryland* suggests that the married couple were given the position of honor at this meal, both by receiving gifts without returning them and by their seating location. As stated earlier, the meaning of the bride's presentation of food to her husband and guests was not a sign of drudgery but part of the general pattern of food exchanges that demonstrated the bride's and groom's ability to provide food and marked the new relationship between them.

William Strachey's observations of marriage among the Chesapeake Algonquians were different in some respects but nonetheless centered on food, which again had a highly gendered role. Men, Strachey wrote, "expresse their Loves to such women, as they would make Choyse to live withall, by presenting them with the fruictes of their Labours, as by Fowle, Fish, or Wild Beasts, which by their huntings, their bowes and arrowes, by weeres or otherwise, they obteyne, which they bring unto the young woman, as also of such Sommer fruictes and berryes, which their travell abroad hath made them knowe readily where to gather, and those of the best kinde of their season." The suitor plays a familiar role of hunter and fisherman, who by his skill in these masculine roles demonstrates his ability to provide the sort of food that will sustain his family for much of the year. The inclusion of "Sommer fruictes and berryes" is odd, given that these were foods typically gathered by women. Strachey's quotation suggests that by gathering berries, the would-be husband indicated his ability to find new sources of food for his wife to gather. Assuming his gifts of food were enough to convince the woman, her decision still had to be approved by her family. Their approval rested on the ability of the groom (and presumably his family) to build a house and provide "some platters, morters, and Matts." Henry Spelman, describing quite similar customs, accounted for them in terms of a man purchasing a bride, but Spelman also described the "mirth and feastinge" that followed the marriage ceremony.[53]

A similar marriage tradition was reported by the Dutch official Isaak de

Figure 16. This image from the Drake Manuscript (fol. 113) heightens the association of gender roles with certain foods. An Indian man brings fish and game to a woman's family to prove his suitability as a marriage partner, while on the left a container of grain and a mortar rest near the intended bride and her mother. The caption reads, in part, "He does not drink or eat in the house before having brought meat and venison in abundance, and he brings as much as possible to show that he works hard to provide well for himself, his wife and family." *The Drake Manuscript in the Pierpont Morgan Library: Histoire Naturelle des Indes*, trans. Ruth S. Kraemer, (London: André Deutsch, 1996), 270. Courtesy The Pierpont Morgan Library, New York.

Figure 17. In this image from the Drake Manuscript (fols. 124–124v), a man and woman are given permission to marry by the bride's father, who addresses his daughter with these words: "You need this young man. He will feed you well. You see that he brings a lot of good things for us to eat; he works hard at fishing as well as at catching wild animals; he plants, gathers fruit and firewood, in short, everything needed to feed the whole house." The bride's father then speaks to his future son-in-law, calling attention to his daughter's skill at baking bread, which she shapes into loaves. *The Drake Manuscript in the Pierpont Morgan Library: Histoire Naturelle des Indes*, trans. Ruth S. Kraemer (London: André Deutsch, 1996), 271-72. Courtesy The Pierpont Morgan Library, New York.

Rasieres of the Algonquians near New Amsterdam. The groom presented his bride's friends with *zeewan*, or wampum, and assuming there was agreement on the match, negotiated a mutually satisfactory exchange of wampum. Then, as the bride waited, the groom, "supporting himself by hunting," brought food to this assembly. The bride and groom "then eat together with the friends, and sing and dance together." After the ceremony, "the wife must provide the food for herself and her husband, as far as breadstuffs are concerned, and she must buy what is wanting with her sewan." The highly gendered meanings of certain foods and the "dramaturgy" of weddings combined in these examples to manifest gender relations on ritualized public occasions.[54]

Weddings between English and Indians were very rare. The most famous, that of Wahunsenacawh's daughter Pocahontas and John Rolfe, was unfortunately described only briefly by Ralph Hamor, who did not describe the ceremony or whether a feast was included. Hamor noted only that Wahunsenacawh sent an uncle of Pocahontas's, named Opachisco, to give away the bride but did not attend the ceremony himself. When Rolfe and Pocahontas left for England, Pocahontas was accompanied by several attendants. In 1621, the Virginia Company returned two of these women to America, directing that they return to Virginia via Bermuda. Only one survived the voyage, and when she arrived in Bermuda, this woman was married to an English man. At that wedding, Bermuda governor Nathaniel Butler hosted a lavish feast for more than one hundred guests, a ceremony intended to recognize the bride's status. According to Butler, her "kindred and freindes . . . wer prime commandours, and not lesse than Viceroyes." He suggested that the bride's brother had succeeded Powhatan, requiring a wedding feast commensurate with this station.[55]

On August 14, 1623, Governor Bradford of Plymouth was married. Bradford's wedding feast complements the "first Thanksgiving" of two years earlier, showing the slow evolution of the relationship between Massasoit and Bradford. According to Emmanuel Altham, an investor in the Plymouth settlement, colony official, and captain of a privateer, "Upon the occasion of the Governor's marriage . . . Massasoit was sent for to the wedding, where came with him his wife, the queen, although he hath five wives." It is unclear whether Massasoit was recognizing Plymouth's customs of monogamy by bringing only one wife to the wedding, but it was extremely rare for an Indian woman's presence to be noted at a ceremonial occasion hosted by the English. Altham continues, in language very reminiscent of the "first Thanksgiving": "With him came four other kings and about six score men with their bows and arrows—where, when they came to our town, we saluted them with the shooting off of many muskets and training our men. And so all the bows and arrows was brought into the Governor's house, and he brought the Governor three or four bucks and a turkey."[56]

The Wampanoags' arrival in state—more than a hundred armed men accompanied Massasoit—was met with a military salute by the settlers, who either carried or allowed the Wampanoags to carry their arms into the governor's house. Traditionally masculine gifts of food—deer and turkey—were given directly to Bradford, not distributed to other prominent men as Massasoit had done on the earlier occasion. Then some of the Algonquian guests danced, an awkward custom familiar to both sides at weddings. Altham's description of Bradford's wedding feast concludes with the delicious and high-status meal that celebrated the marriage: "We had about twelve pasty venisons [venison pasties, or pies], besides others, pieces of roasted venison and other such good cheer."[57]

Overall, it is a description of unusual goodwill, mutual understanding, and commensality. But in light of the 1621 "first Thanksgiving" at Plymouth, it is clear that more was at stake at Bradford's wedding for Massasoit than simply celebration. Massasoit was not invited to the earlier celebration, and as the festivities got under way, Plymouth's settlers responded to the unannounced arrival of "their greatest King Massasoyt, with some nintie men" with a military display that was not described as a welcome. Given Plymouth's weakness in 1621, the arrival of Massasoit's men was a possible threat, and Massasoit's decision to leave the settlement and return with gifts of venison was a simultaneous display of friendship and power. The similarities in the two accounts, written by different authors, suggest that the messages Massasoit conveyed to the Plymouth planters on the earlier occasion had been accepted by 1623. Massasoit was invited to Bradford's wedding, and although he was met with a military display on the later occasion as well, his men were allowed to bring their arms into the settlement, even into the governor's house. In 1621, a fusillade was a sign of a testy encounter; in 1623 it had become a ceremonial welcome.[58]

Bradford's wedding celebration evokes intercultural understanding, an evolving relationship characterized by increasing familiarity and punctuated by ritualized occasions. This celebration was a unique opportunity to cement the close relationship between Plymouth and the Wampanoags, and as such it was important to invite Massasoit and impossible for Massasoit to refuse. These points raise a final feature of shared meals. As Indians and English grew familiar with each other and with each other's expectations, invitations were a means to solidify peaceful relationships. But since refusing such an offer was almost unthinkable, invitations to a shared meal also provided a unique opportunity to lure enemies into an ambush, a far more common occurrence in the early period than celebrations.

Although English writers disagreed on the circumstances under which such a stratagem could be justified, English settlers regularly made false offers of hospitality and regularly accepted them. Mutual familiarity and shared expectations, in short, underpinned much of the violence that characterized early encounters. Edward Waterhouse's *Declaration of the State of the Colony and Affaires in Virginia* described the surprise attack of March 22, 1622, based on reports from the colony (Waterhouse himself never traveled to Virginia). On that day, Pamunkeys and other Chesapeake Algonquians attacked the Virginia Company's scattered settlements. Led by Wahunsenacawh's brother Opechancanough, the attack very nearly wiped out the colony: 347 of roughly 1,240 settlers were killed. In retrospect, according to Waterhouse, the English tradition of hospitality had laid the foundation for this disaster. English "houses [were] generally set open to the Savages, who were alwaies friendly entertained at the tables of the English, and commonly lodged in their bed-chambers," Waterhouse wrote. But on the morning of March 22, Indians "came unarmed into our houses . . . with Deere, Turkies, Fish, Furres, and other provisions, to sell, and trucke with us." While there, according to Waterhouse, the Indians "sate downe at Breakfast with our people at their tables, whom immediately with their owne tooles and weapons . . . they basely and barbarously murthered."[59]

Waterhouse's image of betrayal and treachery is obviously in part a fabrication. He notes that many of the English dead were killed in the fields or otherwise far from their breakfast tables, and the account he provides of murders could for obvious reasons not have been derived from firsthand reports. But his rhetorical use of betrayed English hospitality was effective. The Chesapeake Algonquians approached the English under false pretenses, bearing gifts of food that clearly suggested peaceful intentions. Not only did the Indians betray the hospitality of their hosts, but killing English men and women in their homes and with their own tools was, to Waterhouse, an outrage. His arguments were quickly picked up by subsequent writers, who portrayed the English settlers as generous and kindhearted, their Indian counterparts as treacherous. In the New World, among the natives, Waterhouse claimed, this simple generosity was misplaced.

There were earlier examples of similar false invitations in the Chesapeake, in which Indian groups invited parties of English men into their villages for food, and the English were killed. George Percy offered an example, describing how a party of English settlers was "intysed" into Indian homes. The "Salvages," in Percy's account, were "pretendinge to feaste them" and the English settlers "lyke greedy fooles accepted thereof." It is revealing that Percy blamed the English for walking into an ambush, "forgettinge [the Algonquians'] Subtellties." Percy suggested that the false offer of hospitality was a legitimate *ruse de guerre*, not treachery, though whether it was because the false host did the killing and not a false guest or because this invitation took place at a time of heightened alarm and hostility is not clear.[60]

By contrast, in Waterhouse's dramatic account the English were blameless victims, guilty only of generosity and trust. His was a rhetorical effort to change the narrative of English colonialism, clearing away the justifications and concerns of the earlier settlers in favor of a simpler and more violent rationale and code of conduct. In the aftermath of the 1622 attack, the Virginia council suggested that the European laws of war had to be modified to suit their situation. The council wrote to the Virginia Company as follows: "Whereas we are advised by you to observe rules of Justice with these barberous and perfidious enemies, wee hold nothinge injuste, that may tend to theire ruine, (except breach of faith)[.] Stratagems were ever allowed against all enemies, but with these neither fayre Warr nor good quarter is ever to be held." "Stratagems" or "Subtellties" were accepted parts of warfare, under specific circumstances, and an enemy's use of guile was even praiseworthy. But in these accounts, the 1622 attack justified all tactics short of "breach of faith," an interesting exception intended to preserve Jamestown's leaders' claim that they would not stoop to the methods Waterhouse and others deplored.[61]

News of the 1622 attack spread rapidly and made the Plymouth settlers very uneasy about whether their Indian neighbors were actually as generous and friendly as they seemed. In 1623, the Plymouth planters claimed to have uncovered a vast conspiracy among the Algonquians of the Massachusetts Bay area, instigated by a group of Massachusetts led by a man named Wituwamat. Meals and manners played a vital role in convincing the Plymouth leaders that they were in danger. Miles Standish, who commanded Plymouth's militia, became convinced of the reality of this conspiracy through careful observation of the degrees of hospitality offered him at the house of Canacum, sachem of the village of Manomet, as compared to the more favorable treatment afforded Wituwamat. This might seem slender evidence to support a charge that the Indians of the region were massing in a vast conspiracy, but Standish's charge demonstrates how closely meals and manners were scrutinized by the leaders of English settlements.[62]

Plymouth's governor, William Bradford, assembled a war council of the settlement's leading men, including Miles Standish and Edward Winslow. Plymouth's leaders concluded, according to Winslow's account of these events, that "it is impossible to deal with [the Massachusetts] upon open defiance, but to take them in such traps as they lay for others." Winslow's words are strikingly similar to the contemporaneous statements of the Virginia settlers. Despite the fact that false invitations were not reported of New England Algonquians, Winslow and the Plymouth planters were acting in accordance with the lessons learned from the 1622 attack, at least as the Virginia Company interpreted those lessons, and Standish was sent to lure the Massachusetts into an ambush.

Winslow's detailed account of the ambush avoided discussing exactly what kind of trap the English party set. The ruse was necessary to bring the English and their enemies together, Winslow's account suggests, but once the fighting started, the Massachusetts had a chance to fight back. Winslow was not present at the actual fighting, probably relying on Standish himself for his account of the events. In this telling, the struggle between Standish and Wituwamat encapsulated the whole of the conflict, in which superior fighting skill on the English side was bound to prevail: Standish killed Wituwamat in single combat, with his own knife.[63]

Thomas Morton, Plymouth's English rival in the region, told a different story. Morton added one telling detail to Winslow's account of the battle between Standish and Wituwamat, claiming that the Massachusetts had been invited to a feast. Standish's war party was sent from Plymouth, "bringing with them pork and things for the purpose, which they set before the Salvages."[64]

It is suggestive at least that Winslow neglected to mention the form of the ruse Standish employed (presumably with the knowledge or on the instructions of Bradford and Winslow, who would have had to supply him with more than the usual provisions). It is similarly revealing that Morton used this episode to encapsulate what he saw as the Plymouth planters' underhanded dealings with their Indian and English neighbors. Attacking guests at a meal bordered on "breach of faith," the one exception the Virginia planters made to their insistence on a relaxation of the rules of war in their conflict with the Chesapeake Algonquians. Jamestown's settlers also soon crossed, or at the very least blurred, the line they had drawn earlier. At a parley in 1623, the English settlers and leaders of the Chesapeake Algonquians, including Opechancanough,

shared a meal, after which the English proposed a toast, offering the Algonquians poisoned wine. As soon as the Indians had drunk, the English fired a
volley into the sickened crowd. Opechancanough survived the poisoning and
a gunshot wound, although his injuries kept him out of sight for years. At
least one Virginia Company member, the Earl of Warwick, was disgusted by
the English conduct during this episode, although other accounts describe this
false invitation as a legitimate tactic.[65]

After 1622, relations with all Indian groups were colored by the news
of the killings in Virginia, and even those English settlers used to peaceful
relations with their neighbors might consider a preemptive strike justified.
But hospitality remained important throughout the early period, even during
periods of hostility, for the simple reason that there was no clearer way to send
a message of friendship and reciprocity than to extend an invitation and no
clearer way to signal a breach than to refuse one.

Bradford's wedding celebration was perhaps the closest any English group
came to communicating with their Indian neighbors in the terms Palmer laid
out. The wedding feast contained all the right sorts of foods and gestures,
from both sides, to indicate respect for station and for the occasion. Taken
together with the "first Thanksgiving," the example shows how meanings were
conveyed through food in an especially direct way. Also, the two meals suggest
a process: In 1621, both sides' desire for alliance was tempered by fear on the
English part and a helping of resentment on Massasoit's, all of which was on
clear display at the "first Thanksgiving." In 1623, an invitation was extended
and graciously accepted, two leaders honored each other, and the guest lent
special honor to his host's wedding day. Without a doubt sharing a table and
the high-status foods on it, dancing and eating together, these two groups
were closer than any others of the period.

Meals were at once an especially rich form of symbolic communication
and a form of encounter with meanings unique to itself, in all the ways Palmer
noted. Meals could neither be avoided nor emptied of symbolic weight. For
these reasons, when Indians and English in the early period sized each other
up, they paid special attention to meals. These tense encounters, fraught with
the possibility of misunderstanding, violence, or peaceful celebration, were in
many ways the purest expression of the complex relationship between English
and Indians in the early period.

Conclusion

"When Flesh Was Food": Reimagining the Early Period after 1660

The times wherein old Pompion was a Saint
When men far'd hardly yet without complaint
On vilest Cates, the dainty Indian Maize
Was eat with Clamp-shells out of wooden Trayes
Under thatch'd Hutts without the cry of Rent,
And the best Sawce to every Dish, Content,
When Flesh was food, & hairy skins made coats,
And men as wel as birds had chirping Notes.
　　　　　　—Benjamin Tompson, *New Englands Crisis* (1676)

In the 1660s, John Winthrop Jr. carefully but pointedly refuted the great six-teenth-century herbalist John Gerard's claims that maize was "a Graine not so pleasant or fitt to be Eaten by mankind," being "hard of Digestion" and yielding "little or no Nourishment." Winthrop noted that "there had beene yet no certaine proofe or experience" with maize in Gerard's time, but by the 1660s, it had been "found by much Experience" to be "wholesome and pleasant for Food of which great Variety may be made out of it.[1]

Winthrop's remarks signaled a decisive shift from the Atlantic world of his father. "Much Experience" with crops like maize had changed the way English officials in the New World thought about its foods, and new standards for observing and describing the natural world changed the way the same men wrote about them. Stressing his own experience, Winthrop deliberately effaced the Indian knowledge, alliances, and provisions that had sustained earlier generations and informed earlier writers. The image of William Bradford's 1623 wedding, for example—Indians and English sharing a landscape and a table, bound by mutual need—was replaced by Benjamin Tompson's verses extolling a simpler and more honest time, with humbler foods and meals and with no mention of Native Americans except the glancing reference to "the dainty Indian Maize."[2]

The early period of negotiation, trial and error, and mutual dependence gave way after 1660 to a more confident and permanent English presence in the Americas. Rather than stressing their skills in communicating with Indians, understanding their culture, and securing their respect, English writers were increasingly likely after 1660 to portray Indians in a new light: tragic, hungry, and helpless victims of European conquest; or else uncivilized, barbaric, and even bestial. To be sure, these were not accurate descriptions, even though Native American military strength and diplomatic influence had undeniably waned since the first decades of English settlement. Benjamin Tompson's verses reimagined New England's English past without Native Americans even as Wampanoags, Narragansetts, Nipmucks, and other Algonquian groups were burning English towns and seizing English captives in King Philip's War.

Led at least nominally by Massasoit's son Metacom, New England Algonquians hoped that a victory would purge the landscape of its English population, and after their defeat the English set about much the same goal. And yet despite the profound differences that separated Metacom's New England from his father's, English writers in the later seventeenth century still focused their observations on food. Where early accounts stressed common ground, writers after 1660 were more likely to describe what Indians ate and how they ate it with unconcealed disgust, evidence that Indian and English bodies and cultures were wholly distinct. But they still looked to food in making this argument, sharing with earlier writers a sense that food was an especially pure encapsulation of civility, gentility, and status (or the lack thereof). At the same time that English crops, animals, technologies, and laws had transformed the American landscape, new commodities transformed English homes, tables, dishes, and the foods placed on them. Despite the depth and scale of these changes, food remained a unique way to convey meaning, no matter how much those meanings had changed.

In the preface to his 1705 *History and Present State of Virginia*, Robert Beverley wrote, "I am an Indian, and don't pretend to be exact in my Language." By claiming to be an "Indian," Beverley asserted that his conclusions derived from a lifetime of direct, firsthand experience in Virginia, not that they were based in any way on Virginia's native population. In fact, Native Americans are wistfully absent from his account, clearly a part of Virginia's "History," not its "Present State": "Thus I have given a succinct account of the Indians; happy, I think, in their simple State of Nature, and in their enjoyment of Plenty, without the Curse of Labour. They have on several accounts reason to lament the arrival of the Europeans, by whose means they seem to have lost their Felicity, as well as their Innocence. The English have taken away great part of their Country, and consequently made every thing less plenty amongst them. They have introduc'd Drunkenness and Luxury amongst them, which have multiply'd their Wants, and put them upon desiring a thousand things, they never dreamt of before."[3]

In one sense this description of the proud and once-formidable native peoples of Virginia shares certain features with those of the previous century. Beverley's description of "their simple State of Nature, and . . . . their enjoyment of Plenty, without the Curse of Labour" echoed Barlowe's words in 1584: "The earth bringeth foorth all things in aboundance, as in the first creation, without toile or labour. The people onely care . . . to feede themselves with such meat as the soile affoordeth." But overall, Beverley's portrait is overwhelmingly one of Indian "Innocence," their "simple State of Nature" ruined by the English, their goods, and Indians' desires for them. In this way Indians are absent from Beverley's account as actors and informants, and certainly as allies and enemies, in a way that writers of Barlowe's day would have found incredible.[4]

The absence of Indians was a deliberate feature of Beverley's history and his self-presentation, much as it had been for John Winthrop Jr. Beverley wrote that his readers could trust his observations and conclusions because "I have been very scrupulous not to insert any thing, but what I can justifie, either by my own Knowledge, or by credible Information." The similarities to Winthrop's emphasis on the personal experience and observations of elite white men is especially clear in Beverley's description of Indian religion. Beverley wrote that "I think my self oblig'd sincerely to deliver what I can warrant to be true upon my own knowledge" to resolve the question whether Algonquians had a notion of God. Native informants were untrustworthy, and in any case Beverley "cou'd learn little from them, it being reckon'd Sacriledge, to divulge the Principles of their Religion."[5]

Coming upon a "Quioccosan (which is their House of Religious Worship)" at a time he knew he would not be discovered, Beverley entered it. This building, he well knew, was an ossuary in which the Chesapeake Algonquians interred their leaders. Finding rolled mats inside, he "made use of a Knife, and ripp'd them," finding "some vast Bones." To prove they were human, Beverley "measur'd one Thigh-bone, and found it two foot nine inches long." Beverley's effort to pretend that he had "discovered" these bones and "proven" they were human was disingenuous. His descriptions were intended to convey not new knowledge but a new means of acquiring knowledge—not on the basis of earlier accounts or the testimony of native religious leaders, but with a knife and a ruler.[6]

Beverley's self-presentation, like his actions, would have been incomprehensible to Captain John Smith, but epistemological shifts cannot explain why Smith never thought to violate the tomb of Powhatan's ancestors, rip open the mats that held their remains, and describe their contents. Smith knew that he would not have survived this outrage. At the heart of the differences separating John Smith's and Robert Beverley's attitudes toward Algonquian sacred spaces lies the steep decline in Algonquian power over the course of the seventeenth century and the corresponding decline in Indians' centrality to written accounts of British North America.[7]

John Lawson's 1709 *New Voyage to Carolina* shares this melancholy perspective on Native Americans as a vanishing part of America's past, focusing on food and meals, in particular hospitality, as a way to encapsulate this. Echoing Beverley, Lawson wrote: "They are really better to us, than we are to them; they always give us Victuals at their Quarters, and take care we are arm'd against Hunger and Thirst: We do not so by them (generally speaking) but let them walk by our Doors Hungry, and do not often relieve them. We look upon them with Scorn and Disdain, and think them little better than Beasts in Humane Shape, though if well examined, we shall find that, for all our Religion and Education, we possess more Moral Deformities, and Evils than these Savages do, or are acquainted withal."[8]

The change after 1660 is clear. Lawson's remarks on hospitality echo the comments of earlier writers like Thomas Morton and Roger Williams, who praised New England Algonquian hospitality in comparison with the region's English population. But unlike those writers, both Lawson and Beverley portrayed Indians as pitiable, helpless, hungry, and in need of charity. In the early period, terms like these were a more accurate portrayal of the English, not Indians, but hospitality remained the richest symbolic expression of these very different meanings.

Lawson's example is also valuable as a caution against overstating the diminution of Indian power after 1660. Lawson is credited with founding the first European settlement in North Carolina. When Tuscaroras responded to encroachment on their territory by attacking English settlements in 1711, they took Lawson captive and handed him over to the Coree Indians, who had a score to settle with him. Lawson's painful and public execution clearly indicates that although native groups were no longer the primary source of knowledge, provisions, and alliances, not all Indians were pitiable, weak, and hungry.[9]

Lawson's comments on hospitality were not the only way writers in the later seventeenth century drew conclusions from Native American food habits that were starkly different from those of earlier accounts. As European crops, technology, animals, and diseases transformed the ecology of the Americas, written accounts began to describe the differences between English and Indians in new terms. Although they still looked to food and meals as a window on Indian society and culture, fewer accounts stressed similarities in diet and manners, as earlier writers had. Instead, writers like John Josselyn separated Indians from English based on what they ate, how they ate it, and where they drew the line between permissible and proscribed foods.[10]

Josselyn's *New Englands Rarities Discovered* was an herbal, a list of medicinal plants and remedies he collected while in New England from 1663 to 1671. Many of Josselyn's descriptions added a medicinal use for familiar foods like goose (for the bloody flux, Josselyn suggested drinking the drippings from a roasting goose) or for animals not usually considered food, for example osprey's beak as a remedy for toothache.[11]

Josselyn wrote that New England Algonquians regarded certain foods as indicative of status, among them moose tongue, which, "dried in the smoak after the *Indian* manner, is a dish for a *Sagamore*." Josselyn's remarks on the noble dish of moose tongue are in line with earlier descriptions of Indian foods as different but analogous to English customs, and one can be sure that if moose were indigenous to England, moose tongue would have been incorporated into the diet there as well. Homologies like these were especially important in the early period, providing a common language in meals and exchanges, especially those including venison.[12]

Where Josselyn does suggest a change is in his effort to separate Indian foods and those suitable for English bodies based on which animals were commonly eaten and how they were prepared (or not prepared). Eating certain foods, for Josselyn and his contemporaries, was a sign of barbarism or savagery. It took extreme want to drive the English settlers at Jamestown, for example, to eat snakes during the "starving time," but according to Josselyn, Indians ate them simply to sustain themselves: "The *Indians*, when weary with travelling, will take [rattlesnakes] up with their bare hands, laying hold with one hand behind their Head, with the other taking hold of their Tail, and with their teeth tear off the Skin of their Backs, and feed upon them alive; which they say refresheth them." Whereas descriptions of Indian foods from the early period were more likely to stress similarities with English foods and customs, Josselyn's description is one of barbarism or savagery, wholly separate from English norms. Josselyn described Indians grabbing at anything, even a venomous snake, to sate themselves, killing and tearing a live animal apart with their teeth. Without cooking, without sitting to eat or bothering to kill and skin the animal, Indian hunger is ungoverned, ravenous, like that of an animal.[13]

Although he interjected a note of caution regarding whether or not Indians ate snakes, Lawson's detailed account of Indian foods also suggested a clear distinction with the English. To Lawson, certain Indian foods, like bear and squirrel, were agreeable. But a dish of fetal fawns "taken out of the Doe's Bellies, and boil'd in the same slimy Bags Nature had plac'd them in, and one of the Country-Hares, stew'd with the Guts in her Belly, and her Skin with the Hair on" was, like Josselyn's description of rattlesnake, intended to mark the Indians as primitive, unwilling to clean and prepare their foods in the simplest way before cooking and eating them. Descriptions like these carried with them more than a helping of civilized nausea, a bodily disgust at the thought of what less civilized people would eat. This heightened sense of the differences in sensory perception between genteel English men and women and others is still another dimension of the difference between Beverley's and Smith's Virginia.[14]

But no matter how different these accounts and how much time separated them, each writer based his conclusions on observations of Native American foods and meals. Beverley disagreed with Lawson's suggestion of Indian barbarism, for example, but like Lawson he believed that food was a window onto Indian culture and a gauge of civility. Beverley wrote that the Virginia Algonquians did in fact "skin and paunch [i.e., clean or gut] all sorts of Quadrupeds; they draw [again, clean or gut], and pluck their Fowl; but their Fish they dress with their Scales on, without gutting; but in eating they leave the Scales, Entrails and Bones to be thrown away." Beverley also mentioned that Indians ate insects and larvae of various kinds but added that other cultures (especially in Africa) did as well, and concluded his discussion with a recipe similar to the one Lawson described but with a very different meaning. "They make excellent Broth, of the Head and Umbles [entrails] of a Deer," Beverley wrote, "which they put into the Pot all bloody. This seems to resemble the *jus nigrum* of the Spartans, made with the Blood and Bowels of a Hare." Beverley interpreted the same Indian food habits in a way that led his readers to a different conclusion: that the Virginia Algonquians ate foods that an English man or woman would not (or even could not), but that in doing so they were not wholly outside the realm of known experience. The Virginia Algonquians' meal of bloody entrails linked to the noblest features of the European past.[15]

As the seventeenth century gave way to the eighteenth, new styles of eating widened the gap between the tables of elites and the poor and offered new ways to delineate lines of status and precedence. Leaders of early settlements, even elites like Edward Maria Wingfield, had found it difficult to present themselves in the usual manner for men of status in part because their material circumstances were so similar to those of ordinary settlers (Wingfield's memorable squirrel may have been roasted, served, and eaten in a tent). William Bradford pointed to the same difficulty when describing the disagreements in 1623 over Plymouth's "Common Course and Condition." "Upon the point all being to have alike, and all to do alike," Bradford complained that younger and poorer men "thought themselves in the like condition" as their elders and social superiors "and one as good as another."[16]

Even as late as 1680, Virginia's gentry families did not live in qualitatively different circumstances from those of more humble status, but by the mid-eighteenth century, clear shifts were under way. Metropolitan patterns of consumption were adopted by a broader spectrum of men and women in British North America. New dining spaces, set apart from the rest of gentry houses, contrasted sharply with the multipurpose rooms in humbler homes. New objects like ceramic tea sets, silver serving dishes, matched sets of silverware, tablecloths, and napkins embodied wealth, as did tables dedicated solely to dining and matched sets of chairs to accompany them. Coffee, tea, chocolate, sugar, and other exotic commodities began to appear more frequently on these tables in the late seventeenth and eighteenth centuries. Familiarity with these furnishings and foods and the occasions on which they were consumed became crucial markers of gentility.[17]

By the mid-eighteenth century, even middling households in British North America had the ability to buy, display, and use items like tea sets and forks and foods like sugar once associated with elites. And yet despite the new props and scenery available, these households and their homes, which a century earlier Henry Wotton had called the "Theater of Hospitality," hosted familiar performances, with food at center stage.[18]

Hospitality is a recurrent theme in Sarah Kemble Knight's account of her travels from Boston to New Haven and from there to New York in 1704–5. Much of the time Knight stayed in inns and taverns, but she was also offered meals and lodging in private homes. Those of New York received her clear approval, "they'r Tables being as free to their Naybours as to themselves." And Connecticut governor Fitz-John Winthrop's social standing as "A Gentleman of an Ancient and Honourable Family" was marked by his manner ("a very curteous and afable person") and the fact that he was "much Given to Hospitality." His grandfather, Massachusetts Bay governor John Winthrop, also viewed hospitality as an obligation.[19]

The *Itinerarium* of Dr. Alexander Hamilton, based on Hamilton's experiences during a journey from Annapolis to Albany and York, Maine, in 1744, contains similar remarks linking gentility with hospitality. When Hamilton met the wealthy Jeremiah Rensselaer at Albany, he expected generous hospitality and wrote that he received it. At Newport, Rhode Island, Hamilton noted the grand houses of the wealthy and commented favorably on the hospitality they offered. He remarked of Boston that the "better sort are polite, mannerly, and hospitable to strangers."[20]

For Knight and Hamilton, material culture and manners manifested the status of leading men in ways that would have been familiar to earlier generations even though tea and chocolate would not. Equally familiar would have been the opportunity material culture presented for a self-presentation that did not correspond with social status. Encountering a man named Morison, Hamilton described him as "a very rough spun, forward, clownish blade, much addicted to swearing, att the same time desirous to pass for a gentleman." Morison was "much affronted" by a landlady "who, seeing him in a greasy jacket and breeches and a dirty worsted cap, and withall a heavy, forward, clownish air and behaviour, I suppose took him for some ploughman or carman and so presented him with some scraps of cold veal for breakfast." Receiving a meal suitable for a man of his appearance and manner but not his perceived station in life, Morison flew into a rage. And yet even here, Hamilton echoed earlier writers. When Virginia's planters protested in 1620 that Sir George Yeardley's hasty knighthood was a feeble and fruitless effort to elevate the status of a "meane man," they reminded the Virginia Company that "all cannott be select." Both Knight and Hamilton would have agreed.[21]

For different reasons, both writers looked with special disapproval on rural claims to gentility. When Knight described a tablecloth as "a Twisted thing like a cable, but something whiter," she was mocking the pretensions of her rural hostess, who recognized the importance of a tablecloth but was unable to keep it clean and pressed enough for the proper effect. For Knight, consumer goods encapsulated rural poverty in a way nothing else could. Knight described one home as follows: "the doore tyed on with a cord in the place of hinges; The floor the bear earth; no windows but such as the thin covering afforded, nor any furniture but a Bedd with a glass Bottle hanging at the head on't; an earthan cupp, a small pewter Bason, A Bord with sticks to stand on, instead of a table, and a block or two in the corner instead of chairs." The rural cottage Knight described made no pretensions to gentility. Its poverty was clearly marked in the primitive furnishings, and Knight's intention in this passage is to convey all of these meanings through a simply drawn image focused on material culture: "all and every part being the picture of poverty," as she put it.[22]

Hamilton, on the other hand, judged rural households negatively *because of* their efforts at gentility, not the inadequacy of those efforts. When he visited a home in the lower Hudson Valley, Hamilton and his traveling companion, Mr. Milne, noted that their hosts affected gentility through the goods they bought and displayed in their home: "[We] observed severall superfluous things which showed an inclination to finery in these poor people, such as a looking glass with a painted frame, half a dozen pewter spoons and as many plates, old and wore out but bright and clean, a set of stone tea dishes, and a tea pot." Milne objected that items like these "were superfluous and too splendid for such a cottage, and therefor they ought to be sold to buy wool to make yarn." Instead of a fine mirror, "a litle water in a wooden pail might serve," and "wooden plates and spoons would be as good for use and, when clean, would be almost as ornamental." Milne's insistence that this rural family should sell its possessions and display its true station in life with wooden tableware in place of pewter was not motivated by any sacrifices the family made to have these things. There is no indication that the family was hungry but chose to buy pewter spoons, nor is there any indication that they needed yarn more than a tea set. Instead, the very fact of possessing such items was incongruous with the family's rural poverty, an echo of the sumptuary legislation of an earlier time.[23]

Food remained the medium for this message. As Lawson and Josselyn had when describing meals of undressed game, fetal fawns, and live snakes, Knight and Hamilton summed up the differences between themselves and the humble households they visited in the nausea with which they regarded food and meals. Knight wrote of one hostess's meal that "The sause was of a deep Purple, which I tho't was boil'd in her dye Kettle; the bread was Indian," and, she concluded, "every thing on the Table service Agreeable to these." Whether or not her hostess had cooked Knight's supper in her dye kettle, she saw nothing nauseating about it, but Knight's readers could cringe along with her at the thought of such a meal. Cornbread was another way Knight signaled to her readers the difference between foods nourishing to elite bodies and those nourishing to the ordinary sort. In one instance, presented with a dish of mutton that "smelt strong of head sause," Knight simply turned up her nose and refused to eat; on another occasion Knight dramatically vomited up a mixture of molasses and milk offered to her as a medicinal draft. And with a mixture of fascination and revulsion, Knight described Connecticut farmers as "too Indulgent . . . to their slaves . . . permitting them to sit at Table and eat with them, (as they say to save time,) and into the dish goes the black hoof as freely as the white hand."[24]

Hamilton echoed Knight's genteel nausea in his description of the keeper of the Susquehanna Ferry, "a little old man" whom Hamilton encountered "att vittles with his wife and family upon a homely dish of fish without any kind of sauce. They desired me to eat, but I told them I had no stomach. They had no cloth upon the table, and their mess was in a dirty, deep, wooden dish which they evacuated with their hands, cramming down skins, scales, and all. They used neither knife, fork, spoon, plate, or napkin because, I suppose, they had none to use."[25]

John Josselyn's description of Indians eating snakes and John Lawson's nausea at fetal fawns and undressed game conveyed many of the same meanings. But Hamilton's portrait of rustic foods, tableware, and manners also echoes earlier writers. In the sixteenth century, Dionyse Settle described the residents of the Orkney Islands in similar terms: "They take great quantitie of fishe, which they drie in the winde and Sunne. They dresse their meate very filthily, and eate it without salt." Fynes Moryson wrote of the Irish that "they have no tables, but set their meate upon a bundle of grasse, and use the same Grasse for napkins to wipe their hands." Knight expected tablecloths in rural New England and felt justified in criticizing their cleanliness and whether or not they had been properly ironed, in much the same way Settle wrote with disapproval of the fact that Inuits "neither use table, stoole, or table cloth for comelinesse." Despite the vast differences between Settle and Knight, their descriptions are essentially the same, each summing up an entire people, capturing an entire culture, in a single meal.[26]

Only the conclusions drawn from these descriptions had changed. Robert Beverley did not find Indians' organ stew appetizing, but he did connect these Indian meals with Spartan simplicity. The lines from Benjamin Tompson praising the simple virtues and simple foods of the early period—maize eaten from wooden trays with clamshells—made the same point. Concluding his description of the Susquehanna ferryman, so did Hamilton: "I looked upon this as a picture of that primitive simplicity practiced by our forefathers long before the mechanic arts had supplied them with instruments for the luxury and elegance of life." Unlike the family in the Hudson Valley, whose tea set provided an incongruous note of striving for gentility in the midst of rural poverty, the ferryman's family was content to live, and eat, according to their humble station in life. By doing so, they earned Hamilton's respect but not his company. Gentlemen like him "had no stomach" for such a meal.[27]

To conclude with a voice from an earlier age, when sugar was a rare medicinal, the highest reaches of the English nobility regarded forks as a dubious foreign novelty, and a Chinese porcelain cup like that found at Jamestown may have been the only such object in British North America, Sir Thomas Palmer mused on the world he knew. The world in 1606 was also structured by tastes and desires and, above all, foreign things: "being once brought unto civilitie, and to the taste of the World, either to be equall with others, or to be engreatned; there is no Nation or Countrie, but standeth in necessarie neede and want of forraine things: the which being once tasted of generally, it is almost impossible to be left and forgotten." Foreign trade, foreign tastes, and new items of consumption were central to Palmer's view not just of England's place in an earlier "world of goods" but of the everyday displays of status and authority that included those goods at their center. Broadly sketching "the customes and prerogatives of the Nobilitie of a nation," Palmer identified "the chiefe whereof" lying "in their superioritie and preheminence in sitting, going, talking, eating, washing, subscribing, arrogating peculiar phrases, and order of stile in writing, and such like." "Madam Knight," as she styled herself, could not have put it better.[28]

Notes

INTRODUCTION

1. Barlowe, *Discourse of the First Voyage*, in David Beers Quinn, ed., *The Roanoke Voyages, 1584–1590*, 2 vols. (London: Hakluyt Society, 1955), 1:95–6. For Barlowe's account and the events it described, see Michael Leroy Oberg, *The Head in Edward Nugent's Hand: Roanoke's Forgotten Indians* (Philadelphia: University of Pennsylvania Press, 2008), 32–33, 38–50; Karen Ordahl Kupperman, *Roanoke: The Abandoned Colony*, 2d ed. (Lanham, Md.: Rowman and Littlefield, 2007), 14–15, 68–72; David Beers Quinn, *Set Fair for Roanoke: Voyages and Colonies, 1584–1606* (Chapel Hill: University of North Carolina Press, 1985), 24–40.

2. Barlowe, *Discourse*, in Quinn, *Roanoke Voyages*, 1:98.

3. Ibid. Some of Barlowe's party had firsthand knowledge about Indians. The voyage's pilot, Simon Fernandes, a Portuguese native of Terceira in the Azores, claimed to have visited the region with a Spanish expedition. John White, who may have been on the 1584 voyage, had visited the Arctic on the second of Martin Frobisher's voyages, in 1577, and painted portraits of Inuits there and of captives taken back to England. Such captives were an uncommon sight in England, but others among the carefully chosen members of the expedition, many of whom were close associates of Ralegh, could have seen native men and women in England before the voyage. Quinn, *Set Fair for Roanoke*, 22–24; Oberg, *Head in Edward Nugent's Hand*, 31–35; Alden T. Vaughan, "Sir Walter Ralegh's Indian Interpreters, 1584–1618," *William and Mary Quarterly*, 3d ser., 59 (2002): 341–76; Vaughan, "Powhatans Abroad: Virginia Indians in England," in Robert Appelbaum and John Wood Sweet, eds., *Envisioning an English Empire: Jamestown and the Making of the North Atlantic World* (Philadelphia: University of Pennsylvania Press, 2005), 49–67; Karen Ordahl Kupperman, *The Jamestown Project* (Cambridge, Mass.: Harvard University Press, 2007), 73–108.

4. Barlowe, *Discourse*, in Quinn, *Roanoke Voyages*, 1:98.

5. Ibid. Coll Thrush, "Vancouver the Cannibal: Cuisine, Encounter, and the Dilemma of Difference on the Northwest Coast, 1774–1808," *Ethnohistory* 58 (2011): 1–35, comes to some of the same conclusions regarding shared meanings in a very different context.

6. Barlowe, *Discourse*, in Quinn, *Roanoke Voyages*, 1:98–101.

7. Ibid., 101, 105.

8. Oberg, *Head in Edward Nugent's Hand*, 21–24.

9. Barlowe, *Discourse*, in Quinn, *Roanoke Voyages*, 1:108–9; Robert Appelbaum, *Aguecheek's Beef, Belch's Hiccup, and Other Gastronomic Interjections: Literature, Culture, and Food among the Early Moderns* (Chicago: University of Chicago Press, 2006), 155–200.

10. Barlowe, *Discourse*, in Quinn, *Roanoke Voyages*, 1:107–8.

11. Ibid.

12. Andy Wood, *Riot, Rebellion and Popular Politics in Early Modern England* (New York: Palgrave, 2002), 15–17.

13. Following Appelbaum, *Aguecheek's Beef*, 10–11, I avoid the term "foodways," which connotes a static and closed system of meaning. David Arnold, *Famine: Social Crisis and Historical Change* (Oxford: Basil Blackwell, 1988), 96: "So central have been ideas of the ruler as the ultimate earthly provider that notions of kingly or state legitimacy have often hinged upon this responsibility." See also Appelbaum, *Aguecheek's Beef*, 120.

14. Appelbaum, *Aguecheek's Beef*, 300. See also xii–xiii: "Food in the early modern period . . . was not only a biological function, or an economic reality answering to a biological function, but also the object of a discourse. Or, better yet, it was the object of a multitude of discourses." Making a similar point, Jack Goody has pointed out that in structuralist anthropology "there is a tendency to spirit away the more concrete aspects of human life, even food, sex, and sacrifice, by locating their interpretation *only* at the 'deeper' level, which is largely a matter of privileging the 'symbolic' at the expense of the more immediately communicable dimensions of social action." Jack Goody, *Cooking, Cuisine, and Class: A Study in Comparative Sociology* (Cambridge: Cambridge University Press, 1982), 25. See also Katherine Knowles, "Appetite and Ambition: The Influence of Hunger in Macbeth," *Early English Studies* 2 (2009), http://www.uta.edu/english/ees/ (accessed October 29, 2010); Michael Dietler, "Feasts and Commensal Politics in the Political Economy: Food, Power, and Status in Prehistoric Europe," in Polly Wiessner and Wulf Schiefenhövel, eds., *Food and the Status Quest: An Interdisciplinary Perspective* (Providence, R.I.: Berghahn Books, 1996), 87–125, esp. 89.

15. Thomas Tusser, *Five hundreth points of good husbandry united to as many of good huswiferie* (London, 1587); Keith Wrightson, *Earthly Necessities: Economic Lives in Early Modern Britain* (New Haven, Conn.: Yale University Press, 2000), 51–68, 132–58; Wrightson, *English Society, 1580–1680* (New Brunswick, N.J.: Rutgers University Press, 1984), 89–104. Andrew McRae, "Tusser, Thomas (*c.* 1524–1580)," in *Oxford Dictionary of National Biography*, online ed., ed. Lawrence Goldman (Oxford: Oxford University Press), http://www.oxforddnb.com/view/article/27898 (accessed December 19, 2007).

16. Tusser, *Five hundreth points of good husbandry*, sig. F2r-G1r, G2r, R4r; John Fitzherbert, *Here begynneth a newe tracte or treatyse moost p[ro]fytable for all husba[n]de men* (London, 1530), fol. 50v.

17. Tusser, *Five hundreth points of good husbandry*, sig. H3r–H3v.

18. Ibid., D1r. Madeline Bassnett, "Restoring the Royal Household: Royalist Politics and the Commonwealth Recipe Book," *Early English Studies* 2 (2009), http://www.uta

.edu/english/ees/ (accessed October 29, 2010) argues that during the Restoration period, images of well-ordered households and the meals they produced were an important symbol of royalist politics.

19. David G. Anderson and Marvin T. Smith, "Pre-Contact: The Evidence from Archaeology" and John Brooke, "Ecology," in Daniel Vickers, ed., *A Companion to Colonial America* (Malden, Mass.: Blackwell, 2003), 1–24, 44–75; Felipe Fernández-Armesto, *Near a Thousand Tables: A History of Food* (New York: Free Press, 2002), 76–100; Alfred Crosby, *The Columbian Exchange: Biological and Cultural Consequences of 1492* (Westport, Conn.: Greenwood Press, 1972), 165–202; Charles G. Mann, *1491: New Revelations of the Americas Before Columbus* (New York: Alfred A. Knopf, 2006), 191–201; Alice Beck Kehoe, *America Before the European Invasions* (New York: Longman, 2002), 192–206; Peter Nabokov with Dean Snow, "Farmers of the Woodlands," in Alvin M. Josephy, ed., *America in 1492: The World of the Indian Peoples Before the Arrival of Columbus* (New York: Vintage, 1991), 119–45; Daniel K. Richter, *Facing East from Indian Country: A Native History of Early America* (Cambridge, Mass.: Harvard University Press, 2001), 53–59; and Arturo Warman, *Corn and Capitalism: How a Botanical Bastard Grew to Global Dominance*, trans. Nancy L. Westrate (Chapel Hill: University of North Carolina Press, 2003), 1–36.

For specific regions, Richard White, *The Middle Ground: Indians, Empires, and Republics in the Great Lakes Region, 1650–1815* (New York: Cambridge University Press, 1991), 41–49; Daniel K. Richter, *The Ordeal of the Longhouse: The Peoples of the Iroquois League in the Era of European Colonization* (Chapel Hill: University of North Carolina Press for the Omohundro Institute of Early American History and Culture, Williamsburg, Va., 1992), 11–20; and Kathleen DuVal, *The Native Ground: Indians and Colonists in the Heart of the Continent* (Philadelphia: University of Pennsylvania Press, 2006), 13–28, in addition to the sources in note 19.

20. William Cronon, *Changes in the Land: Indians, Colonists, and the Ecology of New England* (New York: Hill and Wang, 1983), 34–53; Helen C. Rountree, *The Powhatan Indians of Virginia: Their Traditional Culture* (Norman: University of Oklahoma Press, 1989), 17–57, 88–89; Michael Leroy Oberg, *Uncas: First of the Mohegans* (Ithaca, N.Y.: Cornell University Press, 2003), 15–33; Oberg, *Head in Edward Nugent's Hand*, 9–16, 23–24; and Kathleen M. Bragdon, *Native People of Southern New England, 1500–1650* (Norman: University of Oklahoma Press, 1996), 55–129.

21. Thomas Harriot, *A briefe and true report of the new found land of virginia* (1588; New York: Dover Publications, 1972, repr. of the 1590 Theodor de Bry Frankfort ed.), 60.

22. Karen Ordahl Kupperman, *Indians and English: Facing Off in Early America* (Ithaca, N.Y.: Cornell University Press, 2000), 14.

23. Mary C. Fuller, *Voyages in Print: English Travel to America, 1576–1624* (Cambridge: Cambridge University Press, 1995), 91–94.

24. Martin H. Quitt, "Trade and Acculturation at Jamestown, 1607–1609: The Limits of Understanding," *William and Mary Quarterly*, 3d ser., 52 (1995): 244.

25. Kupperman, *Jamestown Project*, emphasizes the broad chronological and geographic context of the Jamestown settlement.

CHAPTER I

1. Richard Eburne, *Plaine Path-Way to Plantations* (London, 1624), 68.

2. William Strachey, comp., *For the Colony in Virginea Britannia: Lawes Divine, Morall and Martiall, &c.* (London, 1612), in Peter Force, ed., *Tracts and Other Papers, Relating Principally to the Origin, Settlement, and Progress of the Colonies in North America, from the Discovery of the Country to the Year 1776*, 4 vols. (Gloucester, Mass.: Peter Smith, 1963), vol. 3, no. 2, p. 5.

3. Wrightson, *English Society*, 18–28; Richard Brathwaite, *The English Gentleman* (London, 1630), 155; *A Declaration in Defense of an Order of Court Made in May 1637*, in *Winthrop Papers*, 5 vols. (Boston: Massachusetts Historical Society, 1929–), 3:424; Tusser, *Five hundreth points of good husbandry*, sig. C3r.

4. Eburne, *Plaine Path-Way*, 68; Nathaniel Butler, *The Historye of the Bermudaes, or Summer Islands* ([1622?]; repr., J. Henry Lefroy, ed., London: Hakluyt Society, 1882), 179.

5. Kevin Sharpe, "A Commonwealth of Meanings: Languages, Analogues, Ideas and Politics," in Kevin Sharpe, ed., *Remapping Early Modern England: The Culture of Seventeenth-Century Politics* (Cambridge: Cambridge University Press, 2000), 38–123, quotation on 44; Wrightson, *English Society*, 18–19; Karen Ordahl Kupperman, "The Beehive as a Model for Colonial Design," in Karen Ordahl Kupperman, ed., *America in European Consciousness, 1493–1750* (Chapel Hill: University of North Carolina Press for the Institute of Early American History and Culture, 1995), 272–92. See also Edward Williams, *Virgo Triumphans, or Virginia in Generall, but the South part thereof in particular* (London, 1650), 39–40, for an extended discussion of gardening as a form of government.

6. Tim Harris, introduction to Harris, ed., *The Politics of the Excluded, c. 1500–1850* (New York: Palgrave, 2001), 11. For an overview of local officeholding, see Michael J. Braddick, *State Formation in Early Modern England, c. 1550–1700* (Cambridge: Cambridge University Press, 2000), 27–46. Other examples include Steve Hindle, "The Political Culture of the Middling Sort in English Rural Communities, c. 1550–1700," in Harris, *Politics of the Excluded*, 125–52; Richard Cust, "Honour, Rhetoric, and Political Culture: The Earl of Huntingdon and His Enemies," in Susan D. Amussen and Mark A. Kishlansky, eds., *Political Culture and Cultural Politics in Early Modern England* (New York: Manchester University Press, 1995), 84–111; and Mark Goldie, "The Unacknowledged Republic: Officeholding in Early Modern England," in Harris, *Politics of the Excluded*, 153–94.

7. Braddick, *State Formation*, 68–85; Wrightson, *English Society*, 62–65; 149–73, esp. 155–73 on the efforts of local officeholders to mediate between the desires of those above them and their local communities. See also Goldie, "Unacknowledged Republic"; Michael J. Braddick, "Administrative Performance: The Representation of Political Authority in Early Modern England," in Michael J. Braddick and John Walter, eds., *Negotiating Power in Early Modern Society: Order, Hierarchy, and Subordination in Britain and Ireland* (Cambridge: Cambridge University Press, 2001), 166–87; A. J. Fletcher, "Honour, Reputation and Local Officeholding in Elizabethan and Stuart England," in Anthony Fletcher and John Stevenson, eds., *Order and Disorder in Early Modern England* (Cambridge: Cambridge University Press, 1985), 92–115. For social mobility, see Wrightson, *English Society*, 20–26.

8. Wrightson, *English Society*, 122–48; Braddick, *State Formation*, 47–55. On the "Little Ice Age," see Karen Ordahl Kupperman, "The Puzzle of the American Climate in the Early Colonial Period," *American Historical Review* 87 (1982): 1262–89.

9. A. L. Beier, *Masterless Men: The Vagrancy Problem in England, 1560–1640* (New York: Methuen, 1985), xxii; Braddick, *State Formation*, 150.

10. Wrightson, *English Society*, 149–55; Braddick, *State Formation*, 104–18; Wrightson, *Earthly Necessities*, 215–21; Steve Hindle, "Exhortation and Entitlement: Negotiating Inequality in English Rural Communities, 1550–1650," in Braddick and Walter, *Negotiating Power in Early Modern Society*, 102–22.

11. Wrightson, *Earthly Necessities*, 110–11; Braddick, *State Formation*, 118–28; John Walter, "The Social Economy of Dearth in Early Modern England," in John Walter and Roger Schofield, eds., *Famine, Disease, and the Social Order in Early Modern Society* (Cambridge: Cambridge University Press, 1989), 75–128.

12. Frank Whigham, *Ambition and Privilege: The Social Tropes of Elizabethan Courtesy Theory* (Berkeley: University of California Press, 1984), 45. As Tim Harris has pointed out, both "central and local authorities frequently called on the people to occupy public space in order to endorse their acts and to confirm the legitimacy of their rule," but the "inclusion of ordinary people . . . gave them the potential for subversion, opening up a space for them to exercise their own political power." Tim Harris, introduction to Harris, *Politics of the Excluded*, 13, 14. See also C. Holmes, "Drainers and Fenmen: The Problem of Popular Political Consciousness in the Seventeenth Century," in Fletcher and Stevenson, *Order and Disorder in Early Modern England*, 167–95; Andy Wood, "'Poore Men Woll Speke One Daye': Plebeian Languages of Deference and Defiance in England, c. 1520–1640," in Harris, *Politics of the Excluded*, 67–98; Wrightson, *English Society*, 173–79; John Walter, *Understanding Popular Violence in the English Revolution: The Colchester Plunderers* (Cambridge: Cambridge University Press, 1999), 1–9, 31–68; and John Walter, "Public Transcripts, Popular Agency, and the Politics of Subsistence in Early Modern England," in Braddick and Walter, *Negotiating Power in Early Modern Society*, 123: the term "riot" is "a lazy shorthand for the complexity within crowd actions."

13. Wrightson, *English Society*, 129, 140–48; Wrightson, *Earthly Necessities*, 115–31, 174.

14. Sir Ferdinando Gorges to Sir Robert Cecil, November 16, 1596, in James Phinney Baxter, ed., *Sir Ferdinando Gorges and His Province of Maine* (1890; repr., New York: Burt Franklin, 1967), 3:9. For other mentions of Gorges's refusal to let grain leave Plymouth in a time of scarcity, see 3:4, 17, and 19. Hugh Plat, *Sundrie new and Artificiall remedies against Famine* (London, 1596), A2v, uses similar language to discuss the necessity of elites' remaining in the localities and distributing food in times of scarcity. John Walter and Keith Wrightson, "Dearth and the Social Order in Early Modern England," *Past and Present* 71 (1976): 22–42. For a specific example, see John Walter, "Grain Riots and Popular Attitudes to the Law: Maldon and the Crisis of 1629," in John Brewer and John Styles, eds., *An Ungovernable People: The English and Their Law in the Seventeenth and Eighteenth Centuries* (New Brunswick, N.J.: Rutgers University Press, 1980), 47–84. Cecil was the author of the poor laws and dearth orders in the 1570s and 1580s; see Wrightson, *Earthly Necessities*, 156, 215.

15. Butler, *Historye of the Bermudaes*, 179; Ivor Noël Hume, *The Virginia Adventure, Roanoke to James Towne: An Archaeological and Historical Odyssey* (New York: Alfred A. Knopf, 1994), 306; Carla Gardina Pestana, "A West Indian Colonial Governor's Advice: Henry Ashton's 1646 Letter to the Earl of Carlisle," *William and Mary Quarterly*, 3d ser., 60, no. 2 (2003): 395; John Pory, "A Reporte of the Manner of Proceeding in the General Assembly Convented at James City," in Susan Myra Kingsbury, ed., *Records of the Virginia Company of London*, 4 vols. (Washington, D.C.: U.S. Government Printing Office, 1906–35), 3:160.

16. Quotations from "A Coppie of the Subscription for Maydes" (July 16, 1621), printed in David R. Ransome, "Wives for Virginia, 1621," *William and Mary Quarterly*, 3d ser., 48 (1991): 7; and Richard Whitbourne, *A Discourse Containing a Loving Invitation both Honourable, and profitable to all such as shall be Adventurers, either in person, or purse, for the advancement of his Majesties most hopefull Plantation in the New-found-land, lately undertaken* (London, 1622), 17. For other accounts of the sending of wives for Virginia's planters, see Kathleen M. Brown, *Good Wives, Nasty Wenches, and Anxious Patriarchs: Gender, Race, and Power in Colonial Virginia* (Chapel Hill: University of North Carolina Press for the Institute of Early American History and Culture, 1996), 81–83; Edmund S. Morgan, *American Slavery, American Freedom: The Ordeal of Colonial Virginia* (New York: W. W. Norton, 1975), 95, 111.

17. Wynne's letter in Richard Whitbourne, *A Discourse and Discovery of New-foundland* (London, 1622), 10; also Gillian T. Cell, ed., *Newfoundland Discovered: English Attempts at Colonisation, 1610–1630* (London: Hakluyt Society, 1982), 258. See also Andrew White, "A Briefe Relation of the Voyage Unto Maryland, by Father Andrew White, 1634," in Clayton Colman Hall, ed., *Narratives of Early Maryland, 1633–1684* (New York: Charles Scribner's Sons, 1910), 29–45; and "Notes taken from Letters which came from Virginia in the 'Abigail,' June 19, 1623," in Kingsbury, *Records of the Virginia Company,* 4:231–32.

18. "The Account of A. B. for Furnishing the Ship 'Supply,' September 1620," in Kingsbury, *Records of the Virginia Company,* 3:389; also Richard Berkeley and John Smith, "A Commission to George Thorpe for the Government of the Plantation, September 10, 1620," in Kingsbury, *Records of the Virginia Company,* 3:400: "Markhams and Goouges bookes of all kynd of English husbandry and huswifry, and .2. others for the orderinge of silk and silkwormes are nowe sent." See William S. Powell, "Books in the Virginia Colony Before 1624," *William and Mary Quarterly*, 3d ser., 5 (1948): 179. The Virginia Company also sent over, on request, Gerard's *Herball*, intended to help in the identification of "simples," and therefore the preparation of medicinals. John Gerard, *The Herball; or, Generall historie of plantes* (London, 1597). Doreen Evenden Nagy, *Popular Medicine in Seventeenth-Century England* (Bowling Green, Ohio: Bowling Green State University Press, 1988), 43–81; Rebecca J. Tannenbaum, *The Healer's Calling: Women and Medicine in Early New England* (Ithaca, N.Y.: Cornell University Press, 2002), 3–44.

19. William Bradford and Edward Winslow, *A relation or Journall of the beginning and proceedings of the English Plantation setled at Plimoth in New England, by certaine English Adventurers both Merchants and others* (London, 1622), 24–25 (hereafter cited as Bradford and Winslow, *Mourt's Relation*); Carole Shammas, *A History of Household Government*

in America (Charlottesville: University of Virginia Press, 2002), 24–52; C. Anne Wilson, "Keeping Hospitality and Board Wages: Servants' Feeding Arrangements from the Middle Ages to the Nineteenth Century," in C. Anne Wilson, ed., *Food for the Community: Special Diets for Special Groups* (Edinburgh: Edinburgh University Press, 1993), 51–52; C. Anne Wilson, "From Mediaeval Great Hall to Country-house Dining-room: The Furniture and Setting of the Social Meal," in C. Anne Wilson, ed., *The Appetite and the Eye: Visual Aspects of Food and Its Presentation Within Their Historic Context* (Edinburgh: Edinburgh University Press, 1991), 33; Sara Paston-Williams, *The Art of Dining: A History of Cooking and Eating* (London: National Trust, 1993), 71, 108, 162; Brown, *Good Wives, Nasty Wenches*, 84–85. John Winthrop's "family" was large enough to lose fourteen members in the early months of the Massachusetts Bay settlement (*Winthrop Papers*, 2:320). For Virginia's example, in which colonial officials were directed to distribute tenants among established settlers, "devideing them into families or socyeties," see Virginia Company, "Instructions to the Governor and Council of State in Virginia, July 24, 1621," in Kingsbury, *Records of the Virginia Company,* 3:479.

20. On the historiography of Bradford's land distribution, George D. Langdon Jr., *Pilgrim Colony: A History of New Plymouth, 1620–1691* (New Haven, Conn.: Yale University Press, 1966), 30; George F. Willison, *Saints and Strangers* (New York: Reynal and Hitchcock, 1945), 231; Allan Kulikoff, *From British Peasants to Colonial American Farmers* (Chapel Hill: University of North Carolina Press, 2000), 27–38, 226. On the need for landownership, see Karen Ordahl Kupperman, "Errand to the Indies: Puritan Colonization from Providence Island Through the Western Design," *William and Mary Quarterly*, 3d ser., 45 (1988): 70–99. For Virginia's similar experiments, see "A Breife Declaration of the Plantation of Virginia during the first Twelve Yeares, when Sir Thomas Smith was Governor of the Companie, & downe to this present tyme. By the Ancient Planters nowe remaining alive in Virginia [1623/4]," in H. R. McIlwaine, ed., *Journals of the House of Burgesses of Virginia, 1619–1658/9* (Richmond: Virginia State Library, 1915), 31–32, 36.

21. Mary Beth Norton, *Founding Mothers and Fathers: Gendered Power and the Forming of American Society* (New York: Vintage Books, 1996), 7; William Bradford, *Of Plymouth Plantation, 1620–1647*, ed. Samuel Eliot Morison (New York: Alfred A. Knopf, 1952), 121.

22. Bradford, *Of Plymouth Plantation*, 121.

23. Ibid.

24. Ibid. In 1624, Emmanuel Altham reported a labor shortage at Plymouth resulting from the fact that women refused to farm. Emmanuel Altham to Sir Edward Altham, March 1623/24, printed in Sydney V. James Jr., ed., *Three Visitors to Early Plymouth: Letters about the Pilgrim Settlement in New England During Its First Seven Years* (Bedford, Mass.: Applewood Books, 1997), 36.

25. Eburne, *Plaine Path-Way*, 68. Sir Thomas Smith, *De Republica Anglorum: A Discourse on the Commonwealth of England*, ed. L. Alston (Cambridge: Cambridge University Press, 1906), 39–40.

26. Felicity Heal and Clive Holmes, *The Gentry in England and Wales, 1500–1700* (Stanford, Calif.: Stanford University Press, 1994), 17–18, and on 19, "the gentry were that body

of men and women whose gentility was acknowledged by others"; Michael J. Braddick, "Civility and Authority," in David Armitage and Michael Braddick, eds., *The British Atlantic World, 1500–1800* (New York: Palgrave Macmillan, 2002), 95–98, quotation on 97. See also Dan Beaver, "'Bragging and Daring Words': Honour, Property, and the Symbolism of the Hunt in Stowe, 1590–1642," in Braddick and Walter, *Negotiating Power in Early Modern Society*, 149–65; Cust, "Honour, Rhetoric, and Political Culture"; Kupperman, *Indians and English*, 93–97; D. M. Hadley, "Dining in Disharmony in the Later Middle Ages," in Maureen Carroll, D. M. Hadley, and Hugh Willmott, eds., *Consuming Passions: Dining from Antiquity to the Eighteenth Century* (Stroud, Gloucestershire, U.K.: Tempus, 2005), 101–19.

27. Robert Gray, *A Good Speed to Virginia* (London, 1609), sig. D2r.

28. Butler, *Historye of the Bermudaes*, 14.

29. Michael Lok, "Michael Lok's Testimony" [1579?], in James McDermott, ed., *The Third Voyage of Martin Frobisher to Baffin Island, 1578* (London: Hakluyt Society, 2001), 87, 88; John Nicholl, *An Houre Glasse of Indian Newes* (London, 1607), B3v–B4r for exchange of gunfire.

30. "Instructions for the 1578 Voyage," in McDermott, *Third Voyage of Martin Frobisher*, 60, 62–63.

31. Bradford, *Of Plymouth Plantation*, 370; Richard S. Dunn, James Savage, and Laetitia Yeandle, eds., *The Journal of John Winthrop, 1630–1649* (Cambridge, Mass.: Belknap Press, 1996), 586; "JW's Financial Statement to the General Court," September 4, 1634, *Winthrop Papers*, 3:173.

32. For Yeardley's knighthood, see Kingsbury, *Records of the Virginia Company*, 3:217; for Nathaniel Rich's doubts, see ibid., 4:211; for Warner, see Michael A. LaCombe, "Warner, Sir Thomas (c. 1580–1649)," in *Oxford Dictionary of National Biography*, online ed., ed. Lawrence Goldman (Oxford: Oxford University Press), http://www.oxforddnb.com/view/article/28768 (accessed July 8, 2005); John Featley, *A sermon preached to the nobely-deseruing gentleman, Sir Thomas Warner: And the rest of his companie: bound to the West-Indies* (London, 1629); "Adventurers and Planters: Copy of a Petition to the Counsell for Virginia, 1620 (?)," in Kingsbury, *Records of the Virginia Company*, 3:231–32. See also Council for Virginia, *A Declaration of the State of the Colony and Affaires in Virginia* (London, 1620), 67.

33. Peter Thompson, "William Bullock's 'Strange Adventure': A Plan to Transform Seventeenth-Century Virginia," *William and Mary Quarterly*, 3d ser., 61 (2004): 107–28; William Bullock, *Virginia Impartially examined, and left to public view, to be considered by all Judicious and honest men* (London, 1649), quotations on 17, 10.

34. Eric H. Ash, *Power, Knowledge, and Expertise in Elizabethan England* (Baltimore: Johns Hopkins University Press, 2004), 1–18; Jim Egan, *Authorizing Experience: Refigurations of the Body Politic in Seventeenth-Century New England Writing* (Princeton, N.J.: Princeton University Press, 1999), 3–13, 32–46; Egan refers to experience as "a rhetorical category in need of legitimation" on 7. See also Kupperman, *Jamestown Project*, 131–44.

35. For the biblical injunction, see 2 Thess. 3:10.

36. R. Malcolm Smuts, *Culture and Power in England, 1585–1685* (New York: St. Martin's Press, 1999), 2–3; Sharpe, "A Commonwealth of Meanings"; Kupperman, "Beehive."

37. Braddick, *State Formation*, 107; Andrew Fitzmaurice, *Humanism and America: An Intellectual History of English Colonisation, 1500–1625* (New York: Cambridge University Press, 2003), 3, 14–16, 21–25, 28, 58; Smuts, *Culture and Power in England*, 7–10. For some of the ways criticism of officials' private lives was phrased, see Braddick, *State Formation*, 79–85; John Guy, "The Rhetoric of Counsel in Early Modern England," in Dale Hoak, ed., *Tudor Political Culture* (New York: Cambridge University Press, 1995), 292–310. Proper government of the household was another area that attracted potentially negative scrutiny; see Heal and Holmes, *Gentry in England and Wales*, 96; Cynthia B. Herrup, *A House in Gross Disorder: Sex, Law, and the 2nd Earl of Castlehaven* (Oxford: Oxford University Press, 1999). For the connection between the *vita activa* and diet, see Steven Shapin, "How to Eat Like a Gentleman: Dietetics and Ethics in Early Modern England," in Charles E. Rosenberg, ed., *Right Living: An Anglo-American Tradition of Self-Help Medicine and Hygiene* (Baltimore: Johns Hopkins University Press, 2003), 21–58.

38. Fitzmaurice, *Humanism and America*, 3, 14–16, 21–25, 28, 58; Smuts, *Culture and Power in England*, 7.

39. Fitzmaurice, *Humanism and America*, 157–66; Tacitus, *The Agricola and the Germania*, trans. H. Mattingly, trans. rev. S. A. Handford (New York: Penguin Books, 1970), 62, 63, 73 (quotation) (*Agricola*, chaps. 11, 13, 21); and 106, 111, 114, 119, 121, 123, 139 (*Germania*, chaps. 6, 11, 12, 15, 21, 23, 27, 45). See also Kupperman, *Indians and English*, 27–30.

40. Fitzmaurice, *Humanism and America*, 8–9, 13: "given that humanism provided terms in which colonisation was understood . . . the foundation of colonies was a means through which humanists could pursue their moral and political values." See also Nicholas Canny, "The Origins of Empire: An Introduction," in Canny, ed., *The Origins of Empire*, vol. 1 of *The Oxford History of the British Empire* (New York: Oxford University Press, 1998), 1–33; David Armitage, "Literature and Empire," in Canny, *Origins of Empire*, 99–123.

41. Edward Winslow, *Good Newes from New England* (London, 1624), A3r, 47–48.

42. Winslow, *Good Newes*, 47–8; John Smith, *The Generall Historie of Virginia, New-England, and the Summer Isles*, in Philip L. Barbour, ed., *The Complete Works of Captain John Smith*, 3 vols. (Chapel Hill: University of North Carolina Press for the Institute of Early American History and Culture, 1986), 2:185, 213–14, 224; Edward Maria Wingfield, "Discourse" (1608), in Philip L. Barbour, ed., *The Jamestown Voyages Under the First Charter, 1606–1609* (Cambridge: Hakluyt Society, 1969), 1:213; Butler, *Historye of the Bermudaes*, 40; Silvester Jourdain, *A Discovery of the Barmudas, otherwise called the Ile of Divels* (London, 1610), 23. For other mentions of Plymouth's governors working alongside their settlers, see Bradford and Winslow, *Mourt's Relation*, 27; and Bradford, *Of Plymouth Plantation*, 327. For another example, see George Best, *A True Discourse of the late voyages of discoverie, for the finding of a passage to Cathaya, by the Northweast, under the conduct of Martin Frobisher Generall* (London, 1578), 3: 36.

43. Niccolò Machiavelli, *Discourses on Livy*, trans. Harvey C. Mansfield and Nathan Tarcov (Chicago: University of Chicago Press, 1996), 211 (book 3, chap. 1, sec. 3); the full quotation from Machiavelli reads as follows: "This drawing back of republics toward their beginning arises also from the simple virtue of one man, without depending on any law that stimulates you to any execution; nonetheless, they are of such reputation and so much

example that good men desire to imitate them and the wicked are ashamed to hold to a life contrary to them"; Smith, *Generall Historie*, 224–25.

44. Fitzherbert, *Here begynneth a newe tracte*, A2r.

45. Virginia Company, *A True Declaration of the estate of the Colonie in Virginia* (London, 1610), 20.

46. William Strachey, "A True Reportory of the Wreck and Redemption of Sir Thomas Gates," in Louis B. Wright, ed., *A Voyage to Virginia in 1609* (Charlottesville: University Press of Virginia, 1964), 10, 11 (quotation), 12, 69 (quotation); Strachey, *Lawes Divine, Morall and Martiall*, in Force, *Tracts*, vol. 3, no. 2, p. 30.

47. William Crashaw, *A sermon preached in London before the right honorable the Lord Lawarre* (London, 1610), sig. F1r

48. Butler, *Historye of the Bermudaes*, 59; Strachey, "True Reportory," in Wright, *Voyage to Virginia*, 66–67.

49. "Adventurers and Planters," in Kingsbury, *Records of the Virginia Company*, 3:231–32.

50. Strachey ("True Reportory," in Wright, *Voyage to Virginia*, 80) related De La Warre's procession to church during his stay at Jamestown in the following words: "Every Sunday, when the lord governor and captain general goeth to church, he is accompanied with all the councilors, captains, other officers, and all the gentlemen, and with a guard of halberdiers in His Lordship's livery, fair red cloaks, to the number of fifty, both on each side and behind him; and, being in the church, His Lordship hath his seat in the choir, in a green velvet chair, with a cloth, with a velvet cushion spread on a table before him on which he kneeleth; and on each side sit the council, captains, and officers, each in their place; and when he returneth home again he is waited on to his house in the same manner."

51. "The Governor and Council in Virginia: Letter to the Virginia Company of London, 7 July 1610," in Edward Wright Haile, ed., *Jamestown Narratives* (Champlain, Va.: RoundHouse, 1998), 458–59. The supplies were hardly lavish: see "A Breife Declaration," in McIlwaine, *Journals of the House of Burgesses*, 29–30.

52. Alexander Whitaker, *Good Newes from Virginia* (London, 1613), sig. B2r. For biographical information on Whitaker, see Karen Ordahl Kupperman, "Whitaker, Alexander (1585–1617)," in *Oxford Dictionary of National Biography*, online ed., ed. Lawrence Goldman (Oxford: Oxford University Press), http://www.oxforddnb.com/view/article/71159 (accessed July 7, 2005); and Harry Culverwell Porter, "Alexander Whitaker: Cambridge Apostle to Virginia," *William and Mary Quarterly*, 3d ser., 14 (1957): 317–43.

CHAPTER 2

1. Whitaker, *Good Newes from Virginia*, sig. B2r.

2. Carville V. Earle, "Environment, Disease, and Mortality in Early Virginia," in Thad W. Tate and David L. Ammerman, eds., *The Chesapeake in the Seventeenth Century* (Raleigh: University of North Carolina Press, 1979), 109; see also Quitt, "Trade and Acculturation at Jamestown," 227–58, 239 and note.

3. William M. Kelso, Nicholas M. Luccketti, and Beverly A. Straube, *Jamestown Rediscovery IV* (Richmond, Va.: Association for the Preservation of Virginia Antiquities, 1998), 24, 27–28; Mark Nicholls, "George Percy's 'Trewe Relacyon': A Primary Source for the Virginia Settlement," *Virginia Magazine of History and Biography* 113 (2005): 247.

4. Nicholls, "George Percy's 'Trewe Relacyon,'" 248; Don Alonso de Velasco to Philip II, June 14, 1610, in Alexander Brown, ed., *The Genesis of the United States* (1890; Bowie, Md.: Heritage Books, 1994), 392; see also Appelbaum, *Aguecheek's Beef*, 263–65.

5. Ralph Lane, "Discourse on the First Colony, 17 August 1585–18 June 1586," in Quinn, *Roanoke Voyages*, 1:267; Smith, *Generall Historie*, in Barbour, *Complete Works of Captain John Smith*, 2:166.

6. Nicholls, "George Percy's 'Trewe Relacyon,'" 248; Sir George Somers to the Earl of Salisbury, June 15, 1610, in Brown, *Genesis*, 401. For archaeological evidence that the Jamestown settlers did, in fact, eat all these things and more, see William M. Kelso, *Jamestown Rediscovery II: Search for 1607 James Fort* (Richmond: Association for the Preservation of Virginia Antiquities, 1996), 37; and William M. Kelso and Beverly A. Straube, *Jamestown Rediscovery VI* (Richmond: Association for the Preservation of Virginia Antiquities, 2000), 23–26.

7. Velasco to Philip II, in Brown, *Genesis*, 392; Nicholls, "George Percy's 'Trewe Relacyon,'" 248–49; "A Breife Declaration," in McIlwaine, *Journals of the House of Burgesses*, 29.

8. L. A. Clarkson and E. Margaret Crawford, *Feast and Famine: Food and Nutrition in Ireland, 1500–1920* (New York: Oxford University Press, 2001), 136; Julia Marvin, "Cannibalism as an Aspect of Famine in Two English Chronicles," in Martha Carlin and Joel T. Rosenthal, eds., *Food and Eating in Medieval Europe* (London: Hambledon Press, 1998), 80–82 (quotation); Anthony Pagden, *The Fall of Natural Man: The American Indian and the Origins of Comparative Ethnology* (New York: Cambridge University Press, 1982), 87–89; for biblical accounts, see Lev. 26:29 and 2 Kings 6:25, 28–29. For the "custom of the sea" that condoned cannibalism among survivors of a shipwreck, see Samuel Purchas, *Purchas His Pilgrimage* (London, 1614), 747; and Butler, *Historye of the Bermudaes*, 65.

9. Kupperman, *Jamestown Project*, 210–40.

10. David Cressy, *Coming Over: Migration and Communication Between England and New England in the Seventeenth Century* (Cambridge: Cambridge University Press, 1987), chap. 4. See, for example, "Instructions for the 1578 Voyage," in McDermott, *Third Voyage of Martin Frobisher*, 58; Christopher Levett, *A Voyage into New England* (London, 1624), 38; Emmanuel Altham to Sir Edward Altham, September 1623, in James, *Three Visitors to Early Plymouth*, 28; and Francis Higginson, "Some Brief Collections out of a letter that Mr. Higginson sent to his friends at Leicester," in *New-Englands Plantation with the Sea Journal and Other Writings by Rev. Francis Higginson* (Salem, Mass.: Essex Book and Print Club, 1908), 120–21; both Altham and Higginson suggested twelve months' provision. For other sixteenth-century sources, see David B. Quinn, Alison M. Quinn, and Susan Hillier, eds., *New American World: A Documentary History to 1612*, 5 vols. (New York: Arno Press, 1979), 4:94 ("April 22, 1552: Charter party for a ship of La Rochelle victualed at Bordeaux for a voyage to Newfoundland"), 4:193 ("1576: Accounts for the purchase and fitting out of the

Gabriel and *Michael*), and 3:205–6, 208–9 ("February 3 to July 10, 1580: A Chancery case arising out of Sir Humphrey Gilbert's 1578 voyage").

11. Janet MacDonald, *Feeding Nelson's Navy: The True Story of Food at Sea in the Georgian Era* (London: Chatham Publishing, 2004), 9–44; Jennifer Stead, "Navy Blues: The Sailor's Diet, 1530–1830," in Wilson, *Food for the Community*, 69; N. A. M. Rodger, *The Safeguard of the Sea: A Naval History of Britain, 660–1649* (New York: W. W. Norton, 1998), 235; N. A. M. Rodger, "Guns and Sails in the First Phase of English Colonization, 1500–1650," in Canny, *Origins of Empire*, 79–98; James Watt, "The Influence of Nutrition upon Achievement in Maritime History," in Catherine Geissler and Derek J. Oddy, eds., *Food, Diet and Economic Change Past and Present* (Leicester: Leicester University Press, 1993), 62–82.

12. Virginia Company, *The inconveniencies that have happened to some persons which have transported themselves from England to Virginia; without provisions necessary to sustaine themselves* (London, 1622); "Account of a Small Supply Sent to Virginia in the 'Bonny Bess,' April 1623," in Kingsbury, *Records of the Virginia Company,* 4:79; "Invoice of Goods Sent to Virginia by John Harrison in the 'Marmaduke,' September 16, 1623," in Kingsbury, *Records of the Virginia Company,* 4:278–82; E. S., *Britaines Busse; or, A Computation as well of the Charge of a Busse or Herring-Fishing Ship* (London, 1615); Thomas James, *The Strange and Dangerous Voyage of Captaine Thomas James, in his intended Discovery of the Northwest Passage into the South Sea* (London, 1633), 72; William Wood, *New England's Prospect* (London, 1634), 49–51; *A proportion of provisions needfull for such as intend to plant themselves in New England, for one whole yeare* (London, 1630); Richard Ligon, *A True & Exact History of the Island of Barbadoes,* 2d ed. (London, 1673; repr., London: Frank Cass, 1970), 110, 119–20, 121; Robert Harcourt, *Relation of a Voyage to Guiana* (London, 1613), ed. Sir C. Alexander Harris (London: Hakluyt Society, 1928), 121, 125–26; Dunn, Savage, and Yeandle, *Journal of John Winthrop,* 734–36, which includes the *Arbella's* provisions for the 1629 voyage; "Agreements for Bread and Meat," November 19, 1629, in *Winthrop Papers,* 2:171–72; "April 3, 1613: Provisioning of a ship for Newfoundland" and "May 26, 1610: Instructions from the Council to John Guy," in Quinn, Quinn, and Hillier, *New American World,* 4:126, 140; "26 August 1611: An Inventory of the Provisions Left with the Settlers at Cupids Cove" and "Advice on Planting in Newfoundland, Given to Sir Henry Salusbury," in Cell, *Newfoundland Discovered,* 65–67, 246–49.

13. See, for example, "Instructions for the 1578 Voyage," in McDermott, *Third Voyage of Martin Frobisher,* 66ff. for lists of provisions. Here, the ration on the four meat days was one pound of meat; on the three fish days, three fish plus a pound of cheese. Rations were supplemented with beer, peas, and bread (both meal and biscuit). Robert Evelyn, *A Direction for Adventurers* (London, 1641), sig. A3v, offered provisions for seven months as follows: "Pease, Oatemeale, and Aquavite," "five bushells of meale, of which two to be baked into Biskets, and five bushells of Mault, some must be ground and brewed for the voyage," "a hundred[weight] of beefe, and Pork," "two bushels of roots," "salt fish," and "five pound of Butter." This list was reprinted verbatim in Beauchamp Plantagenet, *A Description of the Province of New Albion* (London, 1648), 29–30. The anonymous *Relation of Maryland*

(London, 1635), 42 (misnumbered 26), suggested the following supplies for one year: eight bushels meal, two bushels oatmeal, one bushel peas, one gallon oil, two gallons vinegar, one gallon aqua vitae, one bushel bay salt, sugar, spice, and fruit. Francis Higginson, *New England's Plantation* (London, 1630), D2v; Whitbourne, *Discourse and Discovery*, 27, 81, 84.

14. John Rolfe to Sir Edwin Sandys, January 1619/20, and Sir George Yeardley to Sir Edwin Sandys, June 7, 1620, in Kingsbury, *Records of the Virginia Company*, 3:246, 263, 298–99. Elsewhere the ration is calculated at two pounds of meal per day, which is given as the usual ration, although there is no way to calculate the relationship between weight and volume measures. It was clear that one and one-half pints per day of meal was an insufficient ration and raised complaints; see, for example, Kingsbury, *Records of the Virginia Company*, 3:226, 534.

15. Jay Allan Anderson, "A Solid Sufficiency: An Ethnography of Yeoman Foodways in Stuart England" (Ph.D. diss., University of Pennsylvania, 1971), 262. Sara Pennell criticizes Anderson's reliance on normative literature in composing his portrait of yeoman foodways and what she sees as his oversimplified notion of the yeomanry; see Sara Pennell, "The Material Culture of Food in Early Modern England, circa 1650–1750" (Ph.D. diss., St. Catherine's College, Oxford, 1997), 3. See also James W. Baker, "Seventeenth-Century English Yeoman Foodways at Plimoth Plantation," in Peter Benes and Jane Montagu Benes, eds., *Foodways in the Northeast* (Boston: Boston University Press, 1984), 105–13; Henry M. Miller, "An Archaeological Perspective on the Evolution of Diet in the Colonial Chesapeake, 1620–1745," in Lois Green Carr, Philip D. Morgan, and Jean B. Russo, eds., *Colonial Chesapeake Society* (Chapel Hill: University of North Carolina Press for the Institute of Early American History and Culture, 1988), 176–99; J. C. Drummond and Anne Wilbraham, *The Englishman's Food: A History of Five Centuries of English Diet*, rev. ed. Dorothy Hollingsworth (London: Jonathan Cape, 1958), esp. chaps. 3–5; Sarah F. McMahon, "A Comfortable Subsistence: The Changing Composition of Diet in Rural New England, 1620–1840," *William and Mary Quarterly*, 3d ser., 42 (1985): 26–65.

16. Kupperman, "Puzzle of the American Climate," 1262–89; Karen Ordahl Kupperman, "Fear of Hot Climates in the Anglo-American Colonial Experience," *William and Mary Quarterly*, 3d ser., 41 (1984): 229–30; Karen Ordahl Kupperman, "Climate and Mastery of the Wilderness in Seventeenth-Century New England," in David D. Hall and David Grayson Allen, eds., *Seventeenth-Century New England* (Boston: Colonial Society of Massachusetts, 1984), 3–37; Joyce Chaplin, *Subject Matter: Technology, the Body, and Science on the Anglo-American Frontier, 1500–1676* (Cambridge, Mass.: Harvard University Press, 2001), chap. 4.

17. Roger Williams, *A Key into the Language of America* (London: 1643), 90; Thomas Morton, *New English Canaan; or, New Canaan, Containing an Abstract of New England* (Amsterdam, 1637), reprod. in *"New English Canaan" by Thomas Morton of "Merrymount": Notes and Text*, ed. Jack Dempsey (Scituate, Mass.: Digital Scanning, 1999), 42–43; Karen Ordahl Kupperman, *Settling with the Indians: The Meeting of English and Indian Cultures in America, 1580–1640* (Totowa, N.J.: Rowman and Littlefield, 1980), 82.

18. Warman, *Corn and Capitalism*, chap. 10 (pellagra); Reay Tannahill, *Food in History*

(New York: Crown Trade Paperbacks, 1989), 203–6; Fernández-Armesto, *Near a Thousand Tables*, 30, 94. Much of the early modern medical literature was based on observation of a given food's effects on the digestive system, which no doubt contributed to the low opinion of maize. See Appelbaum, *Aguecheek's Beef*, 60.

19. Kupperman, "Puzzle of the American Climate," 1266; Kupperman, "Fear of Hot Climates," 213–17; Nancy G. Siraisi, *Medieval and Renaissance Medicine: An Introduction to Knowledge and Practice* (Chicago: University Chicago Press, 1990), 97–106; Ken Albala, *Eating Right in the Renaissance* (Berkeley: University of California Press, 2002), chap. 2; Michael C. Shoenfeldt, *Bodies and Selves in Early Modern England: Physiology and Inwardness in Spenser, Shakespeare, Herbert, and Milton* (New York: Cambridge University Press, 1999), chap. 1; Trudy Eden, *The Early American Table: Food and Society in the New World* (DeKalb: Northern Illinois University Press, 2008), 9–20.

20. Kupperman, "Fear of Hot Climates," 229; Chaplin, *Subject Matter*, chaps. 4–5; Eden, *Early American Table*, 49–82; Joshua B. Fisher, "Digesting Falstaff: Food and Nation in Shakespeare's Henry IV plays," *Early English Studies* 2 (2009), http://www.uta.edu/english/ees/ (accessed October 29, 2010).

21. Thomas Gage, *The English-American, His Travail by Sea and Land; or, A New Survey of the West-India's* (London, 1648), 143.

22. Ibid., 42–43; Kupperman, "Fear of Hot Climates," 230.

23. Bradford, *Of Plymouth Plantation*, 26; Bradford wrote about his fear of "hot countries," which "are subject to grievous diseases and many noisome impediments which other more temperate places are freer from, and would not so well agree with our English bodies" (28). See also Kupperman, "Fear of Hot Climates," 225–27; Chaplin, *Subject Matter*, 311; Crosby, *Columbian Exchange*, 152–55; Albala, *Eating Right in the Renaissance*, 86–87; Siraisi, *Medieval and Renaissance Medicine*, chap. 5, esp. 121, 147. For contemporary accounts, see T. Bright, *A Treatise: Wherein is declared, the sufficiencie of English Medicines, for cure of all diseases, cured with Medicine* (London, 1580); John Josselyn, *New Englands Rarities Discovered* (London, 1672), 39; Smith, *Generall Historie*, in Barbour, *Complete Works of Captain John Smith*, 2:168–69.

24. John Gerard, *The Herball; or, Generall historie of plantes: Gathered by Iohn Gerarde of London Master in Chirurgerie very much enlarged and amended by Thomas Iohnson citizen and apothecarye of London* (London, 1633), 83. Of course, given its deficiencies in the amino acids lysine and tryptophan and in the B vitamin niacin, Gerard was not entirely wrong about the nutritional qualities of maize. Kupperman, "Climate and Mastery of the Wilderness," 14–15; Kupperman, "Puzzle of the American Climate," 1270; Stanley Brandes, "Maize as a Culinary Mystery," *Ethnology* 31, no. 4 (1992): 331–37; Trudy Eden, "Food, Assimilation, and the Malleability of the Human Body in Early Virginia," in Janet Moore Lindman and Michele Lise Tarter, eds., *A Centre of Wonders: The Body in Early America* (Ithaca, N.Y.: Cornell University Press, 2001), 37; Albala, *Eating Right in the Renaissance*, 234–35.

25. Kupperman, *Indians and English*, 144, 159–60; *Relation of Maryland*, 9; Bradford, *Of Plymouth Plantation*, 85. See also Gabriel Archer, "A relatyon of the Discovery of our River," in Barbour, *Jamestown Voyages*, 1:89; Barlowe, *Discourse*, in Quinn, *Roanoke Voyages*,

1:105; Smith, *A Map of Virginia* (1612), in Barbour, *Complete Works of Captain John Smith*, 1:157–59; Lynn Ceci, "Fish Fertilizer: A Native American Practice?" *Science* 188 (1975): 26–30; and Nanepashemet, "It Smells Fishy to Me: An Argument Supporting the Use of Fish Fertilizer by the Native People of Southern New England," in Peter Benes, ed., *Algonkians of New England: Past and Present* (Boston: Boston University, 1993), 42–50.

26. Harriot, *A briefe and true report*, 14, 15; Edward Waterhouse, *A Declaration of the State of the Colony and Affaires in Virginia* (London, 1622), 4; Bradford and Winslow, *Mourt's Relation*, 64. For other remarks about maize, see Henry Spelman, *Relation of Virginia* [1613?], in Edward Arber, ed., *Travels and Works of Captain John Smith* (New York: Burt Franklin, 1910), 1:cxi–cxii; William Strachey, *The Historie of Travell into Virginia Britania*, ed. Louis B. Wright and Virginia Freund (London: Hakluyt Society, 1953), 118–19; Virginia Company, *True Declaration*, 27–28; *Relation of Maryland*, 22; Andrew White, "An Account of the Colony of the Lord Baron of Baltamore, 1633," in Hall, *Narratives of Early Maryland*, 10; "Ralph Lane to Richard Hakluyt the Elder, and Master H—— of the Middle Temple" (September 3, 1585), in Quinn, *Roanoke Voyages*, 1:207–10; Smith, *Map of Virginia*, in Barbour, *Complete Works of Captain John Smith*, 1:157–59; Gabriel Archer, "Description of the River and Country," in Barbour, *Jamestown Voyages*, 1:100; Emmanuel Altham to Sir Edward Altham, September 1623, in James, *Three Visitors*, 28; Kupperman, *Indians and English*, 158–61.

27. Ralph Hamor, *A True Discourse* (London, 1615), 43; Archer, "A relatyon of the Discovery of our River," in Barbour, *Jamestown Voyages*, 1:89; James Rosier, *A True Relation* (London, 1605), in David B. Quinn and Alison M. Quinn, eds., *The English New England Voyages, 1602–1608* (London: Hakluyt Society, 1983), 272; "Occurrents in Newfoundland" (September 1, 1612, to April 1, 1613), in Quinn, Quinn, and Hillier, *New American World*, 4:162; Henry Crout to Sir Percival Willoughby, April 10, 1613, in Cell, *Newfoundland Discovered*, 85; Peter C. Mancall, *Deadly Medicine: Indians and Alcohol in Early America* (Ithaca, N.Y.: Cornell University Press, 1995), 43–48; Wood, *New England's Prospect*, 63; Dionyse Settle, *A true reporte of the laste voyage into the West and Northwest regions, &c. 1577 worthily atchieved by Capteine Frobisher of the sayde voyage the first finder and Generall* (London, 1577), sig. C4r; and Kupperman, "Fear of Hot Climates," 229–30, and "Puzzle of the American Climate," 1266.

28. Eden, *Early American Table*, 24–28.

29. Drummond and Wilbraham, *The Englishman's Food*, chaps. 3–5; Anderson, "A Solid Sufficiency," esp. 262; Gondomar to Philip II, October 5, 1613, in Brown, *Genesis*, 660; Smith, *A True Relation* (1608), in Barbour, *Complete Works of Captain John Smith*, 1:33; Sir Thomas Dale to the Earl of Salisbury, August 17, 1611, in Brown, *Genesis*, 505; Butler, *Historye of the Bermudaes*, 159.

30. Richard Frethorne to his parents, March 20, April 2 and 3, 1623, in Kingsbury, *Records of the Virginia Company*, 4:58.

31. Thomas Dudley to the Countess of Lincoln, March 1631, in Force, *Tracts*, vol. 2, no. 4, p. 8; see Virginia Company, *For the Plantation in Virginia; or, Nova Britannia* (London, 1609), which claimed that servants and tradesmen journeying to the settlement "shall

have houses to dwell in, with Gardens and Orchards, and also foode and clothing at the common charge of the Joynt stocke"; *Grievances of the Servants at Saybrook, ca. July 1636*, in *Winthrop Papers*, 3:281; Dunn, Savage, and Yeandle, *Journal of John Winthrop*, 303 (see also 311, which mentions another master charged with providing his servant with insufficient food); Edward Johnson, *Wonder-Working Providence of Sions Saviour in New-England* (London, 1654), ed. J. Franklin Jameson (New York: Charles Scribner's Sons, 1910), 204; Wood, *New England's Prospect*, 51; "Instructions orders and constitutions by way of advise sett downe declared and propounded to Sr Thomas Gates knight Governor of Virginia . . . " (1609), in Kingsbury, *Records of the Virginia Company*, 3:21; Margaret Pelling, "Food, Status and Knowledge: Attitudes to Diet in Early Modern England," in Pelling, ed., *The Common Lot: Sickness, Medical Occupations and the Urban Poor in Early Modern England* (New York: Longman, 1998), 45.

32. Henry Wilkinson, *The Adventurers of Bermuda* (London: Oxford University Press, 1933), 50–61; Wesley Frank Craven, *An Introduction to the History of Bermuda* (Williamsburg, Va., 1938), 15–19; Jean Kennedy, *Isle of Devils: Bermuda under the Somers Island Company, 1609–1685* (London: William Collins Sons, 1971), 26–53; Stephen Greenblatt, *Shakespearean Negotiations: The Circulation of Social Energy in Renaissance England* (Berkeley: University of California Press, 1988), chap. 5; and Peter Linebaugh and Marcus Rediker, *The Many-Headed Hydra: Sailors, Slaves, Commoners, and the Hidden History of the Revolutionary Atlantic* (Boston: Beacon Press, 2000), chap. 1.

33. Wilkinson, *Adventurers of Bermuda*, 1–48.

34. Jourdain, *Discovery of the Barmudas*, 109–11.

35. Strachey, "True Reportory," in Wright, *Voyage to Virginia*, 31; Somers to the Earl of Salisbury, June 15, 1610, in Brown, *Genesis*, 401.

36. Appelbaum, *Aguecheek's Beef*, 123–29; Piero Camporesi, *Bread of Dreams: Food and Fantasy in Early Modern Europe*, trans. David Gentilcore (Chicago: University of Chicago Press, 1989), 78ff.; Massimo Montanari, *The Culture of Food*, trans. Carl Ipsen (Cambridge, Mass.: Blackwell, 1994), 90–100; Lynne Rossetto Kasper, *The Splendid Table: Recipes from Emilia-Romagna, the Heartland of Northern Italian Food* (New York: William Morrow, 1992), 308, 310, 313.

37. Sir William Alexander, *An Encouragement to Colonies* (London, 1624), 27; John Hall, *The Discovery of a New World*, ed. Huntington Brown (Cambridge, Mass.: Harvard University Press, 1937, orig. publ. in Latin ca. 1605, trans. John Healey, London, 1609).

38. Edward Winslow, *Good Newes from New England* (London, 1624), 47–48; John Smith, *Advertisements for the Unexperienced Planters of New England* (1631), in Barbour, *Complete Works of Captain John Smith*, 3:273.

39. Strachey, "True Reportory," in Wright, *Voyage to Virginia*, 40–41, 44.

40. Ibid., 44.

41. Ibid., 46 (quotation), 49–55; Greenblatt, *Shakespearean Negotiations*, 147–55.

42. Strachey, "True Reportory," in Wright, *Voyage to Virginia*, 51–52. See also Robert Johnson, *The New Life of Virginea: Declaring the former successe and present estate of that plantation* (London, 1612), 16–17; Kupperman, *Jamestown Project*, 255.

43. For more on the Mayflower Compact, see Bradford, *Of Plymouth Plantation*, 75–76 (includes text); and William Hubbard, *A General History of New England, from the Discovery to 1680*, in *Massachusetts Historical Society Collections*, 2d ser., 5 (1815): 53.

44. Wilkinson, *Adventurers of Bermuda*, 59.

CHAPTER 3

1. Alexander, *An Encouragement to Colonies*, 11; see also David Reid, "Alexander, William, first Earl of Stirling (1577–1640)," in *Oxford Dictionary of National Biography*, online ed., ed. Lawrence Goldman (Oxford: Oxford University Press), http://www.oxforddnb .com/view/article/335 (accessed November 11, 2006).

2. Kupperman, *Indians and English*, 41–76.

3. John Guy, "John Guy's Journal of a Voyage to Trinity Bay" (1612), in Cell, *Newfoundland Discovered*, 73.

4. Settle, *A true reporte*, sig. C3r–C3v; George Best, "The thirde voyage of Captayne Frobisher," in *True Discourse*, 3:64.

5. Guy, "Journal," in Cell, *Newfoundland Discovered*, 73–75; William Gilbert, "'Divers Places': The Beothuk Indians and John Guy's Voyage into Trinity Bay in 1612," *Newfoundland Studies* 6 (1990): 147–67. There are many other mentions of white flags as a signal of peaceful intentions, which may have led to Guy's mistaken inference. One example is the 1582 account of David Ingram, who claimed to have walked from the Gulf of Mexico to Cape Breton Island in seven months. Ingram mentioned an Indian custom of a white flag as a prelude to exchanges. *The Relation of David Ingram* (1582), published in Hakluyt, *Principall Navigations* (1589) and reprinted in David Beers Quinn, ed., *The Voyages and Colonising Enterprises of Sir Humphrey Gilbert* (London: Hakluyt Society, 1940), 2:286. See also George Best, "A true Report of such things as hapned in the second voyage of Captayne Frobysher," in *True Discourse*, 2:10, 31: "with a white flagge of blathers, sowed togyther wyth the guttes and sinewes of beastes, waftes us amayne unto them"; and White, "Briefe Relation," in Hall, *Narratives of Early Maryland*, 38. For another example that postdates Guy, see "Occurrents in Newfoundland," in Quinn, Quinn, and Hillier, *New American World*, 4:162–63. By 1650, in the Chesapeake, Edward Bland noted that white flags were clearly understood by the Algonquians of the region; see Edward Bland, *The Discovery of New Brittaine* (London, 1651), 1.

6. Guy, "Journal," in Cell, *Newfoundland Discovered*, 73–76.

7. Ibid., 74.

8. Settle, *A true reporte*, sig. B5v; Quinn, Quinn, and Hillier, *New American World*, 4:29; John Janes, "The first voyage of Master John Davis, undertaken in June 1585," in Quinn, Quinn, and Hillier, *New American World*, 4:235. The quotation continues "At length one of them pointing up to the Sunne with his hand, would presently strike his breast so hard that we might heare the blow." Other mentions of this custom of striking one's breast appear on 236, 240, and 290. Although the English had no custom similar to this, they repeatedly returned the gesture.

9. Wilcomb E. Washburn and Bruce G. Trigger, "Native Peoples in Euro-American Historiography," in Trigger and Washburn, eds., *The Cambridge History of the Native Peoples of the Americas*, vol. 1, *North America*, part 1 (Cambridge: Cambridge University Press, 1996), 61–124, esp. 104. The terms are a slight elaboration of those Trigger used in his earlier historiographical overview, Bruce G. Trigger, "Early Native North American Responses to European Contact: Romantic Versus Rationalistic Interpretations," *Journal of American History* 77 (1991): 1195–1215.

10. Richter, *Ordeal of the Longhouse*, 28; Neal Salisbury, "The Indians' Old World: Native Americans and the Coming of Europeans," *William and Mary Quarterly*, 3d ser., 53 (1996): 435–58. Bruce G. Trigger and William R. Swagerty, "Entertaining Strangers: North America in the Sixteenth Century," in Trigger and Washburn, *Cambridge History of the Native Peoples of the Americas*, vol. 1, part 1, pp. 375–76; Christopher L. Miller and George R. Hamell, "A New Perspective on Indian-White Contact: Cultural Symbols and Colonial Trade," *Journal of American History* 73 (1986): 311–28; George R. Hamell, "The Iroquois and the World's Rim: Speculations on Color, Culture, and Contact," *American Indian Quarterly* 16 (1992): 451–69; Bruce M. White, "Encounters with Spirits: Ojibwa and Dakota Theories about the French and Their Merchandise," *Ethnohistory* 41, no. 3 (1994): 369–405; Daniel H. Usner Jr., *Indians, Settlers, and Slaves in a Frontier Exchange Economy: The Lower Mississippi Valley Before 1783* (Chapel Hill: University of North Carolina Press for the Institute of Early American History and Culture, 1992), 26; and James Axtell, *After Columbus: Essays in the Ethnohistory of Colonial North America* (New York: Oxford University Press, 1988), esp. chap. 9, "At the Water's Edge: Trading in the Sixteenth Century."

11. Calvin Martin, "The Four Lives of a Micmac Copper Pot," *Ethnohistory* 22, no. 2 (1975): 111–33; Laurier Turgeon, "The Tale of the Kettle: Odyssey of an Intercultural Object," *Ethnohistory* 44 (1997): 1–29, esp. 8; Axtell, *After Columbus*, 154, 167–71.

12. Gilbert, "Divers Places," 164, interprets the headless arrow as "obviously a sign of peace."

13. Hamor, *A True Discourse*, 45.

14. Sir Ferdinando Gorges, *A Briefe Narration of the Originall Undertakings of the Advancement of Plantations into the parts of America*, printed in Ferdinando Gorges, *America Painted to the Life* (London, 1659), 4; Levett, *Voyage*, 20.

15. Pierre Bourdieu, *Outline of a Theory of Practice*, trans. Richard Nice (New York: Cambridge University Press, 1977), 15: "The fact that there is no 'choice' that cannot be accounted for, retrospectively at least, does not imply that such practice is perfectly predictable, like the acts inserted in the rigorously stereotyped sequences of a rite; and this is true not only for the observer but also for the agents, who find in the relative predictability and unpredictability of the possible ripostes the opportunity to put their strategies to work."

16. White, "Briefe Relation," in Hall, *Narratives of Early Maryland*, 44; Barlowe, *Discourse*, in Quinn, *Roanoke Voyages*, 1:98.

17. Whigham, *Ambition and Privilege*, 68–69.

18. Linda Levy Peck, *Consuming Splendor: Society and Culture in Seventeenth-Century England* (New York: Cambridge University Press, 2005), 18; Linda Levy Peck, *Court Patronage and Corruption in Early Stuart England* (Boston: Unwin Hyman, 1990), 15–21.

19. Whigham, *Ambition and Privilege*, 68–69; David Murray, *Indian Giving: Economies of Power in Indian-White Exchanges* (Amherst: University of Massachusetts Press, 2000), chap. 2.

20. Quinn, Quinn, and Hillier, *New American World*, 4:239. This reference is to Davis's second voyage, in 1586; Sir George Peckham, *A true reporte of the late discoveries* (London, 1583), reprinted in Quinn, *Gilbert*, 2:452; Dunn, Savage, and Yeandle, *Journal of John Winthrop*, 50.

21. Levett, *Voyage*, 14–15.

22. Barlowe, *Discourse*, in Quinn, *Roanoke Voyages*, 1:100.

23. Ibid., 103; Rosier, *A True Relation*, in Quinn and Quinn, *English New England Voyages*, 287; George Percy, "Observations gathered out of a Discourse of the Plantation of the Southerne Colonie in Virginia by the English, 1606" [before April 12, 1612], in Barbour, *Jamestown Voyages*, 1:137; "A relatyon . . . written . . . by a gent. of the Colony" (May 21 to June 21, 1607), in Barbour, *Jamestown Voyages*, 1:80–98, quotations from 84 and 91; Bradford and Winslow, *Mourt's Relation*, 40; Hamor, *A True Discourse*, 14. On Percy's fabric, see John W. Shirley, "George Percy at Jamestown, 1607–1612," *Virginia Magazine of History and Biography* 57 (1949): 241. For other examples of red as a valuable color for trade items, see John Winthrop to John Winthrop Jr., March 28, 1631: "if you could bring two or three hundred sheepskins and lambs skins with the wooll on, dyed redd, it would be a good Comodytye heere, and the coursest woollen clothe (so it be not flockes,) and of sadd Colours, and some redd" (*Winthrop Papers*, 3:21); and Edward Howes to John Winthrop Jr., March 26, 1632: "I understand there is greate hopes of Jo: Sagamore, to be civilized and a christian; I conceive it were very good, to bestowe respect and honor unto such as he (petty kings) by giving them a scarlet coate I meane a red coate to weare; or some other vestment in token of his place and dignitie, which other Sachems (of greater command then he) hearinge and seeinge, may thereby be allured to love and respect the English in hope and expectation of the like, or in theire conceite more glorious clothinge" (*Winthrop Papers*, 3:74).

24. Smith, *True Relation*, in Barbour, *Complete Works of Captain John Smith*, 1:148, 150. Marshall Sahlins has made this point in the following terms: "Direct and equivalent returns for food are unseemly in most social settings: they impugn the motives both of the giver and of the recipient. . . . [O]ne does not exchange things for food, not directly that is, among friends and relatives. Traffic in food is traffic between foreign interests." Marshall Sahlins, *Stone Age Economics* (Chicago: Aldine Atherton, 1972), 215–18. For two recent efforts to stress the overlapping meanings of exchange, see Natalie Zemon Davis, *The Gift in Sixteenth-Century France* (Madison: University of Wisconsin Press, 2000); and Murray, *Indian Giving*.

25. Guy, "Journal," in Cell, *Newfoundland Discovered*, 74. The Beothuk leader's knife in this quotation is further evidence that he had been exposed to European goods through exchange.

26. "John Davis on the search for the Northwest Passage" (1595), in Quinn, Quinn, and Hillier, *New American World*, 4:232; Harcourt, *Relation of a Voyage to Guiana*, 71; Smith, *True Relation*, in Barbour, *Complete Works of Captain John Smith*, 1:29. See also

Archer, "A relatyon of the Discovery of our River," in Barbour, *Jamestown Voyages*, 1:83, 87, 92; *Captain Charles Leigh his voyage to Guiana and plantation there*, in Samuel Purchas, *Hakluytus Posthumous; or, Purchas his Pilgrimes* (London, 1625; repr. ed., 20 vols., Glasgow, 1905–7), 16:310, 312; Nicholl, *An Houre Glasse*, sig. B3r.

27. Richter, *Ordeal of the Longhouse*, 9.

28. Strachey, *Historie of Travell*, ed. Wright and Freund, 103.

29. See Smith, *Generall Historie*, in Barbour, *Complete Works of Captain John Smith*, 2:109 (for *pawcohiccora*) and 113 (for *ustatahamen*); see also Percy, "Observations," in Barbour, *Jamestown Voyages*, 1:140. While waiting at Bristol to sail for Virginia, William Tracy responded to an offer to share a meal of "shepes mogets [or muggets, meaning intestines]" in Bristol with a reciprocal offer of a meal of "*pokahikiti*" in Virginia. Apparently *pokahichary* had become identified as a sort of national dish. William Tracy to John Smyth, September 1, 1620, in Kingsbury, *Records of the Virginia Company*, 3:395.

30. William Morrell, *New-England; or, A Briefe Enarration of the Ayre, Earth, Water, Fish, and Fowles of that Country* (London, 1625), 20; see also 19.

31. Smith, *Generall Historie*, in Barbour, *Complete Works of Captain John Smith*, 2:205. On the drought, see Dennis B. Blanton, "Drought as a Factor in the Jamestown Colony, 1607–1612," *Historical Archaeology* 34, no. 4 (2000): 74–81; David W. Stahle et al., "The Lost Colony and Jamestown Droughts," *Science* 280 (1998): 564–67.

32. Josselyn, *New Englands Rarities Discovered*, 20; Morton, *New English Canaan*, ed. Dempsey, 38, 71–73, 85; Isaak de Rasieres to Samuel Blommaert, ca.1628, printed in James, *Three Visitors to Early Plymouth*, 71 (quotation), 78. Patrick M. Malone, *The Skulking Way of War: Technology and Tactics among the New England Indians* (Baltimore: Johns Hopkins University Press, 1993), discusses native hunting techniques.

33. Whitbourne, *Discourse and Discovery*, 11; William Harrison, *The Description of England* (1587), ed. Georges Edelen (Ithaca, N.Y.: Cornell University Press for the Folger Shakespeare Library, 1968), 129. For other mentions of noble fishes, see Josselyn, *New Englands Rarities Discovered*, 26; and in the Maryland charter, appended to the *Relation of Maryland*, 4, the monarch granted the colonists fishing rights to "Whales, Sturgeons, and all other royal fishes."

34. Roger B. Manning, *Hunters and Poachers: A Social and Cultural History of Unlawful Hunting in England, 1485–1640* (New York: Cambridge University Press, 1993); P. B. Munsche, "The Gamekeeper and English Rural Society, 1660–1830," *Journal of British Studies* 20 (1981): 82–105; Nathaniel V. Shurtleff, ed., *Records of the Governor and Company of the Massachusetts Bay in New England* (Boston, 1853), 1:208 (November 15, 1637). For gifts to Adam Winthrop, see *Winthrop Papers*, 1:258; see also Henry Talbot to the Earl of Shrewsbury, October 16, 1585, in Quinn, Quinn, and Hillier, *New American World*, 3:294.

35. Sir George Yeardley to [Sir Edwin Sandys, 1619], in Kingsbury, *Records of the Virginia Company*, 3:127. The context is unclear, but these appear to be live deer, not preserved venison. See "At a Virginia Court [held] the 19th of June 1622," in Kingsbury, *Records of the Virginia Company*, 2:41–42, for John Martin's later efforts to have James I name him steward of the "royal forest" of Virginia.

36. Dudley to the Countess of Lincoln, March 1631, in Force, *Tracts*, vol. 2, no. 4, p. 12; Frethorne to his parents in Kingsbury, *Records of the Virginia Company*, 4:58; Strachey, *Historie of Travell*, ed. Wright and Freund, 125.

37. Percy, "Observations," in Barbour, *Jamestown Voyages*, 1:138–39; Wingfield, "Discourse," in Barbour, *Jamestown Voyages*, 1:215; Spelman, *Relation*, in Arber, *Travels and Works of Captain John Smith*, 1: cii; Winslow, *Good Newes from New England*, 17. For other examples, see Percy, "Observations," in Barbour, *Jamestown Voyages*, 1:140; Smith, *True Relation*, in Barbour, *Complete Works of Captain John Smith*, 1:49, 67.

38. Winslow, *Good Newes from New England*, 57; John Winthrop to Edward Hopkins, February 10, 1647, and to John Mason, September 19, 1648, in *Winthrop Papers*, 5:128, 255; Dunn, Savage, and Yeandle, *Journal of John Winthrop*, 459; Lion Gardiner, *Relation of the Pequot Warres* (Hartford, Conn.: Case, Lockwood, and Brainard for the Acorn Club, 1901), 24 (8 in original).

39. Archer, "A relatyon of the Discovery of our River," in Barbour, *Jamestown Voyages*, 1:84–85.

40. The most complete account of the "first Thanksgiving" is a very brief mention in Bradford and Winslow, *Mourt's Relation*, 61. An even briefer account can be found in Bradford, *Of Plymouth Plantation*, 90. See also James Deetz and Jay Anderson, "The Ethnogastronomy of Thanksgiving," *Saturday Review of Science*, November 25, 1972, 29–39.

41. Bradford and Winslow, *Mourt's Relation*, 61.

42. Ibid., 36.

CHAPTER 4

1. Laurel Thatcher Ulrich, "It 'went away shee knew not how': Food Theft and Domestic Conflict in Seventeenth-Century Essex County," in Benes and Benes, *Foodways in the Northeast*, 94–104, argues that thefts of food within English communities were signs of a "violation of communal trust," understood differently than other types of theft.

2. Hamor, *A True Discourse*, 11–15.

3. Laurel Thatcher Ulrich, *Good Wives: Image and Reality in the Lives of Women in Northern New England, 1650–1750* (New York: Vintage, 1991), 35–50; Helen C. Rountree, *Pocahontas, Powhatan, Opechancanough: Three Indian Lives Changed by Jamestown* (Charlottesville: University of Virginia Press, 2005), 56.

4. Quitt, "Trade and Acculturation at Jamestown," 227–58.

5. For "dual sachemship," see Bragdon, *Native People of Southern New England*, 140–41, 148–49; and Frederic W. Gleach, *Powhatan's World and Colonial Virginia: A Conflict of Cultures* (Lincoln: University of Nebraska Press, 1997), 34.

6. Smith, *True Relation* and *Generall Historie*, in Barbour, *Complete Works of Captain John Smith*, 1:71 and 2:156.

7. Smith, *Generall Historie*, in Barbour, *Complete Works of Captain John Smith*, 2:194.

8. Nicholl, *An Houre Glasse*, sig. C2r; Smith, *Generall Historie*, in Barbour, *Complete*

Works of Captain John Smith, 2:196, 210; Lane, "Discourse on the First Colony," in Quinn, *Roanoke Voyages*, 2:265–67; Blanton, "Drought as a Factor," 74–81; Stahle et al., "The Lost Colony and Jamestown Droughts," 564–67. Katherine Grandjean, "New World Tempests: Environment, Scarcity, and the Coming of the Pequot War," *William and Mary Quarterly*, 3d ser., 68 (2011): 75–100, suggests that food scarcity was a much more important contributor to the Pequot War than has previously been realized.

9. "John Davis on the search for the Northwest Passage" (1595), in Quinn, Quinn, and Hillier, *New American World*, 4:240–41; Gabriel Archer, "Description of the People," in Barbour, *Jamestown Voyages*, 1:102–3; Smith, *True Relation*, in Barbour, *Complete Works of Captain John Smith*, 1:81. Thomas Shepard, in *The Clear Sun-shine of the Gospel breaking forth upon the Indians in New-England* (London, 1648), wrote that the so-called "praying Indians" were required to sign a pledge abstaining from theft (4). See also Strachey, *Historie of Travell*, ed. Wright and Freund, 75: "they are very thievish, and will as closely as they can convey any thing away from us."

10. *Relation of Maryland*, 31; Smith, *Map of Virginia*, in Barbour, *Complete Works of Captain John Smith*, 1:160; Spelman, *Relation*, in Arber, *Travels and Works of Captain John Smith*, 1: cxi; Morton, *New English Canaan*, 43; Kupperman, *Indians and English*, 77–109.

11. Rountree, *Pocahontas, Powhatan, Opechancanough*, 102, argues that theft from the English was, like warfare, a way for young men to prove their bravery by challenging and triumphing over English men. For discussions of the Nameag incident, see Walter W. Woodward, *Prospero's America: John Winthrop, Jr., Alchemy, and the Creation of New England Culture* (Chapel Hill: University of North Carolina Press for the Omohundro Institute of Early American History and Culture, 2010), 93–137; and Oberg, *Uncas*, 116–22. Seth Mallios, *The Deadly Politics of Giving: Exchange and Violence at Ajacan, Roanoke, and Jamestown* (Tuscaloosa: University of Alabama Press, 2006), argues for a close correlation between violence and violated exchange norms.

12. Quinn, *Roanoke Voyages*, 1:191; Percy, "Observations," in Barbour, *Jamestown Voyages*, 1:138–39; Smith, *True Relation* and *Generall Historie*, in Barbour, *Complete Works of Captain John Smith*, 1:31 and 33 and 2:138. See also Winslow, *Good Newes from New England*, 23.

13. Kupperman, *Indians and English*, 220–21; Smith, *True Relation*, in Barbour, *Complete Works of Captain John Smith*, 1:81, 93; Strachey, *Historie of Travell*, ed. Wright and Freund, 75.

14. John Brereton, *A Briefe and True Relation of the Discoverie of the North Part of Virginia* (1602), in Quinn and Quinn, eds., *English New England Voyages*, 149, 150, 154–55.

15. Archer, "A relatyon of the Discovery of our River," in Barbour, *Jamestown Voyages*, 1:87; Bradford and Winslow, *Mourt's Relation*, 33–34; Winslow, *Good Newes from New England*, 20, 23.

16. Archer, "Description of the People," in Barbour, *Jamestown Voyages*, 1:102–3. See also Smith, *True Relation*, in Barbour, *Complete Works of Captain John Smith*, 1:83, where the return of a stolen hatchet is interpreted as a peace overture; and Bradford, *Of Plymouth Plantation*, 80, where the return of stolen tools is a prelude to a treaty between Plymouth's leaders and Massasoit.

17. Roger Williams to John Winthrop [ca. October 1638], in *Winthrop Papers*, 4:67; Percy, "Observations," in Barbour, *Jamestown Voyages*, 1:143.

18. Settle, *A true reporte*, sig. CIV.

19. Bradford, *Of Plymouth Plantation*, 65–66, 88; Nathaniel Morton, *New Englands Memoriall* (Cambridge, Mass., 1669), 16–17; Bradford and Winslow, *Mourt's Relation*, 8 (quotation), 6–7, 10, 13, 41.

20. Thomas Dermer to Samuel Purchas, December 27, 1619, in Purchas, *Pilgrimes*, 19:129–34; Gardiner, *Relation of the Pequot Warres*, 11 (3 in original); Smith, *Generall Historie*, in Barbour, *Complete Works of Captain John Smith*, 2:144, 179, 191, 215.

21. Smith, *True Relation*, in Barbour, *Complete Works of Captain John Smith*, 1:37–39; Rountree, *Pocahontas, Powhatan, Opechancanough*, 64 ("it was up to the local people, meaning the women who did the farming, to decide whether to hold onto their supply or trade it away for inedible goods"), 13 (women "had considerable say over the corn that was traded"), 116; Smith, *Generall Historie*, in Barbour, *Complete Works of Captain John Smith*, 2:224–25.

22. Shurtleff, *Records of the Governor and Company of the Massachusetts Bay*, 1:82–33, 92, 96, 243; Dunn, Savage, and Yeandle, *Journal of John Winthrop*, 57; Morton, *New English Canaan*, 173–75.

23. For overviews of the Wessagusset story, see Willison, *Saints and Strangers*, 210–30; Neal Salisbury, *Manitou and Providence: Indians, Europeans, and the Making of New England, 1500–1643* (New York: Oxford University Press, 1982), 125–33; Alden T. Vaughan, *New England Frontier: Puritans and Indians, 1620–1675*, 3d ed. (Norman: University of Oklahoma Press, 1995), 82–87; Kupperman, *Settling with the Indians*, 183–84. The major contemporary source is Winslow, *Good Newes from New England*.

24. Charles M. Andrews, *The Colonial Period in American History*, 4 vols. (New Haven, Conn.: Yale University Press, 1934), 1:330–31; Bradford, *Of Plymouth Plantation*, 100–107; Willison, *Saints and Strangers*, 207–10.

25. Willison, *Saints and Strangers*, 214–17.

26. Phineas Pratt, *A Declaration of the Affairs of the English People That First Inhabited New England*, in *Collections of the Massachusetts Historical Society*, 4th ser., vol. 4 (1858): 482.

27. Winslow, *Good Newes*, 14.

28. Glenn W. LaFantasie, "Murder of an Indian, 1638," *Rhode Island History* 38 (1979): 67–77; Bradford, *Of Plymouth Plantation*, 234, 299, 301; Nathaniel B. Shurtleff, ed., *Records of the Colony of New Plymouth*, repr. ed. (New York: AMS Press, 1968), 1:96–97. Jenny Hale Pulsipher, "Massacre at Hurtleberry Hill: Christian Indians and English Authority in Metacom's War," *William and Mary Quarterly*, 3d ser., 53 (1996): 459–86, tells of a similar incident in the Bay Colony. See also Pulsipher, *Subjects unto the Same King: Indians, English, and the Contest for Authority in Colonial New England* (Philadelphia: University of Pennsylvania Press, 2005).

29. Winslow, *Good Newes*, 44. The Plymouth Colony records show several instances of punishment for theft, although none in which the offender was as incorrigible as the Wessagusset man is said to have been. Most of the Plymouth cases were punished with a public

whipping. Some also included a brand on the shoulder, and some called for restitution. Shurtleff, *Records of the Colony of New Plymouth,* 1:74, 143; 2:73, 137, 149, 160–61.

30. Morton, *New English Canaan,* 113.

CHAPTER 5

1. George Percy to the Earl of Northumberland, August 17, 1611, quoted in Shirley, "George Percy at Jamestown, 1607–1612," 239. The full text of the letter (with modernized spelling) can be found in Haile, *Jamestown Narratives* (quotation on 559). Philip Barbour, connecting Percy's statement both to the starvation and warfare at Jamestown and to later English colonial officials, wrote that this passage would be "ludicrous were it not both tragic and portentous." Philip L. Barbour, "The Honorable George Percy: Premier Chronicler of the First Virginia Voyage," *Early American Literature* 6 (1971): 7–17. Rachel B. Herrman, "The 'tragicall historie': Cannibalism and Abundance in Colonial Jamestown," *William and Mary Quarterly,* 3d ser., 68 (2011): 47–74, expresses doubts about the reality of cannibalism at Jamestown, suggesting that the rhetorical significance of these charges are most important.

2. Tusser, *Five hundreth points of good husbandry,* sig. H3r–H3v; George Wheler, *The Protestant Monastery* (London, 1698), 173; Caleb Dalechamp, *Christian Hospitalitie Handled Common-place-wise in the Chappel of Trinity Colledge in Cambridge* (Cambridge, 1632), 7; Felicity Heal, *Hospitality in Early Modern England* (Oxford: Clarendon Press, 1990); Kupperman, *Indians and English,* 104–6; Linda Levy Peck, "'For a King not to be bountiful were a fault': Perspectives on Court Patronage in Early Stuart England," *Journal of British Studies* 25 (1986): 31–61; and Judith M. Bennett, "Conviviality and Charity in Medieval and Early Modern England," *Past and Present* 134 (1992): 18–41.

3. John E. Crowley, *The Invention of Comfort: Sensibilities and Design in Early Modern Britain and Early America* (Baltimore: Johns Hopkins University Press, 2001), 8–11, 13–14; on bread, see Paston-Williams, *The Art of Dining,* 18. See also Drummond and Wilbraham, *The Englishman's Food;* and, for a notable contemporary view, Harrison, *The Description of England,* 133–35.

4. Appelbaum, *Aguecheek's Beef,* 92; on medieval meals and feasts, see Heal, *Hospitality,* 24–25; Wilson, "From Mediaeval Great Hall to Country-house Dining-room," 28–55; Bridget Ann Henisch, *Fast and Feast: Food in Medieval Society* (University Park: Pennsylvania State University Press, 1976), 99–205; Drummond and Wilbraham, *The Englishman's Food,* 47–64; Harrison, *The Description of England,* 126–27; see also Peck, "'For a King not to be bountiful were a fault,'" 34–35.

5. From King James I's speech in Star Chamber, June 20, 1616, printed in Dalechamp, *Christian Hospitalitie,* 126–27. Whitaker, *Good Newes from Virginia,* 6 and 20–21, makes a point similar to this, in the language of Christian charity that Whitaker shared with Dalechamp, both of them ministers; for Whitaker, the social problems demonstrated by the masses of landless and unemployed were evidence that wealthy men either used their

wealth "to the satisfying of their prodigall lusts" (6) or hoarded their wealth; either way, "hard hearted rich men" allowed "multitudes of poore men and women to perish in their quarters for want of their reliefe" (20). Karen Ordahl Kupperman, *Providence Island, 1630–1641: The Other Puritan Colony* (New York: Cambridge University Press, 1993), 4, notes that among the negative characterizations of the puritan gentry was their insistence on associating only with the godly, excluding other gentry from their homes (and presumably their tables); see also Kupperman, *Indians and English*, 23, 27.

6. Brathwaite, *The English Gentleman*, 66; Heal, *Hospitality*, esp. chap. 3; Raymond Williams, *The Country and the City* (New York: Oxford University Press, 1973).

7. King James I, printed in Dalechamp, *Christian Hospitalitie*, 126; Henry Wotton, *The Elements of Architecture* (London, 1624), 71; Harrison, *The Description of England*, 448; Sir Thomas Palmer, *An Essay of the Meanes how to make our Travailes, into forraine Countries, the more profitable and honourable* (London, 1606), 62.

8. Thomas Cooper, *The Art of Giving, Describing the true Nature, and right use of Liberality* (London, 1615), sig. A5v; Michael Sparke, *Greevous Grones for the Poore* (London, 1621), 13; Dalechamp, *Christian Hospitalitie*, 6–7.

9. Wotton, *The Elements of Architecture*, 82; Heal, *Hospitality*; Wilson, "From Mediaeval Great Hall to Country-house Dining-room," 28–55; Bennett, "Conviviality and Charity"; Crowley, *The Invention of Comfort*, 3–78; Paston-Williams, *The Art of Dining*, 63–81, 123–39; Stephen Mennell, *All Manners of Food: Eating and Taste in England and France from the Middle Ages to the Present* (Urbana: University of Illinois Press, 1996), 54–61; and Roy Strong, *Feast: A History of Grand Eating* (London: Jonathan Cape, 2002), 129–267.

10. Dalechamp, *Christian Hospitalitie*, 9; Cooper, *The Art of Giving*, 6; Eburne, *Plaine Path-Way*, 10, 54; Robert Burton, *The Anatomy of Melancholy*, 2d ed. (Oxford, 1624), 56; Harrison, *The Description of England*, 202.

11. Dunn, Savage, and Yeandle, *Journal of John Winthrop*, 15.

12. Ibid., 4, 15, 19, 24, 26, 70; Ligon, *True & Exact History*, 2, 11; James, *Strange and Dangerous Voyage*, 22, 27; Edmund Browne to Sir Simonds D'Ewes, September 7, 1638, in Everett Emerson, ed., *Letters from New England: The Massachusetts Bay Colony, 1629–1638* (Amherst: University of Massachusetts Press, 1976), 226; Francis Higginson to friends in England, July 24, 1629, in Emerson, *Letters from New England*, 16, 22. For examples of English and Spanish commanders sharing a meal, see *The "Tiger" Journal of the 1585 Voyage*, in Quinn, *Roanoke Voyages*, 1:186; and Harcourt, *Relation of a Voyage to Guiana*, 122: upon his arrival at Port-of-Spain, Trinidad, the Spanish commander, "with certaine other Spaniards came aboord us: we gave them the best entertainement that our meanes, the time, and place would affoord." For the Grenville story, see Jan Huyghen van Lischoten, *Itinerario* (Amsterdam, 1596), extract published in Edward Arber, ed., *The Last Fight of the Revenge at Sea*, English Reprints, vol. 8 (New York: AMS Press, 1966), bk. 2, 92: "[Grenville] was of so hard a complection, that as he continued among the Spanish Captaines while they were at dinner or supper with him, he would carouse three or foure glasses of wine, and in a braverie take the glasses betweene his teeth and crash them in peeces and swallow them downe, so that often times the blood ran out of his mouth without any harm at all unto

him." See also [Sir Walter Ralegh], *A Report of the Truth of the fight about the Iles of Açores, this last Sommer* (London, 1591). Grenville for his part observed these customs when he held the upper hand, for example, offering a captured French sailor a glass of wine after seizing his ship and cargo en route to Roanoke in 1586. See Quinn, *Roanoke Voyages*, 1:481.

13. As David Beers Quinn noted, Gilbert "observed the utmost secrecy about his objective from the beginning and it is not possible to envisage clearly what he intended." Quinn argued that Gilbert's destination was not Newfoundland, despite the fact that Gilbert held a royal patent granting him the right to settle there and the fact that Gilbert traveled to Newfoundland in 1583, personally claiming title to the region. Instead, Quinn argued that Gilbert's 1578 voyage was bound for the West Indies and the southern part of North America. His intentions seem to have been to found a settlement as a privateering base from which to plunder Spanish shipping. David Beers Quinn, "Introduction," in Quinn, *Gilbert*, 1:37–38, 40, 44–45. For the "Discourse," see Quinn, *Gilbert*, 1:170–80.

14. Quinn, *Gilbert*, 1:40. For the details of outfitting a privateer and assembling a fleet for a voyage, see Kenneth R. Andrews, *Elizabethan Privateering: English Privateering During the Spanish War, 1585–1603* (Cambridge: Cambridge University Press, 1964), esp. part 1; and Kenneth R. Andrews, *Drake's Voyages: A Re-assessment of Their Place in Elizabethan Maritime Expansion* (London: Weidenfeld and Nicolson, 1967), 97.

15. Sir Francis Knollys held office as a privy councillor and treasurer of the household under Elizabeth. Sir Francis's connections to the monarch were rooted in his own family's service to the earlier Tudors and were strengthened considerably after his marriage. Sir Francis Knollys's wife Catherine was Queen Elizabeth's first cousin. Their daughter Lettice married Walter Devereux, Earl of Essex (and was the mother of Robert Devereux, the second earl), and later married Robert Dudley, Earl of Leicester. Another daughter, Anne, married Thomas West, second Baron De La Warre (and was the mother of the third baron, who served as governor of Virginia); a third, Cecilia, was maid of honor to the queen. For Knollys's family, see Mary Frear Keeler, ed., *Sir Francis Drake's West Indian Voyage, 1585–86* (London: Hakluyt Society, 1981), 21; Wallace T. MacCaffrey, "Knollys, Sir Francis (1511/12–1596)," in *Oxford Dictionary of National Biography*, online ed., ed. Lawrence Goldman (Oxford: Oxford University Press), http://www.oxforddnb.com/view/article/15755 (accessed August 11, 2006). For Sir Francis Knollys's support of Gilbert, see "Memoranda by Sir Francis Knollys" (July 7, 1567) and "Additional Articles of Agreement Between Sir Humphrey Gilbert and the Adventurers, with his Instructions for the Voyage" (December 12, 1582), in Quinn, *Gilbert*, 1:121 and 2:329.

16. Through an aunt who was Elizabeth's governess, Gilbert had been introduced to Elizabeth's household in 1554 or 1555; see Quinn, "Introduction," in *Gilbert*, 1:2–3.

17. Sir Humphrey Gilbert to Sir Francis Walsingham, November 12, 1578, in Quinn, *Gilbert*, 1:203; "Certificate of the reasons why Henry Knollys separated from Sir Humphrey Gilbert" (November 5–[18], 1578), in Quinn, *Gilbert*, 1:208.

18. Gilbert to Walsingham, November 12, 1578, in Quinn, *Gilbert*, 1:204.

19. Ibid.; see also Sir Humphrey Gilbert to Sir Francis Walsingham, November 18, 1578, and "Certificate of the reasons," in Quinn, *Gilbert*, 1:207–8.

20. After his return to England, Knollys was again embroiled with Gilbert over his refusal to surrender two of his men accused of murder to Plymouth authorities who included John Gilbert, Humphrey's older brother. See Quinn, "Introduction," and Gilbert to Walsingham, November 12, 1578, in Quinn, *Gilbert*, 1:40–43 and 204.

21. Gilbert to Walsingham, November 12, 1578, in Quinn, *Gilbert*, 1:204–5. Walsingham was a crucial figure in Gilbert's career, and it was no accident that Gilbert made a particular effort to enlist his support. Bryan Bevan, *The Great Seamen of Elizabeth I* (London: Robert Hale, 1971), 77, suggests that it was Walsingham who arranged for permission for Gilbert to sail, and that Gilbert received his 1578 charter through Walsingham's influence with the queen.

22. Dunn, Savage, and Yeandle, *Journal of John Winthrop*, 93.

23. Michael P. Winship, *Making Heretics: Militant Protestantism and Free Grace in Massachusetts, 1636–1641* (Princeton, N.J.: Princeton University Press, 2002); James K. Hosmer, *The Life of Young Sir Henry Vane, Governor of Massachusetts Bay, and Leader of the Long Parliament* (Boston: Houghton Mifflin, 1888).

24. Winship, *Making Heretics*, 7, 50–51; Louise A. Breen, *Transgressing the Bounds: Subversive Enterprises among the Puritan Elite in Massachusetts, 1630–1692* (New York: Oxford University Press, 2002), 17–56; Janice Knight, *Orthodoxies in Massachusetts: Rereading American Puritanism* (Cambridge, Mass.: Harvard University Press, 1994), 13–71.

25. For Ley, see Pestana, "A West Indian Colonial Governor's Advice," 386, 390 n. 30; and G. G. Harris, "Ley, James, third Earl of Marlborough (1618/19–1665)," in *Oxford Dictionary of National Biography*, online ed., ed. Lawrence Goldman (Oxford: Oxford University Press), http://www.oxforddnb.com/view/article/16620 (accessed July 8, 2005).

26. Dunn, Savage, and Yeandle, *Journal of John Winthrop*, 225; Francis J. Bremer, *John Winthrop: America's Forgotten Founding Father* (Oxford: Oxford University Press, 2003), 242–300; Winship, *Making Heretics*, 138.

27. Dunn, Savage, and Yeandle, *Journal of John Winthrop*, 215, 219, 223, 443. In Plymouth, halberds were not used, but "twelve musketiers" were ordered "to attend the person of the Govnor on the Lord's day, and other tymes when it shalbe required" (Shurtleff, ed., *Records of the Colony of New Plymouth*, 1:62).

28. Eden, *Early American Table*, 49–58.

29. Ash, *Power, Knowledge, and Expertise*, 1–18.

30. Smith, *Generall Historie*, 224–25; John Smith, *The True Travels, Adventures, and Observations of Captaine John Smith* (London, 1630), in Barbour, *Complete Works of Captain John Smith*, 3:156.

31. Philip L. Barbour, *The Three Worlds of Captain John Smith* (Boston: Houghton Mifflin, 1964), 100–105; R. C. Simmons, "Wingfield, Edward Maria (1550–1614?)," in *Oxford Dictionary of National Biography*, online ed., ed. Lawrence Goldman (Oxford: Oxford University Press), http://www.oxforddnb.com/view/article/29735 (accessed August 16, 2006).

32. Barbour, *Three Worlds*, 110–11; Barbour, "The Honorable George Percy," 7–8; Nicholls, "George Percy's 'Trewe Relacyon,'" 214–16; Mark Nicholls, "'As Happy a Fortune as I Desire': The Pursuit of Financial Security by the Younger Brothers of Henry Percy, 9th Earl

of Northumberland," *Historical Research* 65 (1992): 297–98, 301–2, 312; Shirley, "George Percy at Jamestown"; Mark Nicholls, "Percy, George (1580–1632/3)," in *Oxford Dictionary of National Biography*, online ed., ed. Lawrence Goldman (Oxford: Oxford University Press), http://www.oxforddnb.com/view/article/21926 (accessed August 16, 2006).

33. Barbour, *Three Worlds*, 147–49. For a sympathetic description of Wingfield's demotion, see Jocelyn R. Wingfield, *Virginia's True Founder: Edward-Maria Wingfield and His Times, 1550–c. 1614* (Athens, Ga.: Wingfield Family Society, 1993), 234–41.

34. Edward Maria Wingfield, "Discourse" (1608), in Barbour, *Jamestown Voyages*, 1:223. Harold Love, *Scribal Publication in Seventeenth-Century England* (Oxford: Clarendon Press, 1993), 177, suggests that manuscript circulation had the effect of "bonding groups of like-minded individuals into a community, sect or political faction, with the exchange of texts in manuscript serving to nourish a shared set of values and to enrich personal allegiances."

35. Wingfield, "Discourse," in Barbour, *Jamestown Voyages*, 1:229; thanks mostly to the Chesapeake Algonquians, Wingfield claimed, he had "mended the Comon pott," "laid up . . . provision for 3. weekes," and "reared upp xx men able to worke" (ibid., 218). Smith, *True Relation*, in Barbour, *Complete Works of Captain John Smith*, 1:33, supported Wingfield on this point, claiming that the common stores were substantial—sufficient for "13. or 14. weeks"—at the time Newport left. See also Smith, *Generall Historie,* in Barbour, *Complete Works of Captain John Smith*, 2:213: "We had more Sturgeon, then could be devoured by Dog and Man." Percy disagreed (see his "Observations," in Barbour, *Jamestown Voyages*, 1:143).

36. Smith, *True Relation*, in Barbour, *Complete Works of Captain John Smith*, 1:33 and 2:143; Wingfield, "Discourse," in Barbour, *Jamestown Voyages*, 1:219–20, 221, 223; Smith, *Generall Historie*, in Barbour, *Complete Works of Captain John Smith*, 2:143.

37. Wingfield, "Discourse," in Barbour, *Jamestown Voyages*, 1:217, 231. Barbour, *Three Worlds*, 147–50, attributes Wingfield's removal from office in large part to his insistence on precedence at Jamestown. See also Mary C. Fuller, "The First Southerners: Jamestown's Colonists as Exemplary Figures," in Richard Gray and Owen Robinson, eds., *A Companion to the Literature and Culture of the American South* (Malden, Mass.: Blackwell, 2004), 31–33.

38. George Percy to the Earl of Northumberland, August 17, 1611, quoted in Shirley, "George Percy at Jamestown," 239. For Percy's appointment as president, see John Ratcliffe to Lord Salisbury, October 4, 1609, in Barbour, *Jamestown Voyages*, 2:284; for accounts of Percy's role at Jamestown during this period, see Shirley, "George Percy at Jamestown," esp. 236 and 239; Barbour, *Three Worlds*, 271–86; and Hume, *The Virginia Adventure*, 295–310. One source, Emanuel van Meteren, "Commentarien" [1610], in Barbour, *Jamestown Voyages*, 2:278, mentions that Percy was in charge at Jamestown but that he was largely ignored.

39. Wingfield, "Discourse," in Barbour, *Jamestown Voyages*, 1:223.

40. See *Oxford English Dictionary*, 2d ed., s.v. "squirrel" (noun, 1.c.): "Applied to other animals or to persons, usu. with contemptuous force." For claims that squirrels were tasty, see Bullock, *Virginia Impartially examined*, 4; Harriot, *A briefe and true report*, 19; Strachey, *Historie of Travell*, ed. Wright and Freund, 124; and White, "Briefe Relation," in Hall, *Narratives of Early Maryland*, 44 (Chesapeake squirrels were judged "as good as any rabbit"). See also Fuller, "First Southerners," 32.

41. Wingfield's comments on chickens elsewhere in the "Discourse" support this point. Although he claimed to have bred "above 37 and the most part of them of my owne Poultrye," Wingfield only ate one, and that was when he himself was sick. Ratcliffe, on the other hand, had before then "tasted of 4 or 5." Wingfield, "Discourse," in Barbour, *Jamestown Voyages*, 1:231.

42. Ibid., 223; Smith, *Generall Historie,* in Barbour, *Complete Works of Captain John Smith*, 2:145, described seasonal waterfowl migrations, which seem to have coincided with Wingfield's demotion.

43. Wingfield, "Discourse," in Barbour, *Jamestown Voyages*, 1:223; Butler, *Historye of the Bermudaes*, 59–60, 69; Smith, *Generall Historie,* in Barbour, *Complete Works of Captain John Smith*, 2:169, 225; Plat, *Remedies*, A2v–A3r (feasting during famine); Appelbaum, *Aguecheek's Beef*, 239–45. A similar charge is found in "April 17, 1610 to [ ] 1611: The discourse of Abacuk Pricket on Henry Hudson's last voyage," in Quinn, Quinn, and Hillier, *New American World*, 4:289, in which Pricket, one of those who abandoned Hudson, Hudson's son, and several shipmates to die in the Arctic, was accused by other mutineers "of a matter no lesse then Treason amongst us, that I had deceived the company of thirtie Cakes of bread." See also Knowles, "Appetite and Ambition."

44. Virginia Company, "Instructions given by way of Advice," in Barbour, *Jamestown Voyages*, 1:51–53, quotation at 52; Quitt, "Trade and Acculturation at Jamestown," 233; Wingfield, "Discourse," in Barbour, *Jamestown Voyages*, 1:222–23. Smith described "The beginning of Trade abroad" in his *Generall Historie,* in Barbour, *Complete Works of Captain John Smith*, 2:144; see also Smith, *True Relation,* in Barbour, *Complete Works of Captain John Smith*, 1:35.

45. Quitt, "Trade and Acculturation," 243–58; Smith, *Generall Historie,* in Barbour, *Complete Works of Captain John Smith*, 2:153, also 143–46, 154, 205. Making the same point in the negative, Smith made sure his reader connected his departure with the breakdown of trade (Smith, *Generall Historie,* in Barbour, *Complete Works of Captain John Smith*, 2:225–26; see also 1:256 n. 3).

46. Smith, *Generall Historie,* in Barbour, *Complete Works of Captain John Smith*, 2:182, 186 (quotation).

47. Gabriel Archer, from Virginia, to an unknown friend, August 31, 1609, in Barbour, *Jamestown Voyages*, 2:282; Nicholls, "George Percy's 'Trewe Relacyon,'" 244; John Beaulieu to William Trumbull, December 7, 1609," in Barbour, *Jamestown Voyages*, 2:288. A very similar case is recorded in *Captain Charles Leigh his voyage to Guiana*, in Purchas, *Pilgrimes*, 16:322, when a voyage's trade goods were used to buy food from Indians, which in turn was handed over to "Mutinors and monstrous Sailours" to ensure their loyalty.

48. Wingfield, "Discourse," in Barbour, *Jamestown Voyages*, 1:233.

49. Smith, *Generall Historie,* in Barbour, *Complete Works of Captain John Smith*, 2:214, 166; see also 169, for a mention of Smith handing his private stores out to the Jamestown settlers. Richard Pots, who presumably witnessed Smith's announcement, recalled that although Smith "had of his owne private provisions sent from England, sufficient; yet hee gave it all away to the weake and sicke" (Smith, *The Proceedings of the English Colonie in*

Virginia since their first beginning from England in the yeare of our Lord 1606 till this present 1612 [Oxford, 1612], in Barbour, *Complete Works of Captain John Smith*, 1:274); Robert Appelbaum, "Hunger in Early Virginia: Indians and English Facing Off over Excess, Want, and Need," in Appelbaum and Sweet, *Envisioning an English Empire*, 195–216.

CHAPTER 6

1. Michael Dietler, "Theorizing the Feast: Rituals of Consumption, Commensal Politics, and Power in African Contexts," in Michael Dietler and Brian Hayden, eds., *Feasts: Archaeological and Ethnographic Perspectives on Food, Politics, and Power* (Washington, D.C.: Smithsonian Institution Press, 2001), 66.

2. Wood, *New England's Prospect*, 69; Morton, *New English Canaan*, 49; Rosier, *A True Relation*, in Quinn and Quinn, *English New England Voyages*, 302; Williams, *Key into the Language of America*, 16, 17.

3. Shepard, *Clear Sun-shine of the Gospel*, 20; Dermer to Purchas, December 27, 1619, in Purchas, *Pilgrimes*, 19:130; Morton, *New English Canaan*, 21–22.

4. Williams, *Key into the Language of America*, 16, 18; Wood, *New England's Prospect*, 70–71; Morton, *New English Canaan*, 113.

5. Heal, *Hospitality*, 8–9; Strachey, *Historie of Travell*, ed. Wright and Freund, 78; Williams, *Key into the Language of America*, 36.

6. Williams, *Key into the Language of America*, 39; Waterhouse, *Declaration of the State of the Colony*, 16; Smith, *Generall Historie*, in Barbour, *Complete Works of Captain John Smith*, 2:295. For descriptions of Indian dwellings, see Wood, *New England's Prospect*, 94; Williams, *Key into the Language of America*, 82–83, 88–89; Morton, *New English Canaan*, 21.

7. Tacitus, *The Agricola and the Germania*, 113, 119, 121 (*Germania*, chaps. 14, 21, and 23); Fitzmaurice, *Humanism and America*, 3, 21–25, 28, 58, 157–66; Smuts, *Culture and Power in England*, 32–41. The most obvious reference is to the parable of Lazarus and the rich man in Luke 16:19–31, which describes the punishment the rich man suffered in the afterlife for failing to offer hospitality to Lazarus, a poor man dying outside his gate. The rich man's name is usually given as "Dives" (Latin for "rich") in English sources dating back as far as Chaucer's "Summoner's Tale" (ca. 1386). Another clear reference is Matthew 25:31–46, the parable of the sheep and the goats, in which the righteous and the damned are divided based on whether they offer alms and hospitality to the poor.

8. Wood, *New England's Prospect*, 68; Percy, "Observations," in Barbour, *Jamestown Voyages*, 1:137; Kupperman, *Indians and English*, 92.

9. Winslow, *Good Newes from New England*, 27, 57.

10. Barlowe, "Discourse," in Quinn, *Roanoke Voyages*, 1:108.

11. Wood, *New England's Prospect*, 68; *New Englands First Fruits* (London, 1643), 4.

12. Barlowe, "Discourse," in Quinn, *Roanoke Voyages*, 1:109; Smith, *True Relation*, in Barbour, *Complete Works of Captain John Smith*, 1:77.

13. Palmer, *Essay*, 52–53. David Loades, "Palmer, Sir Thomas (1540/41–1626)," in

Oxford Dictionary of National Biography, online ed., ed. Lawrence Goldman (Oxford: Oxford University Press), http://www.oxforddnb.com/view/article/21218 (accessed August 10, 2005), notes that Palmer himself "enjoyed a great reputation for generous hospitality over more than sixty years." Nicholas Canny, "England's New World and the Old, 1480s–1630s," in Canny, *Origins of Empire*, 148–69, suggests that there was a format expected of early travel accounts. For more on Palmer and an account of English distinctions between Irish and Turks through their food habits, see Anna Suranyi, *The Genius of the English Nation: Travel Writing and National Identity in Early Modern England* (Newark: University of Delaware Press, 2008), esp. chap. 4.

14. Palmer, *Essay*, 50–51.

15. Ibid., 67, 110. For an overview of Tudor dining, especially as it related to material culture, see Hugh Willmott, "Tudor Dining: Object and Image at the Table," in Carroll, Hadley, and Willmott, *Consuming Passions*, 121–42.

16. Spelman, *Relation*, in Arber, *Travels and Works of Captain John Smith*, 1:cxiii.

17. Ibid., ciii, cxiii; Wood, *New England's Prospect*, 68, 95; Brown, *Good Wives, Nasty Wenches*, 49–50.

18. Crowley, *The Invention of Comfort*, 15–16, 46; Paston-Williams, *The Art of Dining*, 71; C. Dallett Hemphill, *Bowing to Necessities: A History of Manners in America, 1620–1860* (New York: Oxford University Press, 1999), 7–8; Wilson, "From Mediaeval Great Hall to Country-house Dining-room," 33; Rountree, *Pocahontas, Powhatan, Opechancanough*, 77–78.

19. Kupperman, *Settling with the Indians*, 60–62, and *Indians and English*, 148–52; Wood, *New England's Prospect*, 78, 94–98.

20. Kathleen Bragdon, "Gender as a Social Category in Native Southern New England," *Ethnohistory* 43, no. 4 (1996): 578–79; Bragdon, *Native People of Southern New England*, 45–47.

21. Percy, "Observations," in Barbour, *Jamestown Voyages*, 1:135–36.

22. Oberg, *Uncas*, 74–77, 79–80, 82–85, 88–109; Kupperman, *Indians and English*, 235–38; Vaughan, *New England Frontier*, 155–57, 161–66; and Salisbury, *Manitou and Providence*, 203–15, 231–35. Winship, *Making Heretics*, 194, 242, argues that Miantonomi's close relationship with Henry Vane was another reason he was not trusted.

23. Oberg, *Uncas*, 82–86; Roger Williams to John Winthrop, after September 21, 1638, in Glenn LaFantasie, ed., *Correspondence of Roger Williams* (Hanover, N.H.: Brown University Press and University Press of New England for the Rhode Island Historical Society, 1988), 1:183, 185 n.10.

24. Dunn, Savage, and Yeandle, *Journal of John Winthrop*, 191. The precise meaning of *sanap* is difficult to determine. Dunn, Savage, and Yeandle define *sanaps* as "married males or warriors" (47 n. 82); Wood's glossary (in *New England's Prospect*, O3r) defines *sannup* simply as "man"; Pratt, *Declaration*, 480, uses the word to mean "man" as well. But the word may have had a narrower meaning as well. Wood described the custom of a sachem's annual "progress, accompanied with a dozen of his best subjects, to view his country, to recreate himself, and establish good order" (*New England's Prospect*, 80). If the "best subjects" are *sanaps*, the word would correlate with Winthrop's usage.

25. Dunn, Savage, and Yeandle, *Journal of John Winthrop*, 337; Roger Williams wrote to Winthrop on this occasion that Miantonomi could not be "perswaded to trust to Interpreters whom he fears to trust" and would not go to Massachusetts Bay without Williams as his translator. Roger Williams to John Winthrop, August 21, 1640, in *Winthrop Papers*, 4:269.

26. Dunn, Savage, and Yeandle, *Journal of John Winthrop*, 410–11.

27. Ibid., 461, 47; Oberg, *Uncas*, 87–109.

28. Dunn, Savage, and Yeandle, *Journal of John Winthrop*, 509.

29. Johnson, *Wonder-Working Providence*, 162–63.

30. Archer, "A relatyon of the Discovery of our River," in Barbour, *Jamestown Voyages*, 1:85. For similar descriptions, see Percy, "Observations," in Barbour, *Jamestown Voyages*, 1:135, 137, 140; and Smith, *Map of Virginia*, in Barbour, *Complete Works of Captain John Smith*, 1:167–68.

31. Archer, "A relatyon of the Discovery of our River," in Barbour, *Jamestown Voyages*, 1:92.

32. Smith, *True Relation* and *Generall Historie,* in Barbour, *Complete Works of Captain John Smith*, 1:53 and 2:155.

33. Archer, "A relatyon of the Discovery of our River," in Barbour, *Jamestown Voyages*, 1:84; see also 87, 88; and Smith, *Map of Virginia*, in Barbour, *Complete Works of Captain John Smith*, 1:167.

34. Archer, "A relatyon of the Discovery of our River," in Barbour, *Jamestown Voyages*, 1:86–87.

35. Dudley to the Countess of Lincoln, March 1631, in Force, *Tracts*, vol. 2, no. 4, p. 5. See also Crowley, *The Invention of Comfort*, 6, 73; Paston-Williams, *The Art of Dining*, 71, 130.

36. Rosier, *A True Relation*, in Quinn and Quinn, *English New England Voyages*, 275. The *Relation of Maryland* noted that Algonquians' "conversation each with other, is peaceable, and free from all scurrulous words, which may give offence," while at the same time reporting that Indians scolded their English guests for their tendency to interrupt (31).

37. Rosier, *A True Relation*, in Quinn and Quinn, *English New England Voyages*, 275; Dunn, Savage, and Yeandle, *Journal of John Winthrop*, 47; Higginson, *New England's Plantation*, C4v.

38. Palmer, *Essay*, 61; Morton, *New English Canaan*, 21; Strachey, *Historie of Travell*, ed. Wright and Freund, 84; Archer, "Description of the People," in Barbour, *Jamestown Voyages*, 1:103; Wood, *New England's Prospect*, 67.

39. Robert Cushman, "Reasons & considerations touching the lawfulnesse of removing out of England into the parts of America," in Bradford and Winslow, *Mourt's Relation*, 71–72; Tusser, *Five hundreth points of good husbandry*, sig. C2v; *Relation of Maryland*, 30; Harriot, *A briefe and true report*, 61; Morton, *New English Canaan*, 49; Kupperman, *Indians and English*, 23, 27, 161–62; Shapin, "How to Eat Like a Gentleman," 21–58; Peter Burke, "*Res et Verba*: Conspicuous Consumption in the Early Modern World," in John Brewer and Roy Porter, eds., *Consumption and the World of Goods* (London: Routledge, 1994), 148–61;

and Todd A. Borlik, "'The Chameleon's Dish': Shakespeare and the Omnivore's Dilemma," and Emily E. Speller, "'For Knowledge Is as Food': Digesting Gluttony and Temperance in Paradise Lost," both in *Early English Studies* 2 (2009), http://www.uta.edu/english/ees/ (accessed October 29, 2010).

40. Williams, *Key into the Language of America*, 11; Robert Beverley, *The History and Present State of Virginia* (1705), repr. ed. Louis B. Wright (Chapel Hill: University of North Carolina Press, 1947), 185. See also Bradford and Winslow, *Mourt's Relation*, 34; and the English translation of Jean de Lery, in Joannes Boemus, *The Manners, Lawes, and Customes of All Nations* (London, 1611), 500; David Allan, "Manners and Mustard: Ideas of Political Decline in Sixteenth-Century Scotland," *Comparative Studies in Society and History* 37 (1995): 245.

41. Spelman, *Relation*, in Arber, *Travels and Works of Captain John Smith*, 1:cxiii; *Relation of Maryland*, 31. See also Higginson, *New England's Plantation*, C4r; Wood, *New England's Prospect*, 67; Kupperman, *Indians and English*, 161–62.

42. Mennell, *All Manners of Food*, 86; Strong, *Feast*, 194–99; Anderson, "A Solid Sufficiency," 161–62, 237–39; Gerard Brett, *Dinner Is Served: A Study in Manners* (Hamden, Conn.: Archon Books, 1969), 60–62; Henisch, *Fast and Feast*, 170–74; Paston-Williams, *The Art of Dining*, 45, 67, 74–76, 133 (fork), 138, 189; James Deetz, *In Small Things Forgotten: An Archaeology of Early American Life* (New York: Anchor Books, 1996), 168–69; Peter Brears, "Decoration of the Tudor and Stuart Table," in Wilson, *The Appetite and the Eye*, 66–67, 72, 74, 91; C. Anne Wilson, "Ritual, Form and Colour in the Mediaeval Food Tradition," in Wilson, *The Appetite and the Eye*, 9; Alison Sim, *Food and Feast in Tudor England* (Stroud, Gloucestershire: Sutton, 1997), 91–99; Ken Albala, *Food in Early Modern Europe* (Westport, Conn.: Greenwood, 2003), 103–4; William M. Kelso, Nicholas M. Luccketti, and Beverly A. Straube, *Jamestown Rediscovery V* (Richmond, Va.: Association for the Preservation of Virginia Antiquities, 1999), 48 (wine cup); Nicholas Luccketti and Beverly Straube, *1998 Interim Report on the APVA Excavations at Jamestown, Virginia* (Richmond, Va.: Association for the Preservation of Virginia Antiquities, 1999), 17–19 (ear picker).

43. Smith, *Map of Virginia*, in Barbour, *Complete Works of Captain John Smith*, 1:171; Spelman, *Relation*, in Arber, *Travels and Works of Captain John Smith*, 1:cxiii; Wood, *New England's Prospect*, 79. See also Strachey, *Historie of Travell*, ed. Wright and Freund, 98; *Relation of Maryland*, 33; Winslow, *Good Newes*, 33. Harriot, *A briefe and true report*, 56, claimed that the Algonquians near Roanoke never said grace.

44. Guy, "Journal," in Cell, *Newfoundland Discovered*, 74; Sir Anthony Weldon, *The Court and Character of King James* (London, 1651), 165; see also Joseph Marshall and Sean Kelsey, "Weldon, Sir Anthony (*bap.* 1583, *d.* 1648)," in *Oxford Dictionary of National Biography*, online ed., ed. Lawrence Goldman (Oxford: Oxford University Press), http://www.oxforddnb.com/view/article/28988 (accessed August 10, 2005); Kupperman, *Indians and English*, 93–96, 161–62.

45. Settle, *A true reporte*, sig. C5v; Virginia Company, *True Declaration* (1610), 15.

46. Settle, *A true reporte*, sig. C5v; Fynes Moryson, *An itinerary containing his ten yeeres travell through the twelve dominions of Germany, Bohmerland, Sweitzerland, Netherland,*

Denmarke, Poland, Italy, Turky, France, England, Scotland & Ireland, 4 vols. (Glasgow: J. MacLehose, 1907–8), 4:201–2; Wood, *New England's Prospect*, 67. Settle had similarly unflattering comments about the living standards in the Orkney Islands, which he visited en route to America (*A true reporte*, sig. B3v).

47. Best, *True Discourse*, 1:49, 2:24, 3:65–66. Best's conclusions often fly in the face of his own evidence, as for example in book 3, page 65, where he noted that the Inuits "do sometime parboyle their meate a little and seeth the same in kettles made of beasts skins: they have also pannes cutte and made of stone very artificially," which suggests that their foods were not, or not always, raw.

48. Crowley, *Invention of Comfort*, 5–6; Henisch, *Fast and Feast*, 152, 165ff.; Paston-Williams, *Art of Dining*, 74, 76, 134, 138, 191; Brears, "Decoration of the Tudor and Stuart Table," 94; Wilson, "Ritual, Form and Colour," 9, 12; Sim, *Food and Feast*, 103.

49. Smith, *Map of Virginia* and *Generall Historie*, in Barbour, *Complete Works of Captain John Smith*, 1:174 and 2:181; Strachey, *Historie of Travell*, ed. Wright and Freund, 65.

50. Weldon, *Court and Character of King James*, 165; Kupperman, *Settling with the Indians*, 51; David Harris Willson, *King James VI and I* (London: Jonathan Cape, 1956), 386; Wood, *New England's Prospect*, 67.

51. Ivan Day, "Bridecup and Cake: The Ceremonial Food and Drink of the Bridal Procession," in Laura Mason, ed., *Food and the Rites of Passage* (Totnes, Devon, U.K.: Prospect Books, 2002), 33–61; Simon R. Charsley, *Wedding Cakes and Cultural History* (London: Routledge, 1992); Tony Green, "Ritual Structure and the Dramaturgy of Food in the Context of the Late Twentieth-Century Wedding," in Mason, *Food and the Rites of Passage*, 15–32. In 1637, in order to conserve supplies of wheat flour, the Massachusetts authorities forbade anyone to "sell any cakes or buns," except those "made for any buriall, or marriage, or such like speciall occation" (Shurtleff, *Records of the Governor and Company of the Massachusetts Bay*, 1:214).

52. *Relation of Maryland*, 29.

53. Strachey, *Historie of Travell*, ed. Wright and Freund, 112; Spelman, *Relation*, in Arber, ed., *Travels and Works of Captain John Smith*, 1:cvii. See also Wood, *New England's Prospect*, 81.

54. Isaak de Rasieres to Samuel Blommaert, ca. 1628, printed in James, *Three Visitors to Early Plymouth*, 70–71; Kupperman, *Indians and English*, 144–47.

55. Hamor, *True Discourse*, 11; Butler, *Historye of the Bermudaes*, 284; Kupperman, *Indians and English*, 200.

56. Emmanuel Altham to Sir Edward Altham, September 1623, printed in James, *Three Visitors to Early Plymouth*, 29.

57. Ibid.

58. Bradford and Winslow, *Mourt's Relation*, 61; Bradford, *Of Plymouth Plantation*, 90.

59. Waterhouse, *Declaration*, 12–14.

60. Nicholls, "George Percy's 'Trewe Relacyon,'" 255; Smith, *True Relation*, in Barbour, *Complete Works of Captain John Smith*, 1:91, mentions a report from a captive Algonquian that Powhatan intended to surprise Newport at a feast in a similar way; Strachey, *Historie of Travell*, ed. Wright and Freund, 64.

61. Council in Virginia to the Virginia Company of London, January 30, 1623/24, in Kingsbury, *Records of the Virginia Company,* 4:451; Peter Hulme, *Colonial Encounters: Europe and the Native Caribbean, 1492–1797* (London: Methuen, 1986), 172. See also Fuller, *Voyages in Print;* Salisbury, *Manitou and Providence,* 123–25; Kupperman, *Indians and English,* 219–38; Barbara Donagan, "Atrocity, War Crime, and Treason in the English Civil War," *American Historical Review* 99, no. 4 (1994): 1137–66; and James Drake, "Restraining Atrocity: The Conduct of King Philip's War," *New England Quarterly* 70, no. 1 (1997): 33–56, which owes much to Donagan's work. Other sources include Theodor Meron, *Henry's Wars and Shakespeare's Laws: Perspectives on the Law of War in the Later Middle Ages* (Oxford: Oxford University Press, 1993), which discusses the nuanced distinction between legitimate guile and illegitimate treachery on 44; Maurice Hugh Keen, *The Laws of War in the Late Middle Ages* (London: Routledge and Kegan Paul, 1965).

62. Winslow, *Good Newes from New England,* 24–25. Ralph Hamor made similar observations about hospitality offered him by Powhatan, at first meager and then, after an agreement had been reached, more ample (*True Discourse,* 40–43).

63. Winslow, *Good Newes from New England,* 34–44.

64. Morton, *New English Canaan,* 110. See also Salisbury, *Manitou and Providence,* 154–62; Edith Murphy, "'A Rich Widow, Now to Be Tane Up or Laid Downe': Solving the Riddle of Thomas Morton's 'Rise Oedipeus,'" *William and Mary Quarterly,* 3d ser., 53 (1996): 755–68; Michael Zuckerman, "Pilgrims in the Wilderness: Community, Modernity, and the Maypole at Merry Mount," *New England Quarterly* 50 (1977): 255–77; Karen Ordahl Kupperman, "Thomas Morton, Historian," *New England Quarterly* 50 (1977): 660–64.

65. *Calendar of State Papers, Colonial: America and West Indies, 1574–1739,* ed. Karen Ordahl Kupperman, John C. Appleby, and Mandy Banton (London: Routledge, in association with the Public Record Office, 2000), CD-ROM, vol. 1 (1574–1660), p. 48 (Dephebus Canne to John Delbridge, July 2, 1623) and p. 69 (Robt. Earl of Warwick to Sec. Conway, August 9, 1624); Robert Bennett to Edward Bennett, June 9, 1623, in Kingsbury, *Records of the Virginia Company,* 4:221–22; Rountree, *Pocahontas, Powhatan, Opechancanough,* 220.

CONCLUSION

1. John Winthrop Jr., *On Indian Corne,* ed. Fulmer Mood, *New England Quarterly* 10 (1937): 125. Winthrop quoted from the 1633 edition of Gerard, *The Herball; or Generall Historie of Plantes,* enlarged and amended by Thomas Johnson. The entry on maize is essentially the same in both editions.

2. Benjamin Tompson, *New Englands Crisis* (Boston, 1676), 5.

3. Beverley, *History and Present State of Virginia,* 233.

4. Ibid., 9; Barlowe, *Discourse,* in Quinn, *Roanoke Voyages,* 1:108–9.

5. Beverley, *History and Present State of Virginia,* 11, 195.

6. Ibid., 196. In addition to the descriptions of Chesapeake burial practices by Captain John Smith, which Beverley clearly knew, the illustrations in Beverley's own text were

copies of those Theodor de Bry prepared for the 1590 edition of Harriot's *A briefe and true report*, and they include a depiction of just this sort of ossuary.

7. Henry Lowood, "The New World and the European Catalog of Nature," in Kupperman, *America in European Consciousness*, 295–317 (quotation on 316); see also Christian F. Feest, "The Collecting of American Indian Artifacts in Europe, 1493–1750," in Kupperman, *America in European Consciousness*, 324–60. Egan, *Authorizing Experience*, 32–46, discusses Smith's effort to revise "the traditional aristocratic bases of authority in favor of 'experience' for the very limited purpose of influencing colonial policy" (35). There were occasions on which English travelers and settlers robbed Indian graves; see Virginia Company, *True and Sincere Declaration* (London, 1610), 18; Bradford and Winslow, *Mourt's Relation*, 6, 11. Thomas Morton commented that such practices deeply offended the New England Algonquians, who viewed desecration of graves as "impious and inhumane" (*New English Canaan*, 43–44, 106–7). For desecration of graves, see Kupperman, *Settling with the Indians*, 125.

8. John Lawson, *A New Voyage to Carolina* (London, 1709), ed. Hugh Talmage Lefler (Chapel Hill: University of North Carolina Press, 1967), 243.

9. Hugh Talmage Lefler, "Introduction," in Lawson, *New Voyage to Carolina*, xxiv–xxxvi; Beverley, *History and Present State of Virginia*, 154.

10. Until roughly 1660, Joyce Chaplin has argued, English dependency on Indians for survival and profit led to a description of Indian cultures as analogous to that of the English. After that point, Chaplin argues, English writers described their bodies as superior to those of the Indians, principally because of the effects of disease on native populations. Dismissing fears of hybridity, these writers, including Winthrop, asserted that their bodies were unchanged by the New World plants and animals they ate and the environment they lived in. Chaplin, *Subject Matter*, 8, 16–23, 175.

11. Gerard, *The Herball* (1633); Agnes Robertson Arber, *Herbals, Their Origin and Evolution: A Chapter in the History of Botany, 1470–1670*, 3d ed. (New York: Cambridge University Press, 1986), 129–35, 157 on Gerard; Eleanour Sinclair Rohde, *The Old English Herbals* (London: Longmans, Green, 1922), chaps. 4 and 5.

12. Josselyn, *New Englands Rarities Discovered*, 20.

13. Ibid., 38–39. Lawson also addressed the subject, claiming that some Indians he encountered ate snakes, but not all of them (*New Voyage to Carolina*, 182). Appelbaum, *Aguecheek's Beef*, 246–74, traces a similar apprehension of unrestrained appetite among Indians with roots in the early period. Although the most dramatic example of this is cannibalism, early modern writers gave almost equal weight to the claim that Indians demonstrated uncontrolled hunger. For European views of rattlesnakes, see Karen Ordahl Kupperman, "Natural Curiosity: Curious Nature in Early America," *Common-place* 4, no. 2 (2004), http://www.common-place.org/vol-04/no-02/kupperman/ (accessed January 23, 2005). The only analogous examples from the early period were Dionyse Settle's and George Best's descriptions of the Inuits.

14. Lawson, *New Voyage to Carolina*, 58; Beverley, *History and Present State of Virginia*, 180.

15. Beverley, *History and Present State of Virginia*, 178–80.

16. Bradford, *Of Plymouth Plantation*, 121.

17. Richard L. Bushman, *The Refinement of America: Persons, Houses, Cities* (New York: Knopf, 1992); Rhys Isaac, *The Transformation of Virginia, 1740–1790* (New York: W. W. Norton, 1988), 72–74. See also Lorena S. Walsh, "Urban Amenities and Rural Sufficiency: Living Standards and Consumer Behavior in the Colonial Chesapeake, 1643–1777," *Journal of Economic History* 43 (1983): 109.

18. T. H. Breen, "An Empire of Goods: The Anglicization of Colonial America, 1690–1776," *Journal of British Studies* 25 (1986): 472, 496; T. H. Breen, "Baubles of Britain: The American and Consumer Revolutions of the Eighteenth Century," *Past and Present* 119 (1988): 75–76; Sidney W. Mintz, *Sweetness and Power: The Place of Sugar in Modern History* (New York: Penguin Books, 1986); Carole Shammas, "Changes in English and Anglo-American Consumption from 1550 to 1800," in Brewer and Porter, *Consumption and the World of Goods*, 177–205.

19. Sarah Kemble Knight, *The Journal of Madam Knight*, ed. Sargent Bush Jr., in William L. Andrews et al., eds., *Journeys in New Worlds: Early American Women's Narratives* (Madison: University of Wisconsin Press, 1990), 104–5.

20. Alexander Hamilton, *Gentleman's Progress: The Itinerarium of Dr. Alexander Hamilton, 1744*, ed. Carl Bridenbaugh (Chapel Hill: University of North Carolina Press for the Institute of Early American History and Culture, 1948), 63, 146, 72–74. Hamilton echoes a long-standing negative judgment of the Dutch in this regard. See, for example, Palmer, *Essay*, 63: "Be not the Dutchmen most slovenly and sluttish in their apparell, & feeding?" For other examples, see Hamilton, *Itinerarium*, 103, 156, 169.

21. Hamilton, *Itinerarium*, 13–14; Kingsbury, *Records of the Virginia Company*, 3:231–22.

22. Knight, *Journal*, 91, 99.

23. Hamilton, *Itinerarium*, 55.

24. Knight, *Journal*, 94, 102–3, 106–7, 110–11.

25. Hamilton, *Itinerarium*, 8.

26. Settle, *A true reporte*, sig. C5v, B3v; Moryson, *Itinerary*, 201–2.

27. Hamilton, *Itinerarium*, 8; Appelbaum, *Aguecheek's Beef*, 144–46, argues that the medieval peasant fantasies of abundance like Cockaigne began to be replaced in the early modern period by measured utopias of moderation, even frugality; in what he describes as the "food of regret," Appelbaum traces a pervasive desire for a golden age of rustic simplicity and dietary moderation of the sort Hamilton describes in this passage (*Aguecheek's Beef*, 155–200).

28. Palmer, *Essay*, 94, 110.

Index

Acknowledgments

My greatest debt is owed to Karen Ordahl Kupperman, who generously offered her comments, assistance, and support throughout the process of writing and publishing this book. She is the model of a historian and mentor, and without her faith in the early stages of a somewhat unorthodox topic, this book would not have been written.

I owe a special debt to the CANS, especially to Kimberly Gilmore and Betsy Esch, for help and support in many matters both academic and not.

In the history department at New York University, Tom Bender and the members of his seminar, especially Stephen Mihm, generously read draft after draft as I refined my sense of what and how food meant. Walter Johnson and Lauren Benton each helped clarify the argument through excellent questions and suggestions. Amy Bentley introduced me to NYU's food studies department, which has contributed a great deal to my scholarship and teaching. The "Feast and Famine" colloquium there read a draft of one chapter and has provided me with a consistently interesting academic community and equally wonderful lunches.

My high-school friend and now fellow early Americanist Christopher Bilodeau has given me his very valuable comments on the manuscript, on early American history, on the Boston Red Sox, and on many other subjects over the years. It's a very odd thing to have known Chris for so many years and to have ended up working on such closely related subjects, and I consider myself very fortunate on both fronts.

A fellowship at the John Carter Brown Library in 2002 came at a most opportune moment, and it was there that the project took on what would be its final form. At a fellows luncheon, of all places, I shared my ideas on cannibalism and roast squirrel to a helpful and supportive group whose appetites visibly diminished during my talk. At the Harvard Atlantic History Seminar in 2007, I presented a far more polished version of that paper, this time before lunch. Many thanks to Bernard Bailyn, the seminar's participants, and those invited to comment.

Thanks also to my colleagues at Adelphi University, especially Lou Starkey and Marty Haas. Both are model citizens of a university, and their example has greatly eased my transition into their ranks, with all that transition entails.

A portion of Chapter 5 appeared as "'A continuall and dayly Table for Gentlemen of fashion': Humanism, Food, and Authority at Jamestown, 1607–1609," *American Historical Review* 115 (June 2010): 669–87 ©2010 American Historical Association, all rights reserved. Thanks to the *AHR* and the University of Chicago Press for permission to include that material here.

Many thanks to Bob Lockhart of the University of Pennsylvania Press, who has been a wonderful and supportive editor throughout the process, from the time we met in sweltering Williamsburg through the many stages that followed.

Last of all, my family. Whatever gestational metaphors might spring to mind as one labors to bring a book into the world simply cannot compare with the real thing. My lovely wife, Christa, warm and generous and sweet, has given me her comments, support, and love throughout the process of finishing this book, in our shared academic joys and tribulations, and in every other way. Sophia was born around the time this project started, woke up extra early to help me with my writing, did her best to understand my outrage at Disney's version of early America, and will now finally see the book in print. Vivian arrived in the world two days after I delivered the final draft, and her dad cannot wait to experience predawn mornings, puppies, books, empty boxes, and the rest of the amazing world through her eyes. To frame this period of my life in this way places all the rest in perspective. I am truly fortunate.

CPSIA information can be obtained
at www.ICGtesting.com
Printed in the USA
LVHW091510110920
665711LV00005B/20/J